Service provision within the forensic context is complex, forensic work and some clients can be demanding and harmful. Effective supervision has the capacity to enhance knowledge and skills and to positively impact practitioners' professional and personal integrity. Jason Davies' book is comprehensive and accessible. Written with a practical focus, this excellent text provides practical guidance and thoughtful consideration of important process issues. It is an invaluable and complete resource to guide supervisors, supervisees and those with the capacity to ensure effective supervision within forensic settings.

Professor Michael Daffern, *Centre for Forensic Behavioural Science, Swinburne University of Technology, Australia*

This book is extremely well composed and written, and a masterclass in all aspects of the supervision of forensic practitioners of all kinds. It contains exceptional wisdom and guidance on this essential supportive activity – and is a vital resource for those providing, receiving, planning, and researching supervision. Indeed, it is incomprehensible that such a comprehensive and invaluable text as this has not been written before now. Without doubt, this book will become a necessary guide to the support and nurturance of forensic practitioners and the services in which they work for years to come.

Dr. Caroline Logan, *Lead Consultant Forensic Clinical Psychologist, Greater Manchester West Mental Health NHS Foundation Trust and Associate MSc Programme Director, University of Manchester, UK*

Supervision for Forensic Practitioners

Forensic practitioners work in a diverse range of settings, with a wide variety of groups and with a large number of agencies. Their work, whilst rewarding, is challenging, demanding and often undertaken in highly stressful situations. Ensuring that the workforce is trained and supported is essential in order to maintain skilful, knowledgeable, responsive and effective practitioners. Whilst training, self-directed learning and peer support all play a role, the need for supervision for practitioners is increasingly being recognised.

This text is aimed at all those working in forensic settings who have direct contact with the perpetrators and victims of crime and is written for both those new to supervision and those with many years' experience. Specific chapters focus on knowledge and skills for the supervisor and the supervisee and on those responsible for developing supervision systems for staff groups. This includes a focus on risk, boundaries, approaches to learning and the evidence base for supervision practice. Attention is also given to developing supervision competence and combatting harmful or 'lousy' supervision. The core text is supplemented by ten special topics addressing single themes common in supervision practice, such as ethical issues and reflective practice.

The combination of comprehensive chapters and a focus on specific themes through ten special topics provides those involved in supervision with an essential resource. This book is essential reading for supervisors, students, managers and researchers who are involved or interested in the supervision process.

Jason Davies is a Consultant Forensic and Clinical Psychologist with Abertawe Bro Morgannwg University Health Board and Honorary Professor of Forensic Clinical Psychology with Cardiff Metropolitan University. He has worked as a practitioner in a range of forensic mental health settings and is co-editor of the book *Research in Practice for Forensic Professionals* (2011).

Issues in Forensic Psychology
Edited by Richard Shuker, HMP Grendon

Issues in Forensic Psychology is a book series which aims to promote forensic psychology to a broad range of forensic practitioners. It aims to provide analysis and debate on current issues and to publish and promote the work of forensic psychologists and other associated professionals.

The views expressed by the authors/editors may not necessarily be those held by the Series Editor or NOMS.

1. **Research in Practice for Forensic Professionals**
   Edited by Kerry Sheldon, Jason Davies and Kevin Howells

2. **Secure Recovery**
   Approaches to recovery in forensic mental health settings
   Edited by Gerard Drennan and Deborah Alred

3. **Managing Clinical Risk**
   A guide to effective practice
   Edited by Caroline Logan and Lorraine Johnstone

4. **Handbook on the Study of Multiple Perpetrator Rape**
   A multidisciplinary response to an international problem
   Edited by Miranda A. H. Horvath and Jessica Woodhams

5. **Forensic Practice in the Community**
   Edited by Zoë Ashmore and Richard Shuker

6. **Supervision for Forensic Practitioners**
   Jason Davies

Supervision for Forensic Practitioners

Jason Davies

LONDON AND NEW YORK

First published 2015
by Routledge
2 Park Square, Milton Park, Abingdon, Oxfordshire OX14 4RN

and by Routledge
711 Third Avenue, New York, NY 10017

First issued in paperback 2016

Routledge is an imprint of the Taylor & Francis Group, an informa business

© 2015 Jason Davies

The right of Jason Davies to be identified as author of this work has been asserted by him in accordance with sections 77 and 78 of the Copyright, Designs and Patents Act 1988.

All rights reserved. No part of this book may be reprinted or reproduced or utilised in any form or by any electronic, mechanical, or other means, now known or hereafter invented, including photocopying and recording, or in any information storage or retrieval system, without permission in writing from the publishers.

Trademark notice: Product or corporate names may be trademarks or registered trademarks, and are used only for identification and explanation without intent to infringe.

British Library Cataloguing-in-Publication Data
A catalogue record for this book is available from the British Library

Library of Congress Cataloging in Publication Data
Davies, Jason.
 Supervision for forensic practitioners / Jason Davies.
  pages cm. – (Issues in forensic psychology)
 1. Forensic scientists–Supervision of. 2. Forensic sciences. 3. Criminal justice, Administration of–Research–Methodology. 4. Forensic psychology. I. Title.
 HV8073.D289 2015
 363.25068'3–dc23
         2014032640

ISBN 13: 978-1-138-68783-7 (pbk)
ISBN 13: 978-0-415-63205-8 (hbk)

Typeset in Bembo
by Taylor & Francis Books

For Susie, Bryn and Freya ... thank you for your patience – it's finished at last!

Contents

List of illustrations xi
Acknowledgements xiii
Foreword xiv
Using this text xvi

1 An introduction to practice supervision   1

2 The emerging evidence base for practice supervision   16

3 Supervision types, forms and tasks   34

4 Supervision models and frameworks   50

5 Approaches to learning in supervision   75

6 Being supervised   92

7 Core skills and knowledge for supervisors   108

8 Managing risk and boundaries through supervision   130

9 Developing supervision in forensic practice: structures,
   systems and audit   151

10 Supervisor and supervisee training and development   169

Special topics   **181**

   Special Topic 1: The impact of the setting on supervision   183

   Special Topic 2: Ethical issues   186

Special Topic 3: Supervising group work — 194

Special Topic 4: Supervising non-client work: research, leadership and management activity — 198

Special Topic 5: Critiques of supervision and reflective practice — 205

Special Topic 6: Overcoming problems in supervision — 209

Special Topic 7: Creative approaches to supervision — 215

Special Topic 8: Assessments and measures for use in supervision and research — 219

Special Topic 9: Team supervision — 226

Special Topic 10: Reflective practice — 231

11 The end of the beginning: summary, observations and future directions — 240

Author index — 247
Subject index — 253

List of illustrations

Figures

3.1	Representation of power and responsibility in different types of supervision	35
4.1	Functions of supervision	53
4.2	The supervision hour	55
6.1	Minimally adequate forensic supervision	105
8.1	Factors associated with boundary violations	138
8.2	Triangle of boundary maintenance	144
ST3.1	Supervising group work	194

Tables

5.1	Domains of learning goals	83
ST4.1	Practice leader tasks	202
ST8.1	Regular monitoring – the Global Review Form: Supervision Version	223

Boxes

1.1	What happens in practice supervision?	11
1.2	Personal review: where are you at KEN?	12
2.1	Key questions and considerations when evaluating practice supervision research	17
3.1	Individual supervision agreement example	45
3.2	Example of a supervision record	47
4.1	Developmental levels – examples of characteristics, supervisor approach and level	59
4.2	Parallel process	66
4.3	Supervisory roles	69
4.4	The 12 principles of evidence-based supervision	72
5.1	Taking stock	76
6.1	General goals for supervision	98

6.2	Preparing for supervision	101
6.3	Minimally adequate forensic supervision	105
7.1	Qualities of 'good' supervisors	109
7.2	Some useful questions for supervisors	120
7.3	Client-focused supervision questions	122
8.1	Triangle of boundary maintenance	143
8.2	A quick guide to boundary maintenance	147
9.1	Problem alliances	152
9.2	Steps in developing and implementing supervision	154
9.3	Example audit form	164
10.1	Supervision training programme outline	175
ST2.1	Spotting possible ethical dilemmas	191
ST3.1	Supervising groupwork	194
ST6.1	Preventing and responding to problems in supervision	214
ST7.1	Use of flight as a metaphor of a service	215
ST8.1	Regular monitoring – the Global Review Form: Supervision Version	222
ST9.1	Building solutions in 30 minutes	226
ST9.2	Template for client discussions within team supervision	229
ST10.1	Questions to aid reflection	237

Acknowledgements

There are many people who have had an impact on my thinking and development in relation to supervision. Every supervision encounter adds something to understanding the ideas, processes and practice of supervision if you allow it to. This can both inform and be informed by research, theory, models and philosophies.

I have been very fortunate to have the opportunity to learn (and to continue to learn) about the process and practice of supervision from the many people who have given generously of their time and enthusiasm – as supervisor and supervisee. Supervision is an opportunity to draw on both experience and academic ideas and knowledge – it is both a science and an art. There is a great deal more to develop in relation to the science, however it will never replace the intuition, artistry and experimentation required to make supervision work. For me the opportunity to supervise those starting out in their career as assistants, trainees, students and newly qualified staff is a particular privilege and an opportunity to learn and remain alert and curious – thank you to those who make up this group. Although not individually named, hopefully you know who you are – I certainly do!

There are some people who must be recognised by name because of the particular influences they have had on my view and practice of supervision. They are, in alphabetical order: Susie Black, Richard Carter, Andrea Chadwick, Laura Freeman, Neil Gordon, John Hodge, Kevin Howells, Lawrence Jones, Claire Nagi, Sharron Oddie, Kate Oldfield, Margaret O'Rourke, Joyce Scaife, Ann Salmon, Allison Tennant, Sue Walsh and Marie Williams. Thanks also to *Forensic Update* and The British Psychological Society for granting permission to reproduce some material in this book. Finally, thank you to Susie Black, Mark Campisi, Nicola Derrick, Stephen Jones, Claire Nagi and Marie Williams for feedback on drafts of the text and to Heidi Lee, Editorial Assistant at Routledge for her support and guidance during the process of writing this book.

Foreword

This is a book that is sorely needed. Whilst much has been written about supervision in the human services professions more broadly, it is difficult to think of any specialist resources which have been written for the forensic practitioner. Quite why this should be the case is difficult to fathom. Not only do forensic practitioners work with some of the most challenging clients (some of whom may be resentful or distrustful of our service's involvement, let alone have low levels of problem awareness and motivation), but our work in this area attracts a high level of public and judicial scrutiny and ethical and moral issues arise on an almost daily basis. Practice supervision represents one of the main mechanisms by which we can ensure that we maintain the very highest standards in our work.

It is now widely accepted that all professionals, whether experienced or just starting out, will benefit from having regular professional supervision. For some of us who work in criminal justice settings, this is now a formal requirement, creating tension between the aims of our professions and organisations and our own need for personal development. We need to be clear about what it is we are doing in supervision and what it is that we hope to achieve. At its simplest, practice supervision can be understood as a scheduled regular meeting in which a practitioner meets with a fellow professional with the express purpose of examining their work. And yet, as Jason Davies explains throughout this book, it has the potential to be so much more. A good supervisor will act as a mentor, providing emotional support as well as information and guidance. Supervision can help us to understand more about the context in which our professional practice takes place, and develop the skills that we need to work effectively with clients and colleagues.

There is little doubt in my mind that good supervision is one of the most rewarding aspects of forensic practice, whether we are supervising others or reviewing our own practice. It is associated with pivotal moments in the development of any competent practitioner and has the potential to transform the way in which we work. When done badly, however, supervision can be very stressful, contribute to disillusionment and burn out, and sanction poor or even unethical practice. This book provides a practical and insightful guide to the responsibilities facing all those involved in supervision, covering the types, forms and tasks of supervision as well as models and frameworks and approaches to learning. It is evident that anyone who follows the advice contained in this book will avoid these problems. The chapters discuss what it is like to be supervised and to provide supervision as well as addressing a number of factors which impact on the provision of quality supervision, including a lack of time, workload demands, access to a supervisor, management mistrust and culture. These are all important issues which are discussed too rarely.

Jason has done the forensic area a great service in writing this book. By drawing out the best features of the various different approaches to practice supervision that have been proposed, he articulates an approach that will undoubtedly help to improve the quality of forensic practice. He blends academic knowledge with practice wisdom in a way that is both easy to read and engaging. I hope it will soon become an essential resource for supervisors, supervisees and those who are responsible for managing forensic practitioners alike.

Andrew Day
Deakin University, 4 July 2014

Using this text

Most people don't read from the start to the end of a text book like this! As a starter, the following provides a guide to how the different chapters might be combined for different purposes. It is hoped that once you have read the chapters deemed most relevant, you will read others to broaden your knowledge and understanding. The special topics act as shorter reference points, providing a focus on a single issue.

It is suggested that all readers begin with Chapter 1 as this introduction will help with providing a common starting point for all involved in forensic practice supervision. The suggestions below are based on the different types of involvement individuals might have with supervision.

I'm a supervisee

Chapter 1 will provide an orientation to the field of practitioner supervision and act as a foundation for your engagement in supervision. Once completed it is suggested that you read Chapter 6, which discusses many of the factors relevant to being a supervisee using a question and answer format. It also includes essential skills such as how to plan and prepare for supervision. Finally, those wanting to develop more understanding of the processes within supervision and the models that can be used within supervision should consider reading Chapters 3 and 4.

I'm a supervisor

If you are a supervisor then the majority of this text has been written with you in mind, and therefore much of the text will be relevant for most supervisors. However, you might wish to read the chapters in an order that best suits your experience and knowledge of providing supervision. For example, if you are new to supervision you might wish to start with Chapter 7 which discusses planning for and providing supervision; followed by Chapters 3, 4, 5 and 8; before considering which, if any, special topics might be particularly pertinent at this point in time. As you will also be in the supervisee role you might also wish to read Chapter 6, by doing this you can also determine how you might use the contents of this chapter with your own supervisees.

I'm a manager

If you are a manager of a service in which supervision is provided or is being considered, Chapter 9 addresses issues at the system level. It may also be important to be familiar with some of the evidence base for supervision (Chapter 2) and the opportunities for service evaluation and research. Finally, it may be that information regarding staff training and development in relation to supervision are relevant (Chapter 10) especially if there are plans to develop this.

I'm developing a supervision strategy

Those developing a supervision strategy will probably wish to be familiar with all the material within this book. However, Chapter 9 specifically considers what might be needed in a supervision strategy and how this might be developed. The following chapter (10), discusses training supervisors and supervisees which may well form an essential component of a service development and delivery strategy.

I'm planning to conduct supervision research

There is a great deal of scope for engaging in research and evaluation of forensic practice supervision. Chapter 2 provides an overview of the evidence base and some of the novel ways in which researchers are attempting to understand what takes place in supervision and the possible impact it has.

I'm planning to provide training to others

For those developing or providing training, Chapter 10 provides a focus on the training and development of supervisors and supervisees, along with a basic 'contents list' for supervision training. However, if you are in this role, it is likely that you will want a grasp of a wide range of ideas and issues relating to supervision as well as your own experience on which to draw. This text should provide helpful material for this.

In the ethos of practitioner development in which this text is intended, please contact me with ideas, observations, suggestions and experiences – I can't promise but they might make a future edition!

1 An introduction to practice supervision

Forensic practice is a rapidly developing specialism that covers a very wide range of application. Forensic practitioners may find themselves working in a diversity of settings such as custody, hospitals and the community; with a wide variety of groups such as children and adolescents, adults, offenders and victims of crime; and with a large number of agencies for example the courts, police, health service, prisons, probation and the voluntary sector. Despite this plethora of practice settings and services, the challenge of delivering high quality provision, in 'high-stakes' and often high-pressured situations is a common feature. In order to meet this challenge, there is a need for practitioners to be highly competent and able to work safely and effectively. Forensic practitioners need also to ensure that their performance and wellbeing are maintained across the course of hours, days, weeks, years and decades! Given this enormous commitment expected from staff, there is a need to ensure that sufficient attention is paid to the greatest resource in forensic settings – the 'human capital', i.e. all those who make up the workforce. Investment is needed to provide education, training, guidance as well as practical and emotional support for staff whilst developing and sustaining functional teams and responsive services.

Becoming an effective forensic practitioner requires a complex blend of knowledge, skill, self-awareness, responsiveness and on-going learning. For those new to this area of work and those with many years of experience, a range of mechanisms will be employed to develop and maintain skills, knowledge and ability. These are likely to include access to training and opportunities for self-directed learning. However, whilst such learning is a necessary element, the absorption of knowledge and information is not all that is needed for safe and effective practice. In addition to 'collecting' taught knowledge, is the task of learning from experience and integrating these two. The purpose of this chapter is to provide an overview of practice supervision and to 'set the scene' for the remaining chapters of this book. Therefore, the following pages contain several references to other chapters in this book where ideas and evidence are presented in much more detail.

For the purposes of this book, a pragmatic approach has been taken to the definition of a forensic practitioner as, to the best of my knowledge, this 'collective noun' has not been previously used. A forensic practitioner is taken to be anyone working in settings in which they are in direct contact with the perpetrators or victims of crime. Thus the definition would include police and prison officer/custodial staff; a wide range of support staff (e.g. healthcare support practitioners in forensic mental health settings; support practitioners employed in approved premises as used by probation; voluntary and third sector staff working in projects such as domestic violence support) and formal graduate or post-graduate training in a registered profession such as nursing, social work and psychology. For some, identifying yourself as a forensic professional will be easy as 'forensic' forms part of your title (forensic psychologist, forensic psychiatrist, forensic social worker) whilst for others this identity will be new! This broad definition means that individual consideration will be needed when reviewing this text to consider how the ideas might apply to *you* in *your* role. Additionally, the term 'client' has been used to denote all those within or accessing services. This would include prisoners, inmates and convicted offenders subject to probation and patients within forensic mental health services.

The last 30 years has seen significant developments within the field of practitioner supervision, especially in the areas of therapist training and in mental health settings. For example, within the field of nursing, a paper by Cutcliffe noted that, in 2005, supervision has been present for over two decades in the UK and longer elsewhere (Cutcliffe, 2005). Over this time, and especially within the last decade, the literature on supervision has expanded greatly, reflecting the growing interest in and focus on supervision. In addition to the huge number of journal articles, there are now a number of specialist books which draw upon research and best practice guidelines to provide a generic reference for the supervisor or supervisee (e.g. Beddoe and Davys, 2010; Bernard and Goodyear, 2014; Milne, 2009; Scaife, 2013), or explore supervision from the standpoint of a particular professional group (e.g. Bond and Holland, 2011; Fleming and Steen, 2004). Therefore, it is reasonable to conclude that supervision is a rapidly growing field of practice and research (White and Winstanley, 2012) and, as argued by Fowler (1996a), in relation to nursing practice, has the potential to be 'one of the most powerful tools for nursing practice development' (p. 47). In comparison, a focus specifically on guidance for those engaging in supervision or in establishing supervisory practice, training or undertaking supervision research within forensic practice is very limited. For example, a simple search of the literature using PsycINFO with the terms 'supervision' in the title and ('forensic' or 'prison' or 'offend' or 'custody' or 'secure' or 'DSPD') in the abstract between the dates of 2000 and February 2014 revealed only 18 publications in English during this time. Of these, two were dissertations and five were chapters in books. As noted by Day (2012), this is surprising given the ethical, legal and practice issues that arise on a daily basis within forensic settings.

Towards a definition

An important starting point is to consider a definition for practice supervision especially as the term 'practice supervision' is not in common use, whereas phrases such as 'clinical supervision' and 'managerial supervision' are. Although a somewhat obvious starting place, providing a clear definition is necessary to avoid the confusions that can arise when individuals use the term (Freshwater, Walsh and Storey, 2002) and the assumptions that there is already some shared meaning that is used by all (Shanley and Stevenson, 2006). In the allied area of 'clinical supervision' the possibility for ambiguity and confusion is partly due to there being 'as many written definitions of clinical supervision as there are published books and papers on the subject' (Bond and Holland, 2011, p. 13). Therefore, a clear definition is important not only for practice convenience but also as a foundation for research (e.g. Hyrkäs, Koivula and Paunonen, 1999; Kilminster and Jolly, 2000).

Whilst there is much debate in the literature about the definition of supervision, it would appear that there are common aims and values underlying clinical supervision. Supervision is seen as an important factor in delivering safe and effective services (e.g. Department of Health, 1993), and to support professional development and lifelong learning in order to maintain standards and develop care (e.g. Department of Health, 1999). Day (2012), noted that supervision should be framed as a *formalised, rational* and a *goal directed* enterprise, with Hyrkäs *et al.* (1999), stating that any definition of supervision should comment upon the *goals, process* and *participants* of supervision. The multiple functions of supervision are neatly captured by Inskipp and Proctor (1993) who discuss the *formative, normative* and *restorative* functions of supervision. These aspects, which concern training/education; benchmarking and ethics; and emotional support, are considered in more detail in Chapter 4. However, in meeting these functions, it is critical that supervision should remain focused upon its key purpose – how will supervision enhance practice and/or the service being delivered and positively impact on those receiving the service. This can be operationalised in a simple way – how does supervision contribute to ensuring that clients receive safe, appropriate and responsive services.

Authors and researchers have adopted various approaches in their attempts to establish a definition. Although these concern 'clinical supervision' they are helpful to acknowledge. For example, Milne (2009) attempts to use a 'precision' framework in order to arrive at a definition. Although similar in many ways to definitions already in existence, what Milne does is to explicitly state what supervision is (and is not), how it is practised, what its functions are and how these aspects can be measured. This, he argues, provides a foundation for research and investigation into supervision. Others (e.g. Scaife, 2013, pp. 3–10) present a range of definitions and explore the functions that supervision might serve before listing characteristic features found in supervision. For the purposes of this text a simple and inclusive definition will be used which draws upon the definitions and discussions of Bond and Holland (2011); Milne (2009) and Scaife (2013). Thus for this text, practice supervision is defined as:

> A *formalised* relationship (one to one or group) in which regular, protected time is allocated in which a *trained* supervisor supports, develops and

evaluates the *practice* of the supervisee through the use of a *range* of methods and techniques. The primary *outcome* for supervision is improved service provision. Thus supervision is focused on competence, ethical practice, quality and the emotional impact on the practitioner (the formative, normative and restorative functions).

The words in italics need to be considered in a little more depth in order to help understand the nature of the supervision relationship as distinct from other relationships (which may resemble practice supervision in a number of ways but whose function is limited to particular purposes, e.g. teaching, support or management).

Formalised – a defining feature of practice supervision is that the relationship has an agreement in place which defines:

(a) clear goals and purpose;
(b) the format of supervision;
(c) where and when supervision will take place;
(d) how records will be kept; and
(e) how issues such as confidentiality will be managed.

Regular and protected time is a cornerstone of the formality of supervision and it is this aspect (as we will explore in Chapter 9), that requires organisational effort and structures as a foundation for this.

Trained – being a practice supervisor requires a set of skills and competencies over and above those necessary to do the job that is being supervised. Although there is a long history of individuals becoming practice supervisors because of their position or their length of service/experience, such a crude proxy for supervision competence is inadequate for undertaking this specialist role. As we will consider in Chapter 10, training supervisors and supervisees for the task of supervision is an important undertaking.

Practice – in our definition above, 'practice' refers to the work undertaken by the supervisee. Depending on their work role this may include a wide range of activities such as providing clients with skills training, practical support, advice and guidance; delivering individual or group therapy; escorting duties; presenting evidence to courts or tribunals; teaching and research.

Range – the ability to respond to the nature and needs of the supervisee and their practice requires the supervisor to be skilled in the application of a multitude of methods and techniques including reflection, challenge, exploration and teaching. This will be considered further in Chapters 5 and 7 and Special Topic 10.

Outcomes – the ultimate purpose or 'holy grail' for practice supervision is the impact it has on the actions of the supervisee and thus the positive effect on the client or task. Therefore, the content of the supervision session should have a tangible link to practice discernible through the conversations held – there should be a clear link back to the practice setting. As we will see in Chapter 4, there are many models we can use to guide supervision and help the supervisor and supervisee maintain this focus.

It is important to note that in the definition of 'practice supervision' provided above, the idea of the supervisor as a 'more experienced practitioner' is not included. This is a departure from many definitions for supervision which include this notion. In other definitions the focus of supervision is on students or trainees or there is an implicit or explicit argument that, for other practitioners, supervision is based on a power differential. Whilst these elements often and perhaps usually are the case, the definition of practice supervision is intended to cover both novice and experienced practitioners and to include the meetings between peers (see Chapter 3). Others have excluded such practice by labelling these as consultation or supervision-consultation. Another feature of the above definition is the focus on service provision which may be clients (people using the service) as in most definitions but also includes tasks. This broadening allows work other than that relating directly to clients to form part of supervision and reflects a move away from the therapy/nursing/social care origins of many definitions of supervision. Although you may choose to use a different definition, it is important to agree a definition between yourself and your supervisor and ideally with the service as well.

Supervision often has an element of practice oversight and monitoring, however this needs to be balanced against supervision being a personal learning forum (e.g. Beddoe and Davys, 2010). This issue is discussed further in Chapter 5.

Supervision is not therapy or counselling

In trying to identify and clearly state what supervision is, it is also necessary to be explicit about what it is not. Although there may be many distinctions to be made, we will consider one very important demarcation to make ... supervision is NOT therapy! This has been underscored by many writers on supervision (e.g. Ekstein and Wallerstein, 1958; Yegdich, 1998) with others warning that supervision should not slip into therapy (Mothersole, 2000). In order to help ensure this, explicit agreements for supervision should be made and boundaries should be explicit (see Chapters 3 and 8). This is particularly important when using reflection and when the interface between the practitioner and their work is being explored (e.g. impact of events; managing conflict). Another way to help with this is for the supervisor (and supervisee) to regularly and explicitly return to the work being supervised to determine that any focus on the 'personal' remains in relation to the 'professional', i.e. "how might our discussion impact on your practice". Of course it can be very difficult to link a single supervision session to practice change or service development, however paying attention to the 'focus outwards/focus on action' can be useful. Occasionally, it may be that the supervisor's role is to assist the supervisee to identify additional resources they might need (which could include counselling or occupational health support). Where there is any doubt, the supervisor should assist the supervisee to (a) identify what else might be needed and, where possible, (b) to signpost and or support the supervisee to access this.

Supervision as life-long development

The term supervision has a partly troubled history especially amongst some professional groups because of misconceptions about its purpose and relevance. For example, Cheater and Hale (2001), in a study of nurses, found that there were common misconceptions about who supervision was for with a belief that it was 'appropriate only in circumstances of poor performance, or when nurses were experiencing particular problems' (p. 126). Further, some nurses were said to feel threatened by the prospect of supervision and some General Practitioners (Family Doctors) were found to be suspicious about supervision – concerned it was an external process of inspection or a staff-monitoring system. The idea that supervision is only for junior staff has been compounded by the ways in which supervision has been used as a term to cover allied but distinct activities such as mentorship and preceptorship (Fowler, 1996b). Throughout this text practice supervision is seen as a life-long development process aimed at all staff, novice and highly experienced. However, it is important to recognise that over time supervision will need to evolve, adapt and change along with the relationships between the supervisee and supervisor in order to meet the needs of the supervisee and their work (Hair, 2013). As we will see in later chapters, how supervision is 'performed' may change but its purpose and relevance – as outlined in our definition earlier – does not.

Why bother with supervision?

Having considered a definition of practice supervision the next critical issue to address is why bother with practice supervision. Before dissecting this question in more detail it is worth understanding some of the reasons why supervision, practice development and practice governance appear or re-appear 'on the radar'. Perhaps unsurprisingly, it is often the questions asked in the wake of some of the most extreme and distressing cases that prompts service managers and even national governments to ask 'what should have been done (differently)' and 'how might we prevent this occurring again'. In many instances supervision is part of the reply. Supervision is not a fail-safe, however, a brief look at a sample of these cases shows how and why supervision might play a valid role in public protection, practitioner competence and client outcomes. The three high-profile examples are drawn from the UK, however it is likely that similar reviews and conclusions can be found in many other countries.

Victoria Climbie Inquiry – Victoria Climbie was an eight-year-old girl who died following extreme maltreatment and horrific harm suffered at the hands of her great aunt and her great aunt's partner. The inquiry chaired by Lord Laming (The Victoria Climbie Inquiry, 2003), highlighted the catalogue of failures and opportunities missed by professionals. Lord Laming made a number of very clear recommendations including that supervision was to be provided to a range of professionals.

Ashworth Hospital Inquiry – The inquiry into the multiple problems within the Personality Disorder Unit at Ashworth High Security Hospital, chaired by Peter Fallon Q.C. (Fallon et al., 1999), followed serious allegations made about the management of and serious security breaches within the unit. In finding that this was indeed the case, the report contained several noteworthy comments in relation to supervision. It found that clinical supervision was not apparent, was piecemeal, was not systematic or was inadequate in many instances, and recommended that systematic clinical supervision be introduced.

Mid Staffordshire NHS Foundation Trust Inquiry – This inquiry into the very significant failings in a general hospital NHS Trust in England revealed an unacceptable high mortality rate and many significant failings even in relation to the most basic standards of care. In the public inquiry report (Report of the Mid-Staffordshire NHS Foundation Trust Public Inquiry (2013)), Robert Francis Q.C. emphasised the role for leadership, governance and the importance of the service's 'culture', and noted the need for supervision especially for health care support practitioners.

The above, very briefly described examples, serve to highlight some of the ways in which supervision has been identified as playing a role in good practice. They all indicate failing in supervision and the place for supervision, alongside other structures and processes to maintain a safe and progressive service. Across these examples it is possible to see supervision as a quality assurance, monitoring and patient safety mechanism, however equally important is the role for supervision in developing the skills, knowledge and practice of the workforce (an educative component) and in supporting the workforce. These features will be considered further in Chapter 4. It is, of course, true that we can never know what impact, if any, effective supervision would have had in the above cases, however it may be that the presence of effective supervision is one indicator of a client/task centred organisation, willing to scrutinise its performance through supporting individuals to do so.

Returning to the question of 'why bother with supervision?', this will be further answered by considering the possible benefits in relation to the various 'stakeholders', namely the client or task, the practitioner, the team, the supervisor, the profession and the service (Harkness and Hensley, 1991). Although these 'viewpoints' are likely to be interdependent, it is this framework that will be used in this section. A more detailed discussion of the evidence base for supervision, and specific possible effects are considered in Chapter 2.

Benefits to the client/task

From the viewpoint of the client or the task (e.g. completion of a piece of research), supervision, at its most fundamental, is one mechanism through which governance can be achieved and professional standards maintained. This might include ensuring treatment integrity/fidelity. This focus on standards gives rise to some of the critique levelled at supervision (see Special Topic 5), however safety must be the foundation for any practice. From this foundation, the other benefits of supervision can be built. For example, it is logical to assume that functional teams, with competent and resourceful individuals, are more likely to provide higher quality provision to those they work with. Supervision has a key role to play in this. Ultimately the function for supervision, especially where clients are concerned, is 'safe, high quality services resulting in desired outcomes'.

Benefits to the practitioner

For the individual practitioner, supervision is considered to have many positive effects. For the novice practitioner this includes increasing competence through helping develop new skills and knowledge; for more experienced staff, an opportunity to learn from their practice; and for all supervisees, a method for maintaining an ethical approach, standards and to receive support. Therefore, at a basic level supervision could be considered one medium in which 'care can be taken of the caregiver' (c.f. Bégat and Severinsson, 2006).

Benefits to the team

Supervision provided to the individual practitioner can impact on the team through changes to the practitioner's practice. However, the team itself is also a justifiable focus for supervision either through an individual considering team issues within their individual supervision or through the provision of group supervision to a team. Supervision focused on the team or with the team can be important to maximise team coherence and consistency (working to a common goal) whilst reducing and providing an avenue to identify and address possible divides and splits in the team.

Benefits to the service

At the service level, effective supervision may improve the outcomes of those accessing the service, increase the motivation, commitment and capability of the workforce and reduce complaints. At a very general level, supervision can be seen as a feature of a 'learning organisation' (Rolfe and Gardner, 2006). Such an organisation can be defined as one which fosters learning across the workforce in a way that leads to positive outcomes (e.g. Armstrong and Foley, 2003). However, more than this, supervision itself may be characterised by features of a learning organisation such as those articulated by (Phillips, 2003), e.g. innovation and decision making. Therefore, supervision can be a mechanism through which practitioners and the services within which they work develop and evolve. Further, it has been argued that supervision can help to reduce sickness, burnout and ill-health and enhance staff motivation and morale (see Chapter 2).

Benefits to the supervisor

Providing supervision to others may have many positive effects on supervisors. This can include their satisfaction with their work and their employer and the opportunity for supervisor development through learning new practice from the supervisee.

Professional standards and registration

Many professional groups recognise the contribution made by supervision to practitioner development and practice. This can be described through local or national standards for all who work within certain services. By way of an example, the Standards for Low Secure Services (in the UK) state that all practitioners in such settings should have supervision on at least a monthly basis (Quality Network for Forensic Mental Health Services, 2012). This can also be at the level of the profession whereby practitioners from specific groups may have registration or professional bodies who specify supervision requirements in order to be registered or licensed. As an example (again from the UK), guidance for clinical psychologists who are chartered with the British Psychological Society identifies supervision as a lifelong practice and provides requirements in relation to this (Division of Clinical Psychology, 2003). Similarly, the Social Work Task Force in England (2009) reviewed frontline social work practice on behalf of the Department of Health and the Department for Children, Schools and Families. This body made 15 recommendations for the improvement and reform of the profession that included a national requirement for supervision of social practitioners (recommendation 7). Subsequently, the Social Work Reform Board (Social Work Reform Board, 2012) produced 'Standards for employers of social practitioners in England and Supervision Framework' which provided details for the implementation of practice supervision. The reader is encouraged to identify any existing professional and service requirements to ensure they are meeting them and if they don't exist to ask why?

Service and workforce benefits – A forensic perspective

Having drawn on the general arguments made for supervision in other related contexts, we now turn to two examples of issues and factors drawn from forensic settings. Both issues are service level concerns relating to workforce safeguarding, however there are many others.

Practitioner health and trauma – the potential impact of inadequate supervision systems within organisations has been noted in relation to the effect on staff delivering offender programmes. In a case before the High Court in the UK, damages were awarded to a prison officer who delivered a Sexual Offender Programme without adequate preparation and appropriate supervision (Johnston, 2003). Although practice in relation to such offender treatment has changed significantly since then, this case offers an important context for supervision or, more importantly, its absence. More recently, Clarke (2012) has argued that practitioners in forensic settings could be regarded as working in a critical occupation (i.e. at risk of exposure to trauma). She bases this on the fact that practitioners are exposed to individuals who may be hostile and challenging with histories of abuse and of abusing. She argues that although forensic practitioners generally find their work satisfying and rewarding, it is important that they 'take the duty of care to ourselves seriously' (p. 234) to protect their professional effectiveness. Through her 'Model of Dynamic Adaptation', she argues that supervision (alongside 'energy management' and 'mindfulness') is important to developing and maintaining practitioner resilience. Specifically, supervision is important as it builds skills and competence, aids reflection and provides a forum to express and explore emotional reactions to work.

Interpersonal demand and boundaries – the interpersonal demands of working in forensic settings are manifold. First, there is the nature of the offending behaviour which commonly has an interpersonal element (e.g. offences directly against people or indirectly such as burglary or vandalism). For example, according to the Office for National Statistics (n.d.), of the 3.7 million crimes recorded by the police in the year ending September 2013; 3.1 million were classed as victim-based crimes. Of these, there were almost 60,000 sexual offences, slightly more robberies and 604,000 violent offences against the person. Second, there are the high rates of interpersonal difficulties and attachment problems experienced by those who commit offences. This is evidenced, at least in part, by the high rates of personality disorder diagnosis amongst prisoners (e.g. Singleton, Meltzer and Gatward, 1998); one diagnostic feature of which is interpersonal difficulties. Therefore, practitioners are likely, at least at times, to need to focus upon or address interpersonal issues with clients. To further complicate things, it is also possible that the relationship between the client and the practitioner may be based upon or resemble patterns found in previous offending (and may even be part of an Offence Paralleling Behaviour sequence – see Daffern, Jones and Shine, 2010) whilst at other times this may reflect a broader style of problematic relating. Therefore, as suggested by Mothersole (2000), supervision might be important for identifying and responding to such issues, particularly when they are subtle or outside the 'comfort zone' of the practitioner. Additionally, he suggests that there is a greater chance of being able to avoid or at least manage difficult or problematic processes if supervision is provided. Supervision within forensic practice also has a potentially critical role in risk management especially in relation to boundary problems in therapeutic settings. This issue is further discussed in Chapter 8.

What happens in practice supervision?

Practice supervision is sometimes cloaked in unnecessary mystery and intrigue and not only to those who have never experienced it! It is true that through discussion, supervision can lead to 'light-bulb' moments in which new ideas and possible future actions are generated, however the ways in which this happens can be understood through the processes which take place in supervision. Chapters 3 and 4 will discuss supervision types, content and models in much more detail, however some of what happens in supervision needs to be laid out here.

As the most elemental, supervision consists of five simple processes and functions as summarised in Box 1.1. The first process concerns the *discussion* of work (e.g. what is being done, what needs to be done) and the experience of working (e.g. what am I enjoying; what am I struggling with). Discussion can be seen as the medium through which supervision takes place. Discussion requires that the practitioner has the ability to recollect (e.g. what happened, what was done, what were the consequences), describe (e.g. the details of an action) and be aware (e.g. of thought processes, emotions). Discussion should incorporate successes, positive outcomes and what is working well alongside problems, concerns and difficulties. Although generally a purely verbal process, as we will see when we consider 'creative approaches in supervision' (see Special Topic 7) it may also use other media such as drawing. Second, *developing* ideas (possibilities of what could be useful) and new skills (e.g. through formal learning, role play) can be considered an essential purpose of supervision. Developing, in this context, may include learning something new, approaching a situation in a different way, reviewing goals or revisiting one's attitude or style in a given situation. Third, *discovering* important aspects of the work being undertaken (e.g. what has been working, what has been neglected or overlooked) and of the self (e.g. what are my strengths and weaknesses, what aspects of practice do I approach and which do I avoid) are additional functions of supervision. Such discoveries may give rise to identifying new learning that needs to take place or actions that need to be taken in the practice situation. Fourth, the process of *deciding* on what actions to take and how this will be done must be seen as one of the critical purposes of practice supervision – 'knowing is important but action is essential'. In this process it can be helpful to ensure that there is clarity about *why* the action is being taken, *what* is planned and what are the expected outcomes/consequences, *how* it will be done, *who* will be involved, *when* and *where* it will take place. Of course, it is possible that the decision made will be not to act further or not at this time. Finally the task of *documenting* the supervision needs to be undertaken. Who undertakes this and how this is done should be agreed as part of the supervision agreement (see Chapter 4 for more on this and record keeping), however it might include what was discussed, what has been learned, what actions are to be embarked on and how these will be evaluated.

> **BOX 1.1: What happens in practice supervision?**
> a) Supervisees **discuss** their work and experience of working.
> b) Supervisees **develop** ideas and new skills.
> c) Supervisees **discover** important features of their work and themselves.
> d) Supervisees **decide** on ways of dealing with problems/challenges.
> e) Supervisees **document** plans to evaluate.

As we will see in Chapter 7 where we consider supervisor skills and roles, implicit within practice supervision is the need to manage the dialectic of support and scrutiny.

Taking stock: where are you at?

We will round off this introduction with an opportunity for you to consider your needs, understanding and next steps ... or to think of it in another way, why you have this book and what you need to take from it. In order to help with this, Box 1.2 contains a very basic exercise I often use in training. The KEN exercise can be a useful (and brief) method to take stock. I would encourage you to undertake this task now but also to return to it periodically as a way to both document your development and to monitor your changing needs. However, it is important to be aware that one of the functions of supervision is to help you see what is not obvious to you and consider angles that you might not have thought of or that might not be readily available to you – i.e. we need others to help us consider ourselves and our practice. Thus it may be that your scores would differ from those of an outsider considering your practice and, as suggested in the instructions in Box 1.2, it may be of benefit to ask someone else (maybe your supervisor if you already have one) to also complete the task 'on you'.

> **BOX 1.2: Personal review: where are you at KEN?**
>
> The following exercise is designed to help you identify your **K**nowledge, **E**xperience and **N**eed in relation to supervision. Although this can be undertaken on your own (self reflection) you could discuss your responses in supervision and ask others to complete this task in relation to you.
>
> 1. Rate yourself on a scale 0-10 in relation to how much you **know** about supervision
>
>   (where 0 = nothing and 10 = extremely knowledgeable)
>
> 2. Rate yourself on a scale 0-10 in relation to how much **experience** you have of supervision (providing to others and/or receiving)
>
>   (where 0 = no prior experience and 10 = extremely experienced)
>
> 3. Provide a description/rationale for the scores you have given yourself
> 4. Identify what you might **need** in order to raise your score (if your score is below 8) or maintain your score if you have given yourself a 9 or a 10
> 5. Identify what you **need** to develop (knowledge, skill and/or experience) in relation to supervision
> 6. Draw up a practice supervision action plan based on your answers to questions 4 and 5

> N.B. Next time you return to this exercise start by reviewing your action plan: what you did, what worked, what didn't work, what's outstanding, what new needs has it generated. Then work through the steps as listed.

Conclusion

As outlined by Mothersole (2000) in his paper entitled 'Clinical supervision and forensic work', 'In any work with human beings, the cost of providing a less than optimal service is high in terms of subjective distress. Where offenders are concerned, the costs can be much greater, impacting on the clinician, the offender's victim, the offender, the responsible organisation and on society' (p. 47). However, as Todd and Freshwater (1999) state in discussing clinical supervision in nursing caution, 'The potential idealization of clinical supervision could lead to unrealistic expectations and subsequently feed a nursing culture that breeds disillusionment' (p. 1383). Therefore, practice supervision should be an integral part of forensic service delivery, however it is a tool to foster good practice rather than a panacea to address all difficulties.

References

Armstrong, A. and Foley, P. (2003) 'Foundations for a learning organization: organization learning mechanisms', *The Learning Organization* 10(2): 74–82.

Beddoe, L. and Davys, A. (2010) *Best Practice in Professional Supervision*, London: Jessica Kingsley Publishers.

Bégat, I. and Severinsson, E. (2006) 'Reflection on how clinical nursing supervision enhances nurses' experiences of well-being related to their psychosocial work environment', *Journal of Nursing Management* 14(8): 610–16.

Bernard, J. M. and Goodyear, R. K. (2014) *Fundamentals of Clinical Supervision* (5th edn), International Edition, London: Pearson.

Bond, M. and Holland, S. (2011) *Skills of Clinical Supervision for Nurses: A Practical Guide for Supervisees, Clinical Supervisors and Managers*, Buckingham: Open University Press.

Cheater, F. M. and Hale, C. (2001) 'An evaluation of a local clinical supervision scheme for practice nurses', *Journal of Clinical Nursing* 10(1): 119–31.

Clarke, J. (2012) 'The Resilient Practitioner', in J. Clarke and P. Wilson (eds), *Forensic Psychology in Practice: A Practitioners Handbook*, Basingstoke: Palgrave Macmillan, pp. 220–39.

Cutcliffe, J. R. (2005) 'From The guest editor–clinical supervision: a search for homogeneity or heterogeneity?', *Issues in Mental Health Nursing* 26(5): 471–3.

Daffern, M., Jones, L. and Shine, J. (2010) *Offence Paralleling Behaviour: A Case Formulation Approach to Offender Assessment and Intervention*, Oxford: Wiley.

Day, A. (2012) 'The nature of supervision in forensic psychology: some observations and recommendations', *The British Journal of Forensic Practice* 14(2): 116–23.

Department of Health (1993) *Vision for the Future*, London: HMSO.

Department of Health (1999) *A National Service Framework for Mental Health*, London: HMSO.

Division of Clinical Psychology (2003) *Policy Guidelines on Supervision in the practice of Clinical Psychology*, Leicester: British Psychological Society, pp. 1–4.

Ekstein, R. and Wallerstein, R. S. (1958) *The Teaching and Learning of Psychotherapy*, New York: Basic Books, Inc.

Fallon, P., Bluglass, R., Edwards, B. and Daniels, G. (1999) *Report of the Committee of Inquiry into the Personality Disorder Unit, Ashworth Special Hospital Volumes 1 and 2*, London: The Stationery Office.

Fleming, I. and Steen, L. (eds) (2004) *Supervison and Clinical Psychology: Theory, Practice and Perspectives*, London: Brunner-Routledge.

Fowler, J. (1996a) 'How to use models of clinical supervision in practice', *Nursing Standard (Royal College of Nursing (Great Britain): 1987)* 10(29): 42–7.

——(1996b) 'The organization of clinical supervision within the nursing profession: a review of the literature', *Journal of Advanced Nursing* 23(3): 471–8.

Freshwater, D., Walsh, L. and Storey, L. (2002) 'Prison health care: developing leadership through clinical supervision', *Nursing Management–Harrow* 8(9): 16–20.

GB Social Work Task Force (2009) *Building a safe, confident future*, retrieved from http://webarchive.nationalarchives.gov.uk/20130401151715/. www.education.gov.uk/publications/eOrderingDownload/01114-2009DOM-EN.pdf.

Hair, H. J. (2013) 'The purpose and duration of supervision, and the training and discipline of supervisors: what social workers say they need to provide effective services', *British Journal of Social Work* 43(8): 1562–88.

Harkness, D. and Hensley, H. (1991) 'Changing the focus of social work supervision: Effects on client satisfaction and generalized contentment', *Social Work* 36(6) 506–12.

Hyrkäs, K., Koivula, M. and Paunonen, M. (1999) 'Clinical supervision in nursing in the 1990s–current state of concepts, theory and research', *Journal of Nursing Management* 7(3): 177.

Johnston, P. (2003) '£150,000 award for prison officer on sex wing', *The Telegraph*, 1 April. Retrieved 17 April 2014, from www.telegraph.co.uk/news/uknews/1426270/150000-award-for-prison-officer-on-sex-wing.html.

Kilminster, S. M. and Jolly, B. C. (2000) 'Effective supervision in clinical practice settings: a literature review', *Medical Education* 34(10): 827–40.

Mid Staffordshire NHS Foundation Trust (2013) *Report of the Mid Staffordshire NHS Foundation Trust Public Inquiry*, London: The Stationery Office.

Milne, D. L. (2009) *Evidence-Based Clinical Supervision*, Oxford: John Wiley & Sons.

Mothersole, G. (2000) 'Clinical supervision and forensic work', *Journal of Sexual Aggression* 5(1): 45–58.

Office for National Statistics (n.d.) retrieved 17 April 2014, from www.ons.gov.uk.

Phillips, B. T. (2003) 'A four-level learning organisation benchmark implementation model', *The Learning Organization* 10(2): 98–105.

Quality Network for Forensic Mental Health Services (2012) available at www.rcpsych.ac.uk/pdf/qnfmhsStandards%20for%20Low%20Secure%20Services.pdf.

Report of the Mid-Staffordshire NHS Foundation Trust Public Inquiry (2013) available at www.midstaffspublicinquiry.com/report.

Rolfe, G. and Gardner, L. (2006) '"Do not ask who I am … ": confession, emancipation and (self)–management through reflection', *Journal of Nursing Management*, 14(8): 593–600.

Scaife, J. (2013) *Supervision in Clinical Practice*, Abingdon: Routledge.

Shanley, M. J. and Stevenson, C. (2006) 'Clinical supervision revisited', *Journal of Nursing Management* 14(8): 586–92.

Singleton, N., Meltzer, H. and Gatward, R. (1998) *Psychiatric Morbidity Among Prisoners*, London: The Stationery Office.

Social Work Reform Board (2012) *Standards for employers of social workers in England and supervision framework*, online available at: www.collegeofsocialwork.org/uploadedFiles/TheCollege/_CollegeLibrary/Reform_resources/standards-for-employers(em1).pdf. Retrieved 5 May 2014, from www.local.gov.uk/c/document_library/get_file?uuid=8a333d13-18aa1-44d3-925a-a07682b07190&groupId=10180.

The Victoria Climbie Inquiry (2003) *The Victoria Climbie Inquiry*, London: The Stationery Office.

Todd, G. and Freshwater, D. (1999) 'Reflective practice and guided discovery: clinical supervision', *British Journal of Nursing* 8: 1383–9.

White, E. and Winstanley, J. (2012) 'Clinical supervision for mental health professionals', *Social Work and Social Sciences Review* 14(3): 77–94.

Yegdich, T. (1998) 'How not to do clinical supervision in nursing', *Journal of Advanced Nursing* 28(1): 193–202.

2 The emerging evidence base for practice supervision

In order to understand and establish the possible value of practice supervision it is necessary to consider studies from those areas where researchers have attempted to evaluate and evidence the impacts of supervision. However, what would appear to be a straightforward task is anything but. The highly complex and multifaceted nature of supervision (Proctor, 2010) places high demands on any attempts to evaluate it (Winstanley and White, 2003). As a result, the evidence base for supervision is often difficult to interpret, limited and in many cases methodologically flawed. This chapter will consider how the usefulness and impact of supervision has been studied, what evidence exists and consider some possible avenues for future research. Some of the findings described will provide the reader with the evidence that informs some of the subsequent chapters in this book. However, it will also allow the reader an opportunity to consider for themselves how the evidence base supports or challenges their view of practice supervision. Further, it is hoped that an exploration of some of the existing evidence will encourage the reader to consider how research to enhance our understanding of supervision in forensic settings might be conducted. It may also inspire some to embark on this task! Although this chapter presents some of the emerging evidence in the field of supervision research, this is not intended to be a systematic review of any kind – rather a taster of the research that is available. Readers are therefore encouraged to use this chapter as a springboard from which to develop questions about supervision practice. Some of these may be answered by reading the work of others or may require new research to be carried out.

Much of the research conducted to date, whilst having ambition, has fallen into theoretical and methodological research traps. These include the failure to adopt a clear definition of supervision and the other factors being researched. For example, in some studies supervision is used as a very global term incorporating related yet distinct activities such as mentorship and preceptorship (Hyrkäs, Koivula and Paunonen, 1999). Research has also suffered from problems with measuring the concepts of interest (e.g. client outcomes), the sources of information used (much research is based on supervisee self-report through questionnaires or interviews) and with how the research has been carried out. By way of an example of this latter issue, one study in which significant changes to practice were found, was significantly compromised by the introduction of another intervention (an approach to care planning) alongside the supervision being provided (Berg, Hansson and Hallberg, 1994). Such issues can significantly limit the research, reducing the conclusions to 'an important change took place but we cannot be certain what role supervision played'.

There are many reasons to consider the knowledge and evidence base relating to practice supervision including gathering information about what to do (e.g. models to guide the supervision process) and assessing whether supervision works and, if so, in what ways. Later chapters will consider such aspects as models for supervision and learning; tasks in supervision; and supervisor qualities. In this chapter we will limit ourselves to evidence concerning the possible effects and impacts of supervision. It could be argued that there are three ways we can seek to evaluate supervision namely: (a) supervisee feedback (is it useful?); (b) service impact (is there a healthier, more capable workforce?); and (c) client/task outcomes (are outcomes improved?).

Criteria for evaluating supervision research

In order to be able to use the research that has taken place to inform our understanding and implementation of supervision, it is necessary to develop a way to evaluate the research itself. For general purposes, eight questions are proposed which might act as a starting point when reading research. These are presented in Box 2.1.

> **BOX 2.1: Key questions and considerations when evaluating practice supervision research**
>
> When reading supervision outcome or impact research it is important to have a framework to allow you to judge for yourself the quality of the research and what you should take from it. It is important to remember that not all research is the same – research varies with regard to its purpose (why it was done), the methodology (how it was done), rigour (how well it was done) and utility (its relevance to me). The eight questions below help consider these points. It can sometimes be helpful to work with others to undertake this evaluative process.
>
> 1. Who did and didn't take part?
>
> It is important to understand the nature of the group participating (e.g. profession; level of experience; purpose of supervision) and how many of the total possible participants took part. This may be 'uptake figures' (e.g. 90% of staff were receiving supervision) or figures relating to how many returned a questionnaire (e.g. 30% of the questionnaires were returned). It may also be relevant to know specific details such as the gender, age or race/cultural setting of the participants as these have been

shown to influence certain factors within supervision and thus could impact upon the transferability of outcomes.

2. What was the setting?

The nature of the setting is relevant especially when we are trying to determine how the findings are to be used/should be applied. Factors such as the workplace of those who took part (e.g. community vs. inpatient/custody; criminal justice vs. health) and the nature of the work they were engaged in (e.g. therapy; education; practical skills development) might be relevant.

3. What was the format of supervision?

This covers a range of 'facts' about the supervision encounter such as whether it was individual or group and if the latter what format the group took; where it took place (in or outside the workplace), for how long and how frequently. Research has indicated that some of these factors might form 'minimum standards' for research practice.

4. Who were the supervisors?

Here we need to consider the training and experience of the supervisors as well as their profession, as research indicates that these factors may be associated with how effective supervision is.

5. What outcomes were explored/measured and how?

Outcomes may take many forms including descriptions and perceptions of impact and outcomes measured in some way, e.g. through monitoring of client progress or changes in service delivery. Additionally, some outcome measures may be more useful or appropriate than others – for example Butterworth *et al.* (1999) found that some instruments were more sensitive to change than others.

6. What research approach was used?

This can be a complex question but it considers a number of related issues such as: was the research method appropriate, was the design adequate and have the analyses been used correctly. For quantitative supervision research, a framework such as that of Ellis *et al.* (1996) – discussed later in this chapter – might be helpful.

7. What were the key findings?

In order to make sense of the findings it is necessary to consider both what was found (the results section of a journal article) and how these are discussed (the discussion section). Of added interest is what the author of the paper notes as the limitations of the research and how they draw conclusions. It is important to pay attention to those findings that demonstrate no relationship between supervision and an outcome as this helps understand what supervision 'isn't' or 'doesn't do'.

8. How are these findings relevant to my setting/practice?

The final question is the transfer of the results from the study to the setting in which you work and how you engage in supervision. In some instances this 'translation' will be easy as the context (questions 1–4 above) may be very closely aligned to yours. However in other instances more work may be necessary to see what, if anything, this evidence has for you or your service.

It is worth noting at this point that the majority of the research on supervision is drawn from social care and clinical contexts and relates to 'clinical supervision'. This means that research relating to particular groups, such as psychological therapists, social practitioners and nurses, dominates the existing research base. However, in accordance with step eight of the key questions and considerations framework (Box 2.1), the suggestion here is that these studies contain information which is worthy of consideration in relation to practice supervision in forensic settings.

Supervision quality

In order to be able to evaluate the outcome of something – in this case practice supervision – we need to be able to make some basic assumptions concerning the quality of what is being provided. Although assessing the quality of supervision is difficult, it is unsurprising that the quality of supervision may be particularly important (Carpenter, Webb and Bostock, 2013) and perhaps more important than the quantity of supervision. This distinction is necessary because the latter may be easier and therefore more commonly assessed. In many of the studies considered in this chapter, formal tools are used to assess aspects of supervision, for example the Manchester Clinical Supervision Scale (MCSS) (e.g. Winstanley and White, 2011) used to assess the quality of supervision as perceived by the supervisee. It is outside the scope of this chapter to consider the measures themselves, however some examples are presented in Special Topic 8 later in the book. Further, interested readers should review the evidence base for measures used in supervision research for themselves.

Supervision quality is likely to be linked to a number of factors. For example, in relation to supervisors, the training they have received would be expected to impact on supervision quality, however the evidence for this is largely circumstantial at present. In one study, Hall-Lord, Theander and Athlin (2013) reported that those allocated to provide the most regular supervision to student nurses had generally received less training and were less experienced than those scheduled to provide less frequent 'specialist' supervision. The regular supervisors often failed to meet with the student for the length of time expected and were less likely to use evidence-based research within supervision than the other supervisors. The researchers concluded that supervisors may 'serve as a conserving factor' (p. 510) impacting negatively on the development and learning of the supervisee unless selection, training and supervisor development can enhance what supervisors provide. On the 'other side', supervisee factors might also be important, even basic demographic ones. For example, Hyrkäs, Appelqvist-Schmidlechner and Haataja (2006) found that the gender of the supervisee affected the ratings of supervision quality with females giving a more positive evaluation of supervision than males. Finally, a number of features of the supervision process itself have been associated with higher quality. For example, Edwards et al. (2005) found that the highest scores on the MCSS were associated with sessions that lasted longer than one hour and that took place at least monthly. Further, greater quality was associated with supervisees having chosen their supervisor and where sessions were away from work. No differences were noted between group and individual supervision. There were some important limitations with this study such as those who had little belief in supervision might not have had much commitment to supervision or avoided it. This limitation could have been easily overcome by asking participants – 'if you had the chance would you have engaged in more supervision or longer sessions?' etc. Finally, a study exploring the impact of supervision amongst several groups of nurses in Australia found that rather than the provision of supervision per se, it may be that 'only demonstrably efficacious CS [clinical supervision] may make a contribution to the maintenance/improvement of Supervisee's well-being (Proctor's Restorative domain); axiomatically, superficial supervision will not' (White and Winstanley, 2012, p. 89).

Practice supervision – the impact on clients/working practice

The 'holy grail' for supervision research is to be able to demonstrate a link between supervision activity and client/task outcomes. However, being able to show a direct relationship between a supervisory 'intervention' and a client outcome is very difficult (Kilminster and Jolly, 2000) and, as a consequence, research on the effects of supervision on clients/work practice is limited (e.g. Schoenwald et al., 2013). Despite this, a review of the literature by Kilminster and Jolly (2000), showed that supervision did have a positive effect on client outcome and that an absence of supervision could be detrimental to clients. Furthermore, Cheater and Hale (2001), in a study of supervision in a community health setting found that over half the staff who were engaged in supervision were able to give clear evidence of how supervision had impacted their practice. This included identifying things that the practitioner had changed in their direct client work. They also found significant 'indirect changes' such as an increase in practitioner confidence leading them to feel sufficiently empowered to make changes that they had previously felt unable to do (e.g. to a system of practice). Similar findings have been reported elsewhere. For example, a study based on a children's psychiatric ward (Hallberg, 1994) reported that nurses receiving supervision reported acting 'more consciously, and actively and were more goal-orientated' (p. 47) as a result of supervision. This study also noted some wider impacts of direct relevance to clients and practice. These included staff reporting that they were more able to support and constructively criticise each other which they believed had led to an increase in the quality of care provided.

Some might argue that changes to confidence are changes to the practitioner, that has no bearing on the client. However, if we consider the goal of practice supervision being to improve service provision, then a supervision process which 'shores-up' or develops a supervisee's self-esteem, confidence and emotional well-being/functioning which itself leads to a supervisee taking action that is beneficial to the client might be considered an important practice outcome. Manthorpe et al. (2013) found that the vast majority of social practitioners claimed that supervision helped them improve their practice and manage their workload; conversely those with less supervision reported having a less manageable workload, thought their job conditions were poorer and were less engaged with their work. However, they also note that informal supervision provided by other members of the team might also have a positive impact.

The findings reported above could be criticised for relying largely on practitioner reports of the impact of supervision. There have, however, been some direct evaluations of the impact of practice supervision on client outcomes. In the first example, Bradshaw, Butterworth and Mairs (2007) undertook a simple yet innovative study investigating the impact (on staff and clients) of workplace supervision. They found that training in a particular approach to treatment led to improved outcomes – for staff there was evidence of learning; for clients there was evidence of changes in symptoms and wellbeing. However, in the group who also received workplace supervision, some of the outcomes were enhanced. These included better outcomes on overall symptom reporting and in 'positive' symptoms associated with psychosis (e.g. voice hearing). The supervised students also showed greater learning/knowledge gains.

The second example is taken from social work, and investigated the impact of introducing a form of 'client-focused' supervision. In this generally well-designed study, Harkness and Hensley (1991) assigned four practitioners to receive supervision as usual during the first eight weeks and a client focused supervision during the next eight. Two individuals did not have the 'client-focused' supervision and became a comparison group. In all, 161 clients were seen by the six practitioners. They found that client-focused supervision produced improvements in (a) client satisfaction with goal attainment, (b) client satisfaction with practitioner helpfulness, and (c) client satisfaction with the level of partnership working between client and practitioner. The average effect size across practitioners and measures was .44.

Probably the best example of a study investigating the impact of supervision on client outcomes was conducted by Bambling et al. (2006) who investigated the impact of supervising therapists treating people with depression. They were principally interested in the impact of supervision on two features – the working alliance (i.e. the bond between the client and the practitioner coupled with agreements about goals and how to work towards these e.g. Bordin, 1983) and client outcomes (i.e. drop out, symptom reduction and client evaluation of treatment). In their study, two different forms of 'alliance focused supervision' were provided alongside a group receiving no supervision. The outcomes for the no supervision group were as good as previous studies of the treatment approach, however those in both forms of supervision had better alliance and client outcomes (i.e. lower drop out, lower end of treatment symptom rates and a more positive view of treatment). In all groups the adherence to the specific treatment model was no different. The authors identify some important limitations to their study, however they conclude that 'supervision can play a role in developing the working alliance and enhancing treatment outcome' (Bambling et al., 2006, p. 327).

Impact on staff

There is more research in relation to the impact of supervision on staff as an outcome. In this section we will look at three impacts: general; workplace well-being; and boundaries, whilst the impact on learning and training is presented in Chapter 5. In their meta-analysis of supervision research, Mor Barak and colleagues (Mor Barak et al., 2009), propose a conceptual model of the impacts of supervision on practitioners. In this model, they outline three supervision dimensions and highlight the factors that should increase as a result of supervision (e.g. practitioner effectiveness) and those which should decrease (e.g. burnout). They found that effective supervision was associated with positive practitioner outcomes such as well-being, job satisfaction and the practitioner's sense of competence and accomplishment. Effective supervision was also found to mitigate against negative outcomes for the practitioner such as depression, burnout and wishing to leave their job. In particular, they found that although all three aspects of supervision in their model were moderately associated with the desired outcomes, task-assistance (i.e. supporting supervisees in their learning and development) had the strongest link.

General impact on staff

Studies have reported the many ways in which supervision has a general impact on staff. Staff have reported that supervision provides them with a sense of feeling valued and appreciated (Scanlon and Weir, 1997) whilst a review of the supervision literature by Butterworth et al. (2008) noted that some of the most important advantages of supervision reported by study participants are those that are restorative (i.e. support and emotional wellbeing focused). In a study within a forensic mental health setting, almost three-quarters of the staff surveyed believed that supervision helped them work effectively with the main function of supervision again being the restorative function (Long et al., 2013).

In another study, Carpenter et al. (2013) reviewed studies concerning child welfare services. They reported that supervision had a positive impact on supervisees, for example in relation to job satisfaction; empowerment; ability to make decisions; and intention to stay. It was also reported to impact on the organisation, for example practitioners considering their work to be more manageable; practitioners staying in their jobs; and practitioners feeling valued by the organisation. Although they concluded that the evidence base for supervision in child welfare is weak, they argue that 'effective supervision is an important element of an organization's duty of care to its employees, and to the consumers it serves' (p. 1851). In their systematic review of the literature Wheeler and Richards (2007) found that supervision enhanced supervisee self-awareness and helped to develop skill.

A Swedish study of district nurses and mental health care practitioners noted a number of important practice differences between those being supervised and those not (Magnusson, Lützén and Severinsson, 2002). Those not being supervised were found to be more insecure in their role when they needed to make decisions whilst those in the supervised group (60 per cent of the staff group) were more secure when they were dealing with the patient and more ready to wait for patient's to participate in their care. Interestingly, those practitioners receiving supervision reported that they felt like an intruder when they were in a person's home even though they were more likely to report an equal relationship. Further, those in the supervised group were more likely to visit patients in pairs which they reported as being used to promote a sense of patient security.

Work-place wellbeing

Research into the impact of supervision on work-place wellbeing, stress, burnout and job satisfaction probably makes up the largest proportion of supervision outcome research. Despite this volume, there are some serious limitations with much of this research – the most common of which is the use of study designs which test the relationship between supervision and these factors at a single time point (either through correlation studies or by comparing groups made up from those who meet a certain supervision experience threshold and a group who don't). This means that (a) whilst people receiving more supervision might also report X or Y outcome we cannot know that supervision is the cause, and (b) unless the study is very well designed (and the researchers cautious in their analyses) it is possible to have spurious findings which reflect chance rather than fact.

Studies of nurses and other mental health professionals have shown that practice supervision can positively impact upon reported well-being and the practitioner's satisfaction with their psychosocial work environment (Bégat, Ellefsen and Severinsson, 2005). Further, efficient supervision has been linked to lower burnout whilst in the same study ineffective supervision was related to job dissatisfaction (Hyrkäs, 2005). However, studies that investigate multiple factors and conduct numerous analyses can result in a highly complex study that can be difficult to disentangle because of support for some expected associations and a lack of evidence for others.

Burnout and job-satisfaction: Burnout (or compassion fatigue) can be viewed as the negative reaction to stress which can arise through the exhaustion of resources (both physical and mental). This can be caused by prolonged and unsuccessful attempts to achieve certain outcomes or through vicarious trauma (e.g. Azar, 2000). Several studies have linked supervision with lower burnout and higher job-satisfaction than those who are not receiving supervision. For example, in a study on a ward for patients with dementia, Berg *et al.* (1994) found that the introduction of group supervision was associated with an increase in 'creativity and innovation' whilst tedium and burnout decreased significantly over the one-year study period. Whilst this is very encouraging, the study had a serious weakness in that supervision was introduced in conjunction with a new approach to care planning. Thus it is impossible to know what contribution was made by supervision to the outcomes over and above the care planning changes also introduced. Other studies have tried to avoid such confounding factors. For example, in a study of community mental health nurses, Edwards *et al.* (2006) found that respondents with a higher score on the MCSS reported lower burnout and especially less emotional exhaustion. They also found that those with lower burnout scores reported being more able to discuss sensitive and confidential issues in supervision. Similar findings in relation to burnout have been reported through a large-scale survey in Finland by Hyrkäs *et al.* (2006), however in this particular study, they also found positive associations between supervision and job satisfaction. Evidence for lower levels of emotional exhaustion being associated with higher quality supervision has also been shown in a study of substance abuse counsellors (Knudsen, Roman and Abraham, 2013). These authors also found that individuals who reported a more positive relationship with their supervisor reported higher levels of occupational commitment and organisational commitment. From this, they suggest that these two factors may therefore mediate the link between supervision and exhaustion, i.e. supervision increases occupational and organisational commitment which in turn leads to the experience of less exhaustion.

It is worth bearing in mind, however, that some settings may be more inherently stressful than others. For example, Butterworth *et al.* (1999) reported that staff working in community settings found their work more emotionally draining than their hospital colleagues although they reported less depersonalisation (a cynical and detached response). Therefore, it is worth considering the possibility of 'setting effects' when you intend to transfer findings from one setting to another. On a similar note, features of the supervisee/practitioner might also be a factor in the experience of stress and burnout. In a supervision study concerning the impact of supervision on burn-out and job satisfaction, Hyrkäs et al. (2006) found that those with 10+ years of experience were less likely to report exhaustion but more likely to report depersonalisation compared with less experienced colleagues.

Trauma: As we saw in Chapter 1, researchers and authors have made a case for supervision in relation to preventing practitioner trauma. As noted by Pross (2006), collegial and external supervision is important for those working with clients who have experienced trauma, however they argue that this should not be in place of training and 'self-awareness'. Despite this argument, in a study investigating a range of factors which might reduce trauma experience amongst practitioners, Bober and Regehr (2006) found no link between supervision, self-care (or leisure activity) and trauma symptoms amongst staff. However, they did find that the number of hours per week spent working with traumatised people was associated with practitioner trauma and that those who believed in self-care were more likely to engage in supervision. As with many studies, the data was self-report and collected at a single time point and no detail was provided about the nature and quality of the supervision being received. Nevertheless, this research highlights another important factor for research – establishing what other factors might account for findings and that need to be accounted for (e.g. amount of exposure to trauma, quality of supervision, length of experience).

Effects on supervisors

A number of studies have found positive associations for those who provide supervision to others. For example, Hyrkäs (2005) found that acting as a supervisor to others resulted in higher job satisfaction and lower burnout scores when compared to other practitioners who did not undertake this role. Similarly, a review of the literature by Butterworth *et al.* (2008) revealed a number of positive effects on supervisors including improvements to their practice and increases in their confidence.

Researching practice supervision – lessons from the literature

Even though there is a wealth of material published in the field of supervision, there remain many opportunities for undertaking good quality research in order to advance knowledge and understanding in this area. Whatever one wishes to investigate in practice supervision, it is clear that the lessons from research conducted to date, such as those described above, should be borne in mind. Additionally, a number of authors and researchers have provided detailed observations and clear guidelines and suggestions for those wishing to engage in research in this area.

Several authors have identified limitations with the existing research base and barriers to supervision research. For example, Goodyear and Bernard (1998), in their review of the supervision literature, identified a range of factors which have hampered or negatively impacted on supervision research. These included (1) the lack of theory to drive research (and the related issue of limited testing of the theories and models already in existence); (2) the lack of focus on efficacy research (i.e. outcomes for clients); (3) the focus on supervisee satisfaction; (4) the absence of manualisation of supervision; and (5) problems of randomising staff to supervision/no supervision. Research undertaken since they wrote this paper has addressed some of these points through careful research design, whilst others (such as manualising supervision) need careful practical and conceptual consideration. Goodyear and Bernard (1998) also identify a range of factors that might be important to manage or control when undertaking supervision research. These include individual differences within the supervisee and supervisor such as personal style, stage of development, and ethnicity as well as factors relating to the supervision context including the supervisory relationship itself. Specific issues have also been raised. For example, in their review of the literature, Bogo and McKnight (2006) note that supervision research is often characterised by relatively small convenience samples (i.e. those easy to access) and that the robust measurement of client outcomes needs to become a focus for investigation.

Other authors have considered how supervision effectiveness might be measured and have advocated a pluralist approach to supervision research. For example, in their work to identify competencies in psychology supervision, Falender et al. state that:

> demonstration of effectiveness should take into consideration the impact, both immediate and long term, on the supervisee, clients ... supervisory relationships and processes, and the outcomes ... A range of research procedures should be employed, including, ... self-report, experimental, single subject repeated measures, qualitative, ... to assess the multiple dimensions of the supervision process.
>
> (2004, p. 775)

Finally, authors such as Ellis, Ladany, Krengel and Schult (1996) and Freitas (2002) have produced detailed reviews of the research undertaken in relation to supervision in order to identify the methodological weaknesses and limitations within them and to suggest ways of conducting rigorous supervision research. Anyone planning to undertake research in the field of supervision should consult these methodological critiques before embarking on such research. For example, Ellis et al. (1996) present a comprehensive review of quantitative supervision research and illustrate many of the failings and shortcomings that are present; thus they highlight the pitfalls and errors to which the researcher should be alert. These critiques give rise to a number of fundamental questions to be asked by the researcher such as 'Are we able to assess/measure the things we need to'; 'Do we have enough people in the study to draw conclusions';

'Are we using an appropriate research design'; and 'Do we need to use multiple measures (and perhaps multiple methods) to answer this question'.

Future research in forensic supervision

This introductory review of aspects of the evidence base for supervision allows a number of observations to be made and a range of suggestions for research of practice supervision in forensic settings to be identified. There is now some evidence for the positive effects of supervision, however there is still huge scope for work in this area. Practice supervision appears to be associated with a number of benefits to the practitioner such as lower burnout and greater job satisfaction. There is also small but encouraging evidence concerning the impact of supervision on practice and on the clients that are served by those practitioners receiving supervision. However, it is true that the need and scope for research in this area, especially in forensic settings, is extensive. As a result of the complexity and the methodological difficulties facing research in this field, there are few existing studies that could (or should) be simply replicated within a forensic setting. Some of the more descriptive research, abundant in other areas of supervision research, could be undertaken, however this should not be at the expense of research concerning the impact and effects of practice supervision. There are several areas which are of particular interest or where research could be particularly illuminating; the following paragraphs aim to outline some of these.

Researching the influence of the supervisee and supervisor

There are many factors relating to the supervisor and or supervisee which could impact upon supervision and its outcomes. For example, Goodyear and Bernard (1998) suggest that it would be informative to consider developing supervisee profiles in order to help understand 'effective supervision pairings' and perhaps to elucidate 'what works for whom'. In the same vein, Davies, Salmon and MacDonald (2000) suggest that research should be conducted into the impact of different supervisee and supervisor styles, prior experience and learning, personality and preferred models and frameworks in supervision. It may be that intentionally matching supervisee and supervisor has some merit, based, for example, on need, personality or style. Morgan and Sprenkle (2007) have argued that some models may be especially well matched to some supervisors (or supervisor–supervisee pairings) and that this might be important for effectiveness. Indeed, Nick Black has made a similar argument when highlighting the need for 'observational studies' in health care effectiveness research. He notes that where effectiveness may depend on active participation this will be affected by individual's beliefs and preferences (Black, 1996). This is likely to be the case in supervision and thus this should be investigated. It may be that idiographic approaches such as described for other interventions in forensic settings (Davies, 2010; Davies and Sheldon, 2012; Davies, Howells and Jones,

2007) and in relation to supervision (Milne, Reiser and Cliffe, 2012) are particularly relevant for this.

Practical factors may also be of interest to researchers and should certainly be explicitly considered in forensic supervision research. For example, research has already indicated that sessions of about an hour and at least monthly are associated with greater benefit than those with lower thresholds. Further, timing of supervision (e.g. when it occurs in relation to the piece of work it relates to) may be an important factor (Wheeler and Richards, 2007); this may be particularly relevant in relation to the supervision of individual or group treatments.

Researching the impact of supervision on the supervisee

There are many studies that have investigated links between supervision and other factors such as burnout and supervisee skills acquisition. There is scope for testing the applicability of some of these findings in forensic settings, however there is also scope for undertaking a range of simple yet potentially informative studies to augment such 'replications'. These might include: (a) examining the views of supervisors in relation to who they believe they work best with; (b) which (if any) approaches and frameworks they use explicitly to inform their supervision; (c) the supervisee's awareness of the models and processes being used in supervision; and (d) supervisee reports of how supervision has influenced their practice.

Researching the impact of supervision on client outcomes

Many authors remind us of the need to remain focused on the central purpose of supervision – the work being carried out by the supervisee. In a forensic setting, Day (2012) highlights the need to research whether supervision provides better client outcomes. This has also been identified more generally, for example Mor Barak et al. (2009) identifies the need for research to be undertaken to consider how the impact of supervision on practitioners might be beneficial to clients. A specific question such as 'Does the attainment of a specific skill affect measured client outcomes?' (Lambert and Hawkins, 2001) presents one approach to this. Alternatively, a detailed study of changes to supervisee attitudes, behaviour and practice as revealed in supervision sessions might be another. The qualitative study protocol concerning the impact of supervision on practice amongst health professionals working in oncology described by Dilworth et al. (2013) provides one way in which the latter might be undertaken. Although robust approaches to researching client and task outcomes have yet to be established (Kilminster and Jolly, 2000), the study by Bambling et al. (2006) offers one model for attempting this. How this might be adapted for use in a prison setting, for example, needs careful thought. Bambling et al. (2006) also highlight a number of variations on their study such as testing the effect of different models of supervision on client outcomes. Investigating the impact of manualised supervision on practice outcomes (Goodyear and Bernard,

1998) could allow for some control over what happens in practice supervision. The studies by Bambling *et al.* (2006) and Milne *et al.* (2012) could be seen to have adopted (at least in part) this type of approach.

An interesting proposition is offered by Lambert and Hawkins (2001) who articulate a method for using client outcome feedback and progress to inform supervision. This detailed approach is a logical extension of their previous work where they used a simple colour-coded system to provide feedback to therapists on the progress of their clients. Such research would help place client outcomes at the heart of supervision practice and is certainly warranted within a forensic supervision context.

Researching supervision models and approaches

Carpenter *et al.* (2013) argue that different outcomes might be expected from different models and approaches to supervision and thus research should be undertaken to investigate this. In addition, they suggest that examining the comparative effectiveness of different formats of supervision (e.g. individual and group) on the supervisee and their outcomes is a worthy undertaking. They also argue, as do others such as Jones (2006), for engaging in research into the process of supervision (i.e. what happens in supervision). For example, Jones notes that we know little about what makes supervision work and importantly what its benefits and risks might be, even though Butterworth *et al.* (2008) contend that there is little evidence that supervision is harmful or negative (although others have suggested that it could be harmful – see Chapter 6). Clearly, the links between process and client outcome would be the natural extension of this. In addition, research concerning what occurs within supervision such as whether supervision is experienced as good (Worthen and McNeill, 1996) or contains inadequate or harmful elements (Ellis *et al.*, 2014) is warranted.

Some of the models and frameworks detailed in Chapter 4 could readily lend themselves to closer examination and research. For example, the common-factors approach developed by Morgan and Sprenkle (2007) could be subjected to investigation through the analysis of moments from individual supervision sessions. Similarly, the interactional map presented by O'Donoghue (2014) could be researched in many ways. One simple question would be 'can this model be evidenced within forensic practice supervision?'.

Approaches to researching practice supervision

One fundamental principle in research is that the method is matched to the question being asked (Davies, Sheldon and Howells, 2012). It is beyond the scope of this chapter to discuss this in depth, however in addition to the widely used qualitative and quantitative approaches, some have argued (and demonstrated) that detailed study of individual cases could be relevant to practice supervision research. For example, Milne *et al.* (2012) used a 'single case' design in their detailed investigation of practice supervision approaches. In a forensic context, Mothersole (2000) has also suggested that researchers may wish to consider using single-case approaches in order to investigate the impact of supervision on the work environment and on client-practitioner alliance. These approaches have been argued for in relation to other aspects of forensic practice (Davies et al., 2007; Davies, Jones and Howells, 2010). Another approach is to embed research and evaluation as part of the design and delivery of practice supervision. This could enable data to be collected from 'real world supervision' over time, gathering client outcome data routinely and recording information about such things as the nature, type and quality of supervision. This would help to address questions such as those identified by Butterworth et al. (2008) concerning the impact of supervision on staff and their outcomes.

In his detailed review of ten published supervision research studies, Freitas (2002) comments on the range of methods used. He suggests that future supervision researchers would gain from learning from the strengths and weaknesses of these and he makes a number of suggestions geared particularly to quantitative approaches to research. However, he also makes a number of suggestions for research, e.g. testing the impact of supervision immediately before the practitioner engages in the activity (e.g. client session, teaching session); research involving creative approaches (such as the use of technology in supervision); and the impact of combining administrative and practice supervision. Finally, he suggests trying to standardise as many elements in the research study (e.g. supervisees at similar levels of experience) as possible.

Conclusion

As we have seen, undertaking supervision research is highly complex, however the evidence base for supervision is developing. There is now emerging evidence concerning the impact of supervision on the practitioner, the work they do (client outcomes, task completion) and the service. It remains the case that research and audit of the practice of supervision with a forensic setting needs to be encouraged (Davies et al., 2000) and further, that there are many opportunities for research on supervision especially in the forensic arena. As noted by Freitas (2002), there is reason to be hopeful with regard to future supervision research as there is growing interest; the problems identified with past research can be addressed; and the number of tools available for assessing aspects of supervision and conducting analyses are expanding. Would-be researchers should consult the literature to help develop a sound research design and, above all, should pursue the opportunities to help develop our understanding of practice supervision in forensic contexts.

References

Azar, S. T. (2000) 'Preventing burnout in professionals and paraprofessionals who work with child abuse and neglect cases: a cognitive behavioral approach to supervision', *Journal of Clinical Psychology* 56(5): 643–63.

Bambling, M., King, R., Raue, P., Schweitzer, R. and Lambert, W. (2006) 'Clinical supervision: its influence on client-rated working alliance and client symptom reduction in the brief treatment of major depression', *Psychotherapy Research* 16(3): 317–31.

Berg, A., Hansson, U. W. and Hallberg, I. R. (1994) 'Nurses' creativity, tedium and burn-out during 1 year of clinical supervision and implementation of individually planned nursing care: comparisons between a ward for severely demented patients and a similar control ward', *Journal of Advanced Nursing* 20(4): 742–9.

Bégat, I., Ellefsen, B. and Severinsson, E. (2005) 'Nurses' satisfaction with their work environment and the outcomes of clinical nursing supervision on nurses' experiences of well-being – a Norwegian study', *Journal of Nursing Management* 13(3): 221–30.

Black, N. (1996) 'Why we need observational studies to evaluate the effectiveness of health care', *BMJ: British Medical Journal* 312(7040): 1215.

Bober, T. and Regehr, C. (2006) 'Strategies for reducing secondary or vicarious trauma: do they work?', *Brief Treatment and Crisis Intervention* 6(1): 1–9.

Bogo, M. and McKnight, K. (2006) 'Clinical supervision in social work: a review of the research literature', *The Clinical Supervisor* 24(1–2): 49–67.

Bordin, E. S. (1983) 'A working alliance based model of supervision', *The Counseling Psychologist* 11(1): 35–42.

Bradshaw, T., Butterworth, A. and Mairs, H. (2007) 'Does structured clinical supervision during psychosocial intervention education enhance outcome for mental health nurses and the service users they work with?', *Journal of Psychiatric and Mental Health Nursing* 14(1): 4–12.

Butterworth, T., Bell, L., Jackson, C. and Pajnkihar, M. (2008) 'Wicked spell or magic bullet? A review of the clinical supervision literature 2001–7', *Nurse Education Today* 28(3): 264–72.

Butterworth, T., Carson, J., Jeacock, J., White, E. and Clements, A. (1999) 'Stress, coping, burnout and job satisfaction in British nurses: findings from the clinical supervision evaluation project', *Stress Medicine* 15(1): 27–33.

Carpenter, J., Webb, C. M. and Bostock, L. (2013) 'The surprisingly weak evidence base for supervision: findings from a systematic review of research in child welfare practice (2000–2012)', *Children and Youth Services Review* 35(11): 1843–53.

Cheater, F. M. and Hale, C. (2001) 'An evaluation of a local clinical supervision scheme for practice nurses', *Journal of Clinical Nursing* 10(1): 119–31.

Davies, J. (2010) 'An individual approach to assessing change', in N. Gordon and P. Willmot (eds), *Working Positively With Personality Disorder in Secure Settings: A Practitioner's Perspective*, Oxford: Wiley & Sons.

Davies, J. and Sheldon, K. (2012) 'Single case methodologies', in K. Sheldon, J. Davies and K. Howells (eds), *Research in Practice for Forensic Professionals*, Abingdon: Routledge.

Davies, J., Howells, K. and Jones, L. (2007) 'Evaluating innovative treatments in forensic mental health: a role for single case methodology?', *Journal of Forensic Psychiatry & Psychology* 18(3): 353–67.

Davies, J., Jones, L. and Howells, K. (2010) 'Evaluating individual change', in M. Daffern, L. Jones and J. Shine (eds), *Offence Paralleling Behaviour: A Case Formulation Approach to Offender Assessment and Intervention*, Oxford: Wiley & Sons.

Davies, J., Salmon, A. and MacDonald, F. (2000) 'Supervision: what works for whom?', *Clinical Psychology Forum* 146: 17–20.

Davies, J., Sheldon, K. and Howells, K. (2012) 'Conducting research in forensic settings', in K. Sheldon, J. Davies, and K. Howells (eds), *Research in Practice for Forensic Professionals*, Abingdon: Routledge, pp. 3–15.

Day, A. (2012) 'The nature of supervision in forensic psychology: some observations and recommendations', *The British Journal of Forensic Practice* 14(2): 116–23.

Dilworth, S., Higgins, I., Parker, V., Kelly, B. and Turner, J. (2013) 'Examining clinical supervision as a mechanism for changes in practice: a research protocol', *Journal of Advanced Nursing* 70(2): 421–30.

Edwards, D., Burnard, P., Hannigan, B., Cooper, L., Adams, J., Juggessur, T., et al. (2006) 'Clinical supervision and burnout: the influence of clinical supervision for community mental health nurses', *Journal of Clinical Nursing* 15(8): 1007–15.

Edwards, D., Cooper, L., Burnard, P., Hannigan, B., Adams, J., Fothergill, A. and Coyle, D. (2005) 'Factors influencing the effectiveness of clinical supervision', *Journal of Psychiatric and Mental Health Nursing* 12(4): 405–14.

Ellis, M. V., Berger, L., Hanus, A. E., Ayala, E. E., Swords, B. A. and Siembor, M. (2014) 'Inadequate and harmful clinical supervision: testing a revised framework and assessing occurrence', *The Counseling Psychologist* 42(4): 434–72.

Ellis, M. V., Ladany, N., Krengel, M. and Schult, D. (1996) 'Clinical supervision research from 1981 to 1993: a methodological critique', *Journal of Counseling Psychology* 43(1): 35.

Falender, C. A., Cornish, J. A. E., Goodyear, R., Hatcher, R., Kaslow, N. J., Leventhal, G., et al. (2004) 'Defining competencies in psychology supervision: a consensus statement', *Journal of Clinical Psychology* 60(7): 771–85.

Freitas, G. J. (2002) 'The impact of psychotherapy supervision on client outcome: A critical examination of 2 decades of research', *Psychotherapy: Theory, Research, Practice, Training* 39(4): 354–67.

Goodyear, R. K. and Bernard, J. M. (1998) 'Clinical supervision: lessons from the literature', *Counselor Education and Supervision* 38(1): 6–22.

Hall-Lord, M. L., Theander, K. and Athlin, E. (2013) 'A clinical supervision model in bachelor nursing education – purpose, content and evaluation', *Nurse Education in Practice* 13(6): 506–11.

Hallberg, I. R. (1994) 'Systematic clinical supervision in a child psychiatric ward: satisfaction with nursing care, tedium, burnout, and the nurses' own report on the effects of it', *Archives of Psychiatric Nursing* 8(1): 44–52.

Harkness, D. and Hensley, H. (1991) 'Changing the focus of social work supervision: effects on client satisfaction and generalized contentment', *Social Work* 36(6): 506–12.

Hyrkäs, K. (2005) 'Clinical supervision, burnout, and job satisfaction among mental health and psychiatric nurses in Finland', *Issues in Mental Health Nursing* 26(5): 531–56.

Hyrkäs, K., Appelqvist-Schmidlechner, K. and Haataja, R. (2006) 'Efficacy of clinical supervision: influence on job satisfaction, burnout and quality of care', *Journal of Advanced Nursing* 55(4): 521–35.

Hyrkäs, K., Koivula, M. and Paunonen, M. (1999) 'Clinical supervision in nursing in the 1990s – current state of concepts, theory and research', *Journal of Nursing Management* 7(3): 177.

Jones, A. (2006) 'Clinical supervision: what do we know and what do we need to know? A review and commentary', *Journal of Nursing Management* 14(8): 577–85.

Kilminster, S. M. and Jolly, B. C. (2000) 'Effective supervision in clinical practice settings: a literature review', *Medical Education* 34(10): 827–40.

Knudsen, H. K., Roman, P. M. and Abraham, A. J. (2013) 'Quality of clinical supervision and counselor emotional exhaustion: the potential mediating roles of organizational and occupational commitment', *Journal of Substance Abuse Treatment* 44(5): 528–33.

Lambert, M. J. and Hawkins, E. J. (2001) 'Using information about patient progress in supervision: are outcomes enhanced?', *Australian Psychologist* 36(2): 131–8.

Long, C. G., Harding, S., Payne, K. and Collins, L. (2013) 'Nursing and health-care assistant experience of supervision in a medium secure psychiatric service for women: implications for service development', *Journal of Psychiatric and Mental Health Nursing* 21(2): 154–62.

Magnusson, A., Lützén, K. and Severinsson, E. (2002) 'The influence of clinical supervision on ethical issues in home care of people with mental illness in Sweden', *Journal of Nursing Management* 10(1): 37–45.

Manthorpe, J., Moriarty, J., Hussein, S., Stevens, M. and Sharpe, E. (2013) 'Content and purpose of supervision in social work practice in England: views of newly qualified social workers, managers and directors', *British Journal of Social Work*, available at http://bjsw.oxfordjournals.org/content/early/2013/06/03/bjsw.bct102.abstract.

Milne, D. L., Reiser, R. P. and Cliffe, T. (2012) 'An N = 1 evaluation of enhanced CBT supervision', *Behavioural and Cognitive Psychotherapy* 41(2): 210–20.

Mor Barak, M. E., Travis, D. J., Pyun, H. and Xie, B. (2009) 'The impact of supervision on worker outcomes: a meta–analysis', *Social Service Review* 83(1): 3–32.

Morgan, M. M. and Sprenkle, D. H. (2007) 'Toward a common-factors approach to supervision', *Journal of Marital and Family Therapy* 33(1): 1–17.

Mothersole, G. (2000) 'Clinical supervision and forensic work', *Journal of Sexual Aggression* 5(1): 45–58.

O'Donoghue, K. B. (2014) 'Towards an interactional map of the supervision session: an exploration of supervisees and supervisors experiences', *Practice* 26(1): 53–70.

Proctor, B. (2010) 'Review: a randomised controlled trial of clinical supervision: selected findings from a novel Australian attempt to establish the evidence base for causal relationships with quality of care and patient outcomes, as an informed contribution to mental health nursing practice development', *Journal of Research in Nursing* 15(2): 169–72.

Pross, C. (2006) 'Burnout, vicarious traumatization and its prevention', *Torture* 16(1): 1–9.

Scanlon, C. and Weir, W. S. (1997) 'Learning from practice? Mental health nurses' perceptions and experiences of clinical supervision', *Journal of Advanced Nursing*, 26(2): 295–303.

Schoenwald, S. K., Mehta, T. G., Frazier, S. L. and Shernoff, E. S. (2013) 'Clinical supervision in effectiveness and implementation research', *Clinical Psychology: Science and Practice* 20(1): 44–59.

Wheeler, S. and Richards, K. (2007) 'The impact of clinical supervision on counsellors and therapists, their practice and their clients. A systematic review of the literature', *Counselling and Psychotherapy Research* 7(1): 54–65.

White, E. and Winstanley, J. (2012) 'Clinical supervision for mental health professionals', *Social Work and Social Sciences Review* 14(3): 77–94.

Winstanley, J. and White, E. (2003) 'Clinical supervision: models, measures and best practice', *Nurse Researcher* 10(4): 7–38.

——(2011) 'The MCSS-26©: revision of the Manchester Clinical Supervision Scale© using the Rasch Measurement Model', *Journal of Nursing Measurement* 19(3): 160–78.

Worthen, V. and McNeill, B. W. (1996) 'A phenomenological investigation of "good" supervision events', *Journal of Counseling Psychology* 43(1): 25.

3 Supervision types, forms and tasks

As was outlined in Chapter 1, supervision in its broadest sense is a process in which supervisees can explore, think about and develop their practice with the ultimate goal of enhancing the effectiveness of their work and therefore the outcomes for the client (e.g. Jones, 2006). The purpose of this chapter is to explore the key features associated with supervision and the ways in which it can be delivered. Most of the tasks discussed in this chapter and the models in the next, are relevant to supervision regardless of the form it takes and therefore are important and relevant for all practice supervision.

An introduction to types and forms

There are a range of supervision types (i.e. the nature of the supervisee-supervisor relationship and the reason for supervision taking place) and two broad forms: one-to-one (individual supervision) and group supervision. Thus supervision can be described using these two parameters, for example a group-based peer supervision or individual training supervision. In addition, supervision may be provided from within the service or organisation (*internal*), or by someone who is *external*. Some of the considerations for external supervision such as governance arrangements are noted by Hair (2013).

Types of supervision

In this section we will consider some of the most common types of practice supervision, namely: training supervision; specialist supervision; professional supervision and peer supervision. The first three can generally be conceptualised as forms of 'expert' supervision. Although there are some overlaps between these types, for simplicity they are treated as distinct for our discussion. The main reason for considering these distinctions is to enable the participants (i.e. the supervisee and supervisor) to consider a number of factors relevant to establishing their supervisory relationship and the supervision purpose. It also helps to highlight other factors such as the interaction between power and responsibility. Figure 3.1 provides a simple representation of how these different forms might be conceptualised in relation to power and responsibility. This will be discussed further as we consider each of the supervision types. In broad terms, training supervision, the supervision of support staff and specialist

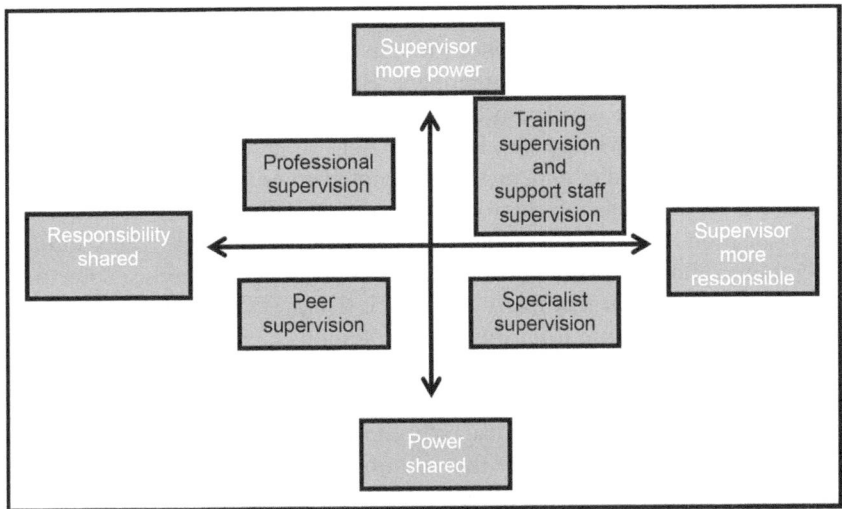

Figure 3.1 Representation of power and responsibility in different types of supervision

supervision (with their focus on acquiring new skills and knowledge, and/or working under the direction of the supervisor) bias these towards the supervisor having greater responsibility than the supervisee. In peer and professional supervision this responsibility is shared. In relation to power, training, support staff and professional supervision can be seen to locate more power with the supervisor whilst in peer and specialist supervision power is more equal. It is important to emphasise that power is relative and that in all relationships, supervisees can be empowered (Cutcliffe and Proctor, 1998) through taking control of processes within supervision such as the agenda, providing feedback and active participation.

Training supervision: this approach to supervision is widely used in practitioner development. In this form of supervision, the supervisee often works 'on behalf of' the supervisor in that they are practising on the basis of the supervisor's professional registration or licence. This form of supervision contains many complexities such as the multiple relationships and 'vested interests' in relation to the supervision provided. Thus the supervisor and supervisee will usually have lines of accountability to a professional training provider (e.g. a university) and the supervisor also has accountability for the work of the supervisee (e.g. accountability to the client). This form of supervision requires that the supervisor be competent in a multitude of areas such as supervision practice, skills training, personal development and competency evaluation. It also requires the supervisor to have specialist knowledge and expertise to guide and oversee the work of others – the supervisor providing a type of apprenticeship in which the supervisee's skills, professional and ethical practice is developed. In training supervision, key outcomes for the supervisee include acquiring essential professional and practice skills and ultimately achieving independent practice status for themselves. The supervisor's role in training supervision almost always includes an explicit evaluative component. Because of this the supervisor holds a great deal of power which can become an impediment to supervision unless the supervisor acknowledges this and takes steps to ensure that this is not misused. Professional bodies and/or training providers usually set criteria for individuals who wish to take on this role and sometimes offer training in supervision and evaluation prior to the supervisor engaging in this role. This form of supervision almost always requires that the supervisor and supervisee come from the same profession, or that the supervision is delegated by (and thus ultimately accountable to) someone from the same profession.

Support staff supervision: support staff are those practitioners who carry out their duties and responsibilities under the guidance of someone else. This group tends to be comprised of individuals who do not have a professional body and are not registered independently thus are not governed by a statutory or professional code of practice. This group comprises many types of practitioner such as assistant and support practitioners in health and criminal justice settings. Within the framework of power and responsibility they are located in the same quadrant as trainee practitioners, although unlike trainee practitioners, support staff may be highly experienced in their roles and the focus of their supervision may well not include a strong focus on training or evaluation. However, a practitioner who is registered to practice directs their work and it is this person or group to which the support practitioner reports. Supervisors providing supervision to support staff need to be clear about their respective responsibilities and the line management arrangements. In many settings, support staff work with infrequent and variable quality supervision and in many respects support staff are an overlooked group both for receiving practice supervision and in supervision research. Further, there tend to be no standards for supervision of this workforce group and therefore it is not unusual for practitioners with limited training and perhaps no interest in supervision to supervise them. However, those supervising this group of practitioners need to take this task seriously and also be aware of the diversity of this group in terms of background, training and experience. Therefore, it is helpful for the supervisor to establish, with the supervisee, their strengths and level of 'functioning' in order to match supervision to the individual's needs. A developmental model (see Chapter 4) may be helpful in order to explore this. As with training supervision, the supervision of support staff is generally 'within discipline'.

Specialist supervision: although specialist supervision can overlap with training supervision, it is used here to denote supervision which concerns only part of the practitioners practice/job role. Such supervision is commonly used where a practitioner is learning a new skill set (such as a therapy model) or where they are providing a specialist service (e.g. a group intervention). In such cases the supervisee should also access professional or peer supervision to focus on other aspects of their practice. In Figure 3.1, the specialist supervisor is described as having more responsibility than the supervisee but power is shared. This is because the supervisor may be responsible for certain tasks such as assisting the supervisee in skills acquisition or monitoring treatment adherence. However, in this relationship power is often shared as the remit for the supervision is limited and the supervisee's main relationship is with someone else. It is common for this form of supervision to be cross-disciplinary which in itself can have an important impact on facilitating power sharing.

Professional supervision: is used in this context to denote the supervision provided to a practitioner from a more senior colleague and it is this differential that results in the power difference in this relationship. In contrast, responsibility is often shared in a professional supervision relationship – the supervisee as an autonomous professional is generally free to use or ignore the 'contents' of their supervision and, as an autonomous practitioner, the supervisee is ultimately accountable to their managers and professional/registering body. In this form of supervision, the supervisee will generally take all aspects of their practice into consideration. Some supervisees find it helpful to supplement this form of supervision with either peer supervision or specialist supervision as part of their on-going development. Many supervisees choose to remain with the same supervisor for a number of years whilst others purposefully seek to change their supervisor periodically. For those choosing to remain with a supervisor for a period of time (possibly years) it is important to plan periodic reviews (in my practice this tends to be about six-monthly) in order to take stock of what is working and helpful in supervision and what needs to change. It can be helpful to use a framework for this such as the ones discussed in Chapter 7 and Special Topic 8.

Peer supervision: encompasses two different forms of supervision and supervisory relationship – 'reciprocal supervision' and 'peer consultation'.

RECIPROCAL SUPERVISION typically involves peers who are highly experienced practitioners (and supervisors) who meet together to provide one another with supervision. In this way, it could equally be called 'peer professional supervision'.

Although the supervision processes may be very similar to those in other forms of professional supervision, the power differential in this relationship is not present. For many highly experienced practitioners, identifying and securing supervision from a more senior colleague or a practice expert is often difficult or impractical and thus a peer approach may become the mainstay for supervision. In reciprocal supervision, each person (in the dyad or group) takes a turn to work through his or her agenda as the supervisee whilst the other(s) take the role of supervisor. It is not uncommon for highly experienced professionals to have a number of similar relationships which they can use 'selectively' – drawing upon different people according to the issue the individual wishes to explore. These may be people with whom they have previously had supervisory relationships or colleagues they have worked/currently work with. However, the availability of 'people who can be called upon' should not replace a regular and planned reciprocal supervision relationship. McCormack and Hopkins (1995) provide an example of this form of peer supervision in which they describe their personal experiences of 'individuals of the same rank or status facilitate [sic] each others' reflection-on-action' (p. 165).

PEER CONSULTATION typically sits alongside other forms of professional supervision and is a 'meeting of professional equals'. Careful negotiation is needed to determine the parameters of peer consultation as it is not designed to facilitate specific learning or decision-making in relation to practice – decisions about practice should remain in the training or professional supervision relationship. As will be discussed in Chapter 8 (in relation to non-disclosure in supervision), how peer consultation might be used for individuals to share concerns and difficulties. In such instances, peers may need to support one another to raise the issues with their professional or training supervisor. Such supervision usually provides a reflective space within which the individual can explore and review their professional development, the impact practice has on them (and vice versa) and wider systemic, service and training issues (for an example see Davies and Coleman, 1999; Hair, 2013). As with reciprocal supervision, the members take turns to lead the discussion. Peer consultation typically has more focus on the restorative component of supervision and provides an opportunity for peers to calibrate themselves in relation to professional development. Peer consultation is often facilitated between individuals going through the same training or amongst new staff. However, those in a peer consultation arrangement need to ensure they have carefully considered the boundaries and purpose of such consultations. Cutcliffe and Proctor (1998) and Davies and Coleman (1999) provide a number of suggestions for establishing peer consultations such as trying to choose someone outside the immediate work setting (e.g. a fellow student on different placements), choosing someone at the same stage of training or development, focusing on successes and the learning to be obtained from these and scheduling regular meetings. As in reciprocal supervision, peer consultation is based upon turn-taking and thus may require the participants to develop a system to ensure some element of equity. Peer consultation can also be a helpful way for practitioners to begin to establish supervision skills in a safe and manageable context.

Several studies have explored forms of peer supervision within nursing, each of which have produced broadly similar findings. In a study of nurse managers, peer supervision was found to promote quality management in their work (Hyrkäs *et al.*, 2003) whilst a study of nursing students, found that peer support had a number of benefits including increasing confidence and providing opportunities for reflection and learning (Aston and Molassiotis, 2003). Similarly, a study of peer 'practice support' for qualified nurses in a rural setting, Willson, Fawcett, and Whyte (2001) found that most participants found it beneficial. However, the issues of finding time and the need for adequate preparation for the role are often raised. Others have also suggested that only providing peer supervision may be limiting as it may stifle innovation and perpetuate existing practice (Devine and Baxter, 1994).

Forms of supervision

Studies generally report that individual supervision is more common than group-based supervision. Both have a role to play in establishing and delivering supervision. In this section we will briefly consider individual supervision before focusing on some specific considerations relevant to group-based supervision.

Individual supervision

In her study of mental health and psychiatric nurses, Hyrkäs (2005) found that of those receiving supervision, 64 per cent participated in individual supervision. Individual supervision requires that the supervisee and supervisor establish a working relationship through which the process of supervision can take place. The majority of the content of this book can be readily applied to individual supervision and much of it is derived from theoretical and empirical work into individual supervision. It is for these reasons that more on individual supervision is not presented at this point.

Group supervision

Group supervision can be defined as three or more people meeting together at regular intervals to discuss, evaluate and reflect upon their practice; such meetings may include a dedicated supervisor (see Bernard and Goodyear, 2014; Bond and Holland, 2011). Groups might be *closed* (i.e. there are the same participants each time), however, some forms of group supervision (e.g. team supervision and peer supervision) lend themselves to being *open* to a wider group with only some attending any given session. Open groups can provide flexibility, however disadvantages noted by Cleary and Freeman (2005) included an absence of focus, a reluctance to self-disclose and repetition of content.

Group supervision has certain efficiencies of scale and provides the supervisees with opportunities to learn from each other and possible exposure to a diversity of clients, problems and ideas (Bernard and Goodyear, 2014). There are several different forms of group supervision commonly used and different ways in which group supervision can be facilitated. Proctor and Inskipp (2013) provide four group typologies: supervision *in* a group (authoritarian) which can be conceptualised as each group member having individual supervision 'in public'; supervision *with* a group (participative) where the supervisor facilitates active participation from members; and two forms of supervision *by* a group – cooperative, in which the supervisor acts as facilitator to enable the participants to consider one another's needs, and peer supervision in which there is no dedicated supervisor facilitating or leading. Group supervision can provide a forum that enables additional ideas and solutions to be generated, and allows some assumptions and preconceptions to be challenged or confirmed which might not have occurred in an individual context (e.g. Arvidsson and Fridlund, 2005). Rankine (2013) notes that because group supervision offers multiple perspectives it can allow for a greater pool of ideas, provides a context for critical reflection in a supportive relationship, can help to promote team spirit and team cohesion and can act as a rich source of learning.

Ideas about ideal group size varies with reports from 3–12 found in the literature (Proctor and Inskipp, 2013). However, they recommend that rather than absolute numbers, 'size must be in ratio with time and function' (p. 161). Commitment also needs to be discussed and a clear agreement should be made from the start to pre-empt 'quitting' and to agree a minimum 'life span' for the group (Hyrkäs et al., 2003). Some have suggested creating groups according to role (Fowler, 1996), whilst others (e.g. Proctor and Inskipp, 2013) also describe 'mixed profession and mixed orientation groups'. Whatever the parameters, it is important that they are explicit and that boundaries and a supervision agreement are discussed and agreed.

Where a supervisor is leading the group supervision, he or she needs to be able to balance three sets of needs – those of the task, the individual and the group (Adair, 2013). Therefore, in addition to being skilled in the processes of supervision, the group supervisor also needs to be skilled in managing groups. This is important as there are many pitfalls and traps which are not present in individual supervision. For example, Magnuson, Wilcoxon and Norem (2000) highlight the problem of 'the squeaky wheel getting all the grease', i.e. a disproportionate amount of time being dedicated to individuals who make the most demand. Therefore, ensuring that attention is paid to all members of the group is essential if members are to get their unique needs met. However, where groups are cooperative or peer led, there is a risk that some may gain more than others (Hyrkäs et al., 2003). Therefore, careful consideration needs to be given to how this might be noticed and addressed.

Groups can often be seen to go through stages over time as they form and set to work. Probably the most widely used framework to understand this process is that of Tuckman (Tuckman, 1965; Tuckman and Jensen, 1977), in which he refers to forming (the group coming together), storming (interpersonal and emotional conflict; resistance), norming (cohesiveness and sharing of opinions), performing (functional and focused on the task) and adjourning (when the group comes to an end). Proctor and Inskipp (2013) identify a number of skills for group supervisors including active leadership, preparation and the skilled use of frameworks. There are many resources for those participating in group supervision as well as those providing group supervision or considering doing so. Those engaging in or offering group supervision may find the chapters by Bernard and Goodyear (2014); Bond and Holland (2011) and Proctor and Inskipp (2013) helpful. There are also useful theories about group processes such as described by Bion (1970) and others who have developed his work (e.g. French and Simpson, 2010).

The group consult model is a special form of group supervision (see Beddoe and Davys, 2010; Rankine, 2013) that has been used in child welfare settings. This approach is designed to be used alongside other forms of supervision at key decision points, when there is an impasse or when progress is stuck. This approach uses a set structure to focus on risk; opening by asking what the purpose for the meeting is and ending by asking if this has been met. The approach is one of 'action-reflection' where risks, dangers and protective factors are explored in order to identify and explore possible solutions. As with other forms of supervision, it is important for the supervisor to have skills in group work (e.g. time keeping and managing participant anxieties and concerns) as well as familiarity with the group consult approach. In this model the supervisor needs to be a role model and foster motivation and enthusiasm.

The reflecting team is a form of group supervision that was developed from a therapeutic approach to working with families (see Reichelt and Skjerve, 2012). The approach uses a structure to lead a process of enquiry, review and decision-making that enables the supervisee to make choices (about client treatment) based on their own preferences, skills and the suggestions offered. Within the framework, being stuck may be a consequence of having a single perspective, thus the team may help by providing new ideas or viewpoints (Anderson, Snow and Wells Parker, 2000). The method has three phases during which supervisees take it in turns to have an opportunity to receive supervision:

(1) A supervisee is interviewed by the supervisor to discover – information about why the case is being brought; information about the system; client information and the supervisee's goals – the rest of the group listen.
(2) The reflecting team process, in which the rest of the group offer thoughts on what they have heard by considering what they like about what is being done; any ideas and observations – during this phase the supervisee and supervisor listen.
(3) The supervisee and supervisor discuss and reflect on what they have heard with the rest of the group being invited to contribute where required. The supervisee may ask for the reflecting team process to consider new issues that have arisen.

In their study, Reichelt and Skjerve (2012) found that when the approach was used some of the format was deviated from which led to some loss of focus and purpose. Further, they found that within the model there appears to be no scope for the supervisor to take on the role of 'teacher'. They therefore suggest that this approach may not be suitable for those who are inexperienced or novices.

Team supervision is a specific form of group supervision that involves members of the same team (Hyrkäs, Appelqvist-Schmidlechner and Paunonen Ilmonen, 2002). This form of group supervision is probably relatively common in forensic settings. In such instances, this form of supervision is likely to help foster team working, improve consistency within the team, reduce splitting and provide a forum to address difficulties within the team. Such supervision requires trust and commitment within the team, and for this reason it is frequently used alongside other forms of supervision (e.g. individual supervision). Team supervision is described in more detail in Special Topic 9 where some useful frameworks for the supervisor are also presented.

Consultation

It is important to make brief mention of consultation as a form of supervision. In this context, consultation is typically a form of specialist supervision provided to an individual or a group (e.g. staff team) and, for example, may relate to a novel client issue, a team difficulty or an event that has happened or is anticipated. As such it is generally provided at the request of the recipient(s) who have usually selected a specific individual to provide the consultation, either because of their knowledge (e.g. of a particular issue or a mode of working) or skill (e.g. in facilitating group reflection or in fostering problem-solving). The defining features of consultation are that it is time limited – most commonly a single meeting, and is focused on a specific question, problem or practice-based concern. It may take various forms (and use various approaches) such as problem-solving, advice-giving, conceptualisation or reflection. The consultation process may draw upon models of, and ideas for, supervision and reflection contained throughout this text (e.g. relating to team supervision, managing boundaries, reflection). However, particular attention is needed to aspects of managing the process, namely: forming a mini-supervision agreement to cover the consultation, agreement of boundaries (including confidentiality), time keeping and note keeping, and opportunities for follow up. Where the consultation is to be in a team, it is important to establish who needs to be present, find a suitable venue and understand factors such as who is 'commissioning' this task, what do they expect and how will the process (and any outcomes) be shared (and with whom).

Supervision tasks

There are several common tasks that are relevant to supervision practice regardless of the type or form it takes. This section will consider in some detail factors in establishing supervision such as the core conditions on which to establish the supervision, basic standards and good practice for supervision such as the use of agreements and record-keeping.

Core conditions for supervision

In order to have a solid base, supervision needs to be founded upon a few basic yet essential core conditions.

Trusting relationship: supervision needs to be underpinned by a trusting relationship. Such a relationship is likely to be more conducive to the supervisee giving an honest appraisal of themselves, their work and their experience of supervision (Ladany, Hill, Corbett and Nutt, 1996).

Safety: in common with a trusting relationship, supervisees need to feel safe within supervision. This is important as supervision will sometimes involve the supervisee 'going beyond their comfort zone' in order to assimilate new skills or to consider their emotional reactions to a client. Supervisees also need to feel safe in order to review their strengths and successes.

Time: this is the factor that probably appears most often as a difficulty in providing supervision (e.g. Freshwater, Walsh and Storey, 2002). If supervision is to be valued and useful it needs sufficient time to be allocated from within 'core working hours' and needs to be prioritised. For practitioners receiving an hour of supervision on a fortnightly basis this represents less than 1.5 per cent of their contracted time, whilst for those receiving an hour monthly this represents less than 1 per cent!

Resources: the resources for supervision are mainly the human resources (in the form of the supervisor) and the space in which supervision can take place. In terms of the supervisor it is important to have someone who can be responsive, is able to support and challenge and can offer opportunities for learning. In relation to space, the basic requirements are simply that the room is comfortable and free from distraction.

A supervision agreement: supervision should be based upon a clear agreement between the supervisor and supervisee. This should include a clear, collaborative and agreed purpose for supervision (Jones, 2006). Supervision agreements will be discussed in more detail later in this chapter.

Regular review: supervision should be founded upon the idea of regular review. A review is important in order for the supervisee to take stock – reviewing their current learning needs, what has worked in supervision and what needs to be different. Such information is relevant whether the supervisee is to continue with the same supervisor (in which case this information can be used to determine the focus for the next period of supervision) or if the supervisee is moving to another supervisor (in which case this information can be used in the initial sessions when establishing the supervision agreement). Each supervision session will normally contain some review, however dedicated time should be allocated to this task periodically.

Basic standards for supervision

There are a few basic standards which should be common to all forms of supervision. First, supervision should be a core activity and therefore should take place at a *pre-arranged time* and within *normal working hours*. Second, the discussions within supervision should be *confidential* with a clear agreement about the limited conditions under which confidentiality may need to be forfeited and how this would be done. As part of establishing the conditions for this, supervision should take place in a *private* and *undisturbed* setting. Finally, there should be an agreed, confidential *record* kept that captures what was discussed and the actions to be taken. Record keeping is discussed in more detail later in this chapter.

Supervision agreements and contracts

Supervision agreements (also often referred to as a supervision 'contract') are an important feature of practice supervision in order to set the boundaries and context within which supervision can take place. Some challenge the use of the term contract (especially between registered practitioners and supervisors) based on the fact that they are not legal documents and not subject to 'contract law', thus in this text the term agreement is used. Supervision agreements need to provide sufficient detail to be useful and to serve as a reminder to both parties. Agreements should be drawn up collaboratively, and may need to include others such as managers or training providers where appropriate. Wilson and Lizzio (2009) suggest that the supervision agreement has four purposes described as: *content* – expressed through clear statements about the 'goals, roles and processes' to ensure shared expectations between supervisor and supervisee; *process* – to establish supervision as a collaborative enterprise with each having some input and control over supervision; *ethical* – enabling the supervisee to make an informed choice based on information about the supervisor and supervision; and *educational* – to ensure that supervision will maximise the supervisee's learning. Care should be taken to ensure that the written agreement resembles the psychological contract held between supervisor and supervisee (i.e. each other's beliefs about the terms of the agreement; Nelson, Barnes, Evans and Triggiano, 2008). Typically this collaborative agreement will need to include the following detail:

(1) *Practical information:* this should identify who the agreement is between and specify key facts such as frequency (how often); duration (how long); and location (where). In addition, the agreement should identify who will be responsible for record-keeping. Either as part of the agreement, or in a supervision policy, there should be minimum standards in relation to the documents kept and where and how these will be stored.
(2) *Boundary information:* there should be a clear statement about what will be/is appropriate for supervision and what would be considered outside the context of supervision. There should also be a statement relating to confidentiality and any limits that might be placed on this.
(3) *Role information:* this should provide information about what the supervisee and supervisor can expect from the other. This might also include information about any specific approach(es)/model(s) being used in supervision and how the session agenda will be agreed.
(4) *Nature of supervision:* there should be a statement concerning whether supervision will be individual or in a group format and another about the focus of the supervision (i.e. does it concern all areas of the professional's work or a specific subset e.g. a specific group being delivered, a specific task or function the supervisee is responsible for).
(5) *Goals:* there should be explicit goals for supervision which should be written in a way that easily allows them to be 'tested' to see if they are being/have been met.
(6) *Review:* a review date should be set and consideration should be given to how supervision will be evaluated/what criteria the supervision will be reviewed against.
(7) *Crisis/emergency support:* it may be appropriate to specify how the supervisee might consult with the supervisor between sessions and other arrangements for supervision e.g. during periods of supervisor leave, in relation to a critical incident. For students and trainees there should be clear information about any circumstances in which the supervisor must be contacted.
(8) *Audit:* the way in which supervision will be monitored and audited should be recorded along with who is responsible for this task.

An example of an agreement can be found in Box 3.1. Creating an agreement should not be an onerous task, however it is a necessary one. The agreement sets the starting point for building a trusting relationship and provides the global boundaries. Although some people make only verbal agreements, a written one is recommended as a concrete statement of collaborative intent. In exceptional circumstances the agreement can be used explicitly to manage supervision, for example when the person responsible for agenda-setting repeatedly omits to undertake this role. The agreement should be a 'live document' that is reviewed and discussed periodically and used to help ensure that the goals and purpose are being met.

> **BOX 3.1: Individual supervision agreement example**
>
> Supervision agreement between _____ and _____
> Supervision will normally take place every _____ (weeks)
> Supervision sessions will normally last for _____ (hours)
> The venue will normally be _____ or _____
> The type of supervision is TRAINING / SUPPORT PRACTITIONER / PROFESSIONAL / SPECIALIST / RECIPROCAL / PEER CONSULTATION (circle as appropriate)
> In the case of specialist/peer please record the name of the main supervisor
> The focus of supervision is _____
> The goals of supervision are _____
> The agenda will be the primary responsibility of _____
> Written records of supervision sessions will be made by _____
> Dates of supervision sessions will be recorded in _____
> The contract and supervision relationship will be reviewed every six months.
>
> 1. A session may be cancelled in exceptional circumstances. In such cases it will be rescheduled at the earliest opportunity.
> 2. Where relevant the service audit form will be completed and submitted by _____
> 3. The sessions will be confidential with the exception of any practice which may breach professional codes or ethics or be illegal or damaging to another individual should confidentiality be broken (in a sensitive and professional manner).
>
> Signature of Supervisee _____ Supervisor _____ Date __/__/__

The supervision agenda

The supervision agenda provides an initial structure to the session. There should be agreement as to who is predominantly responsible for bringing an 'agenda' and, in most instances, this will be the supervisee. Where this is the case the supervisor should add any items to the supervisee's agenda at the start of the session. One 'standing item' for the agenda should be feedback on outcomes or actions generated during the last supervision session. The agenda may be little more than a list of possible topics or issues to be discussed; typically a maximum of half-a-dozen. Chapter 6 discusses preparation for supervision in more detail.

The first task in supervision (after greetings and settling down!) is to briefly go through the agenda to allow an opportunity to prioritise items – an idea late in the list may be worthy of discussion first or there may be a common theme across items that is clarified and prioritised as a result of this brief discussion. The main reasons for using an agenda in supervision are to ensure that important topics are not missed or forgotten; to allow preparation to take place before supervision; to help structure the session and manage time; to start the session on a collaborative footing through negotiating what will be attended to; and to provide a system for linking supervision sessions through prompting for feedback and outcomes from previous sessions.

Record keeping

Record keeping is an essential part of supervision, which provides a 'written memory' of supervision sessions over time. It typically contains a brief account of the session and the actions to be taken/decisions made. At a bare minimum, it provides evidence that supervision took place, however it is generally much more valuable. Making (and reviewing) the written record allows for additional thinking about the issues discussed to be undertaken and can enable common themes discussed (or importantly not identified or discussed) to be highlighted over time. The record should contain sufficient information to facilitate continuity between sessions and to act as an aide memoir for either party to recap on the session at a later date. A supervision record should include the date and time of the session, who was present (in the case of group supervision), what was on the agenda, what was discussed and actions to be taken as a result of the session. It may also include space to record reflections on or additional thoughts about the session afterwards. It does not matter whether it is handwritten or typed, however, there should be clear agreement about who will create the record, how it will be agreed and where it will be kept (i.e. how each party can access it). For many professional groups, supervision is an important part of their evidence of 'fitness to practice' and continued professional development, thus the record is a way to provide evidence for this. In forensic settings it is important to 'have an eye' on issues relating to risk and harm and to record information pertinent to these. A simple example of a supervision record is contained in Box 3.2. This template is intended to foster a discussion between supervisor and supervisee in order to agree a format for and content of the record. It is important to ensure that the record is anonymised as appropriate to maintain confidentiality.

Who makes the record of supervision should be negotiated as part of the initial agreement but may be revisited from time to time. My 'rule of thumb' is that where the supervisee is a registered or licensed practitioner then normally they make the record and make it available or copy it to the supervisor; for other groups it is helpful for the supervisor and supervisee to each make a record which they share with each other. In this way, supervisees develop skills in recording supervision but also differences and discrepancies can be identified and discussed. One variant to this is where the supervisee is experienced and their recording skills have been demonstrated – in such cases it may be appropriate for them to make the sole record which they share with the supervisor. Occasionally, a supervision arrangement has been instigated as part of a disciplinary process. In such circumstances it is helpful for supervisor and supervisee to make a record regardless of the supervisee's experience or qualification.

BOX 3.2: Example of a supervision record

Supervisee's name: A. Trainee
Supervisor's name: T. Supervisor

Date	Time	Topics and discussion outline	Decisions/actions	Post supervision observations
05/03/14	14.00	Client AB Recent violence towards staff – tearful in treatment sessions. Recent history of irritability and 'power play'. Unclear why this behaviour is occurring and how to make sense of it	Update risk assessment and review management plans; undertake functional analysis; consider offence paralleling behaviour	Functional analysis very helpful but need team review of management plan. (10/3/14)
		Confidence re teaching session for staff Discussed and went through session content and some skills re presenting and managing associated anxiety. Discussed group tasks that could be included and a form to collect participant feedback	To meet with peer tomorrow to practice delivering the session	Practice session went well. Good feedback from staff in actual session. Need to do more to build confidence (19/3/14)
		Staff disagreement Staff conflict re how to respond to issues with RA (client). Very polarised views leading to disagreements and different approaches being used	Read handouts re consistency and conflict; identify own position – agenda for next supervision	Mapped own position – surprised by own beliefs about RA. (14/3/14)

Conclusion

Supervision can be provided in a range of ways to groups or individuals. However, there are key features such as creating a supervision agreement, agenda setting and record keeping that are present in all forms and types. Being competent in these key features is a starting point for fostering and developing successful supervision.

References

Adair, J. (2013) *Develop Your Leadership Skills*, London: Kogan Page Publishers.
Anderson, B. J., Snow, R. W. and Wells Parker, E. (2000) 'Comparing the predictive validity of DUI risk screening instruments: development of validation standards', *Addiction* 95(6): 915–29.
Arvidsson, B. and Fridlund, B. (2005) 'Factors influencing nurse supervisor competence: a critical incident analysis study', *Journal of Nursing Management* 13(3): 231–7.
Aston, L. and Molassiotis, A. (2003) 'Supervising and supporting student nurses in clinical placements: the peer support initiative', *Nurse Education Today* 23(3): 202–10.
Beddoe, L. and Davys, A. (2010) *Best Practice in Professional Supervision*, London: Jessica Kingsley Publishers.
Bernard, J. M. and Goodyear, R. K. (2014) *Fundamentals of Clinical Supervision* (5th edn), International Edition, London: Pearson.
Bond, M. and Holland, S. (2011) *Skills of Clinical Supervision for Nurses: A Practical Guide for Supervisees, Clinical Supervisors and Managers*, Buckingham: Open University Press.
Cleary, M. and Freeman, A. (2005) 'The cultural realities of clinical supervision in an acute inpatient mental health setting', *Issues in Mental Health Nursing* 26(5): 489–505.
Cutcliffe, J. R. and Proctor, B. (1998) 'An alternative training approach to clinical supervision: 2', *British Journal of Nursing* 7(6): 346–50.
Davies, J. and Coleman, B. (1999) 'Peer consultation: more than just a trip to the pub?', *Clinical Psychology Forum* 131: 13–16.
Devine, A. and Baxter, T. D. (1994) 'Introducing clinical supervision: a guide', *Nursing Standard* 9(40): 32–4.
Fowler, J. (1996) 'How to use models of clinical supervision in practice', *Nursing Standard* 10(29): 42–7.
Freshwater, D., Walsh, L. and Storey, L. (2002) 'Prison health care: developing leadership through clinical supervision', *Nursing Management* 8(9): 16–20.
Hair, H. J. (2013) 'The purpose and duration of supervision, and the training and discipline of supervisors: what social workers say they need to provide effective services', *British Journal of Social Work* 43(8): 1562–88.
Hyrkäs, K. (2005) 'Clinical supervision, burnout, and job satisfaction among mental health and psychiatric nurses in Finland', *Issues in Mental Health Nursing* 26(5): 531–56.
Hyrkäs, K., Appelqvist-Schmidlechner, K. and Paunonen Ilmonen, M. (2002) 'Expert supervisors' views of clinical supervision: a study of factors promoting and inhibiting the achievements of multiprofessional team supervision', *Journal of Advanced Nursing* 38(4): 387–97.
Hyrkäs, K., Koivula, M., Lehti, K. and Paunonen Ilmonen, M. (2003) 'Nurse managers' conceptions of quality management as promoted by peer supervision', *Journal of Nursing Management* 11(1): 48–58.

Jones, A. (2006) 'Clinical supervision: what do we know and what do we need to know? A review and commentary', *Journal of Nursing Management* 14(8): 577–85.

Ladany, N., Hill, C. E., Corbett, M. M. and Nutt, E. A. (1996) 'Nature, extent, and importance of what psychotherapy trainees do not disclose to their supervisors', *Journal of Counseling Psychology* 43(1): 10.

Magnuson, S., Wilcoxon, S. A. and Norem, K. (2000) 'A profile of lousy supervision: experienced counselors' perspectives', *Counselor Education and Supervision* 39(3): 189–202.

McCormack, B. and Hopkins, E. (1995) 'The development of clinical leadership through supported reflective practice', *Journal of Clinical Nursing* 4(3): 161–8.

Nelson, M. L., Barnes, K. L., Evans, A. L. and Triggiano, P. J. (2008) 'Working with conflict in clinical supervision: wise supervisors' perspectives', *Journal of Counseling Psychology* 55(2): 172–84.

Proctor, B. and Inskipp, F. (2013) 'Group supervision', in J. Scaife (ed.), *Supervision in Clinical Practice*, Abingdon: Routledge, pp. 37–63.

Rankine, M. (2013) 'Getting a different perspective: piloting the "group consult" model for supervision in a community-based setting', *Practice* 25(2): 105–20.

Reichelt, S. and Skjerve, J. (2012) 'The reflecting team model used for clinical group supervision without clients present', *Journal of Marital and Family Therapy* 39(2): 244–55.

Tuckman, B. W. (1965) 'Developmental sequence in small groups', *Psychological Bulletin* 63(6): 384.

Tuckman, B. W. and Jensen, M. A. C. (1977) 'Stages of small-group development revisited', *Group & Organization Management* 2(4): 419–27.

Willson, L., Fawcett, T. N. and Whyte, D. A. (2001) 'An evaluation of a clinical supervision programme', *British Journal of Community Nursing* 6: 614–23.

Wilson, K. L. and Lizzio, A. J. (2009) 'Processes and interventions to facilitate supervisees' learning', in N. Pelling, J. Barletta and P. Armstrong (eds), *The Practice of Clinical Supervision*, Samford Valley: Australian Academic Press, pp. 138–64.

4 Supervision models and frameworks

There are many models of supervision that have been described within the literature which together provide a range of heuristics or guides for undertaking supervision. In each model there are elements which might be helpful to the supervisee or supervisor, however in providing detail of some aspects of supervision others are neglected (Bernard and Goodyear, 2014). As a result, it has been widely acknowledged that there is no single correct way to carry out supervision, nor a 'one size fits all' model or approach that can be adopted (Cutcliffe, 2005; Cutcliffe, Butterworth and Proctor, 2005). It is suggested that supervision should be provided in such a way that the approach fits the problem or issue (not the other way around), that problem solving is used to address difficulties and so that progress can be reviewed (e.g. Schoenwald, Mehta, Frazier and Shernoff, 2013). Furthermore, supervision needs to be responsive and structured to meet individual need (Fowler and Chevannes, 1998). It is common, therefore, for more than one model to be used in supervision, with supervisors often developing their own blend or unique integration of models to guide their practice.

In order to make sense of the many models available for supervision and to appreciate the assumptions and constrictions that have been created within and by them, it is helpful to understand a little of the history. Practice supervision has its roots in psychotherapy from which it has extended to other groups. First, to those in social and mental health services (e.g. nursing and social care) and more latterly across professions where human 'helping contact' of some description is present (e.g. career counselling; Westergaard, 2013, and educational psychology; Atkinson and Woods, 2007; Whitehead, Ward and Collie, 2007). In parallel with this broader use has been the growth of learning and development approaches to describing supervision and models which seek to describe the supervision process itself. This history informs the domains commonly used to categorise supervision models such as the system used by Bernard and Goodyear (2014) of psychotherapy derived models; developmental models; process models; and integrative models.

An overview of the models

In this chapter we will consider four models in some detail. First, a modified 'functions of supervision' model is described based on the work of Kadushin

(1976); Mor Barak et al. (2009) and Proctor (1986). This discusses four tasks that supervision needs to attend to: the supervision relationship; the learning and developmental needs of the supervisee; the professional and ethical needs of the supervisee's practice; and the emotional needs of the supervisee. Second, a session structure is presented to help map the tasks of supervision into the time available for supervision. Based on the work of Wosket and Page (1994), this model leads the supervisee and supervisor through stages in order to maintain a focus on linking supervision to practice within the supervision time available. Third, a developmental model based on Stoltenberg and McNeill (2010) and a forensic application by Davies et al. (2004) is presented which considers how developmental stages of the supervisee and supervisor may be relevant. This model helps anticipate possible supervisee needs, predict some of the potential difficulties in supervision and suggest ways to match elements of the supervisor approach to supervisee developmental level. Forth, a process model of supervision based on Hawkins and Shohet (2006) is described. This model enables the supervisor and supervisee to consider the client or the task from different perspectives. These four models can be seen as complementary to one another – providing the supervisee and supervisor with different foci and information relevant to the supervision endeavour. Finally, the common factors approach and solutions focused supervision are presented. These could be challenged as models as the focus of each is as much on the style and approach to supervision as it is to supervisee development or supervision process. All of the models selected support the assumption that supervision is action orientated and present focused (Schoenwald et al., 2013). Learning theory, which underpins many aspects of supervision, is considered in more detail in Chapter 5 whilst reflective practice is explored in Special Topic 10.

The selection of models and frameworks in this chapter, from the vast array available to the supervisor and supervisee, comes with a warning. These selections are based on the author's exposure to and experience of using them and should not therefore be seen as a particular endorsement or intentional exclusion of any specific model. Indeed, it is useful for the supervisor (and supervisee) to explore the array of models available to identify for themselves which have utility to their practice. Supervision will benefit from supervisors who are able to draw upon an array of models to inform thinking, planning and action. As noted by Fowler (1996), models provide the supervisor with a way of approaching supervision; an idea of 'what to do after saying hello'. It may be that in developing a strategy (see Chapter 9), particular models will be promoted for use within a service or with a particular staff group. Whatever models you adopt, there is a great deal of scope for practice based evaluation and research. As Morgan and Sprenkle (2007) note, 'The field [of practice supervision] will profit from knowing *what* is helpful *with whom* and *when*, in a way that is not limited by the specifics of each model' (p. 6, my italics).

Given the nature of this text, 'treatment or therapy specific' supervision models are not explored, however readers should be aware that most approaches to treatment and therapy have a corresponding framework or approach to supervision. In some cases this includes tools to assess the quality of the supervision based on the presence or absence of features in supervision, which are congruent with the treatment model. Where supervision intentionally resembles the therapy model itself, this may be, at least in part, to promote treatment integrity or adherence, with the expectation that this will enhance outcomes. Those who wish to consider supervision in relation to specific therapies in more detail should consult the very helpful (if a little dated) *Handbook of Psychotherapy Supervision* (Watkins, 1997).

Supervision functions and dimensions

Different authors have described a common triad of core supervision functions in varied but complementary ways. For example, from a social work perspective, Kadushin (1976) describes three functions, namely, educative, managerial and supportive whilst from a counselling perspective, Proctor uses the terms formative, normative and restorative (Proctor, 1986). A related model, based on a meta-analysis of 27 studies, showed three dimensions to be related to effective supervision (Mor Barak et al., 2009). These dimensions were:

(1) task assistance – elements relating to functioning well in one's job (e.g. education, training and practitioner development). This is most similar to the normative and formative functions above;
(2) social and emotional support for the supervisee – e.g. meeting the emotional needs of the practitioner and helping them to respond effectively to work stress. This is most similar to the restorative/supportive function above; and
(3) interpersonal interaction within supervision – based on the supervisee's perception of the supervisory relationship. This can be seen as the medium through which supervision takes place and thus is a critical dimension. This does not have a direct correspondent in the models of Proctor and Kadushin.

The framework provided by Kadushin and Proctor is probably the most widely cited and researched supervision model. For example, Hair (2013) found, both in the literature and in their large-scale survey, strong support for supervision providing emotional support, facilitating knowledge and skills development and addressing the necessary administrative tasks. In an earlier study investigating the implementation of supervision by Ayer et al. (1997), they found the three functions to be evidenced by a range of content and actions:

(1) formative – developing skills and evidence-based practice; managing practice competence; improving staff performance;
(2) normative – improved quality of client care; means of ensuring safe and effective practice; increasing ability to take ethical action; and
(3) restorative – building confidence to discuss anxiety-provoking professional issues; providing a context for constructive challenge; increased confidence in dealing with novel situations (e.g. critical incidents).

Fowler (1996) outlines how the formative role can focus on three differing factors namely: tasks and skills (such as how to do something); decision-making dilemmas and accountability associated with complex ethical and professional judgement (which of the options is best to take); and reflective practice (learning from experiences). To complement this, Playle and Mullarkey (1998) discuss supervision as a method to monitor practice and quality control.

A simple way to represent the functions of supervision is shown in Figure 4.1. In this, the three functions of Proctor and Kadushin are depicted in the three ellipses with the surrounding black text describing some of the ways in which these can be enacted. Two sets of approach are provided in relation to the formative function – those on the right are often associated with the more experienced practitioner (and might be thought of as reflective practice; see Special Topic 10) and those on the left most commonly associated with training. As can be seen, problem solving is a feature of both approaches. The three functions are set within the context of the interpersonal interaction highlighted by Mor Barak and colleagues. This can also be conceptualised as the supervisory working alliance (Bordin, 1983). Based on his earlier work on the working alliance in therapy, Bordin argues that the supervisory working alliance is comprised of three elements: the supervisee's *goals* (i.e. what the supervisee wants from supervision, e.g. mastery of specific skills, enhanced knowledge of certain theory); *tasks* (i.e. how the goals will be met, e.g. supervisor review of taped interactions with a client, supervisor providing coaching); and bond (i.e. the trust, respect and ability to work collaboratively).

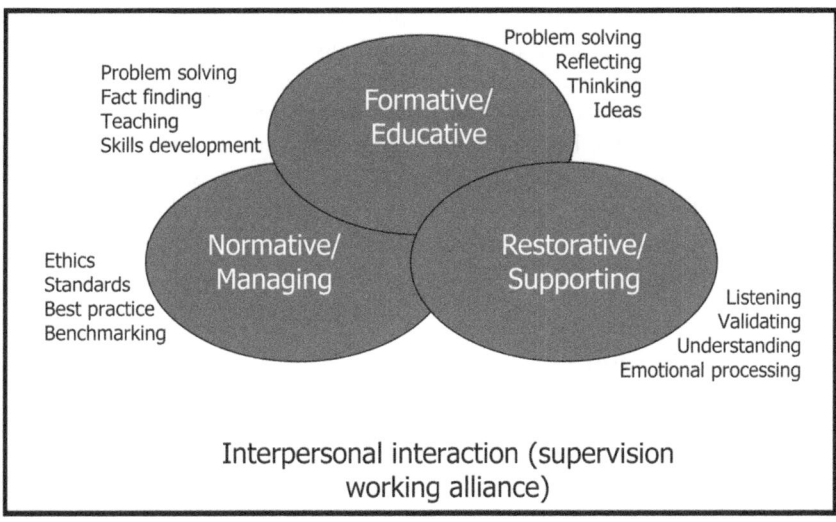

Figure 4.1 Functions of supervision

Getting balance

It is important to remember that supervisors (and supervision) are a finite resource and so time and attention paid to one aspect (e.g. support) will be at the cost of less resource being available for other aspects (Zeni et al., 2013).

It has been argued that within the formative, normative and restorative tasks there may be some form of hierarchy or sequence. For example, Shanley and Stevenson (2006) suggest that support may be the foundation upon which the formative and normative functions are built. Respondents in Jenkins' (2000) telephone-based study highlighted that supervision requires a 'supportive milieu', however it 'must lead to something more than "feeling better". On the other hand, if supervisees do not "feel better", they are unlikely to "come back"' (p. 28). It is worth noting, however, that these might also reflect the establishment of a supervision relationship which is not specifically identified in Proctor or Kadushin's models but is conceptualised as an additional element in Figure 4.1.

Yegdich (1998) challenges the view held by some, of supervision (and specifically nursing supervision) being focused on the emotional needs and wellbeing of the practitioner. She provides a critique of the 'mining metaphor' whereby receiving supervision is likened to practitioners having 'pit head time' in which they engage in supervision to wipe 'off the emotional grime of the job' (p. 194). Although this critique may be a valid reflection for the way in which supervision can be practised, what Yegdich observes is the failure to engage in balanced supervision – in this case a focus on the restorative function at the expense of any others. Therefore, models and frameworks can help supervisors attend to the range of tasks and functions required in order to make supervision a useful and productive process. Specifically, the process is one of development and learning in order to impact on practice, thus 'uncomfortable feelings' can become the trigger for critical analysis resulting in the development of new perspective and consequently new actions or behaviours (e.g. Atkins and Murphy, 1993). Yegdich (1998) also argues that there is a challenge in supervision trying to provide both personal and professional growth. She states that there is a need to demarcate the personal and the professional through the careful use of structure, role boundaries and agreeing a clear purpose for supervision. Without these it is possible that supervision can be seen as a vehicle solely for personal growth.

The supervision hour

Having identified key tasks and dimensions to supervision, the 'supervision hour' model helps to structure the time allocated to supervision. Research has indicated that a supervision session of at least an hour in duration is most beneficial (see Chapter 10). The supervision hour concerns how the time can be used to ensure that the tasks of supervision can be achieved. The structure for the supervision hour is based on work by O'Donoghue (2014) and Wosket and Page (1994) and is represented in Figure 4.2. As can be seen, the model

Supervision models and frameworks 55

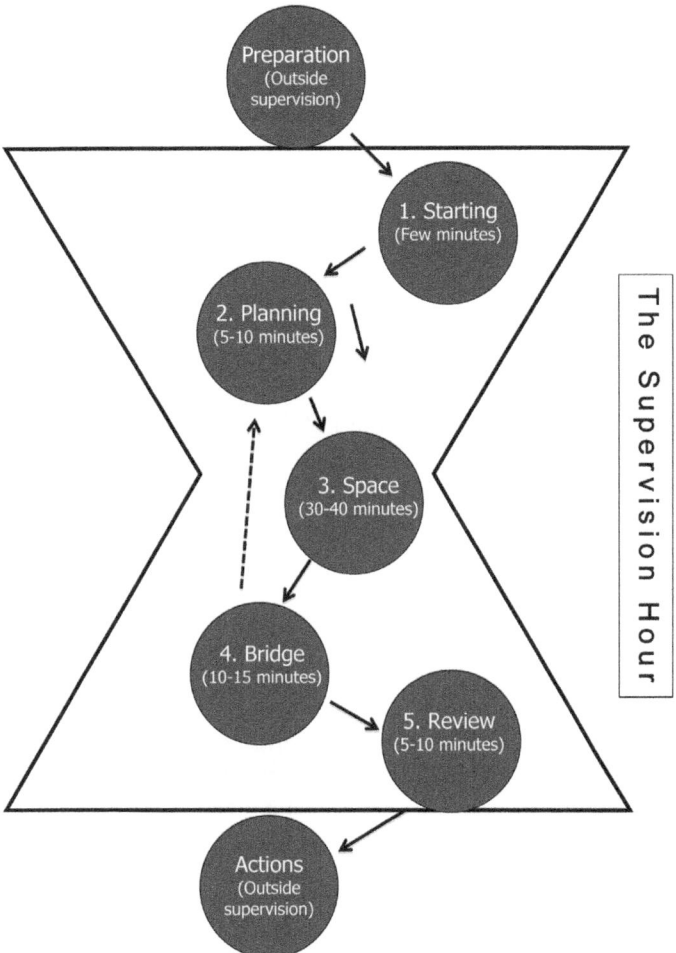

Figure 4.2 The supervision hour
Note: The timings presented with each step are intended as a guide only to help ensure that all steps can be worked through within the session. These timings should not be used slavishly, however it is worth ensuring that sufficient time is allocated to making links to practice and action planning (Step 4).

contains five steps that take place within the supervision hour and two other tasks, namely, preparation before the session, and actions afterwards. Also in the figure are indicative timings from the 60 minutes available for each of the five steps. Focus within the supervision hour can be thought of using the shape of an egg-timer, narrowing from the general to the specific (from 'starting' to 'space') then broadening again (from 'space' to 'review').

Preparation

Prior to the supervision session itself, preparation for supervision needs to be undertaken. The supervisee might keep a log of possible topics for supervision between sessions then review and refine this list prior to supervision and might also review previous actions and supervision notes. Similarly, the supervisor may need to review previous notes and make plans for the session (e.g. things that they may need to bring to the session). Preparing for supervision is discussed more fully in Chapter 6.

Step 1: Starting

At the beginning of each session there are a number of tasks that need to be undertaken to get the session underway. These will include basic greetings, addressing any issues regarding time-keeping or cancellations, discussing any restrictions on the time available or practicalities that may impinge on the session (e.g. anticipated fire alarm) and identification of any supervisor or supervisee factors which may impact on the session. These may be global factors (e.g. issues of physical health, recent life events) and more specific ones (e.g. having just finished a difficult discussion with a client, anxious about delivering a teaching session taking place later in the day). O'Donoghue (2014) refers to this as 'checking in'. As a supervisor, these areas can be discussed by asking questions such as 'how are you?' or 'how has your day been going?' at the start of the session. As the supervisor you should also take a moment to consider the answer to these questions yourself and inform the supervisee of anything relevant. Although the content of this step may not form any later formal focus within the supervision session, it provides important context and may influence some of the thinking and awareness of the supervisor and supervisee. This step can be summarised as 'meet, greet and get settled'. This step might include a brief review of the supervision notes from the last meeting.

Step 2: Planning

This step formalises the agenda for the session. In most instances the supervisee will bring with them a range of items which could form the focus for supervision. The transition from 'starting' to 'planning' may be a simple question by the supervisor such as 'what's on your list for today' or 'what do you need from today'? The planning phase involves a brief discussion of the items on the supervisee's list in order to establish an order of priority and noting any common themes. From this, an agreement should be reached about how things might be discussed. This step will also involve agreeing how much time might be spent on each topic placed on the session agenda. It is worth noting that agenda setting and time allocation can be done in different ways. It may be that the items on the agenda allow for some items to be dealt with at the start simply through discussion of 'fact' or clarification after which other issues are focused on. On other occasions there may be a single significant issue that will take up the whole session. The important aspects of this step are that the agenda is prioritised through discussion and agreement. This step ends when attention moves from considering what needs to be discussed (building the agenda) to discussing the first item on the session agenda.

Step 3: Space

This step might be thought of as the main time of the session and could involve discussion, teaching, clarifying, reflective practice, generating ideas, exploring, making sense, challenge and feedback. Many of the other models such as the developmental model and the process model principally inform the activity within this section of the supervision time. Readers should consider how they might use other models and frameworks within this step. This time might also be allocated to examining supervision itself (e.g. the supervision relationship). Problems can occur when supervision gets 'stuck' in this step or insufficient time is allocated to the subsequent steps.

Step 4: Bridge

This step forms the 'bridge' between the supervision session and the work context. For example, where a client has been discussed, the actions the supervisee will take as a result of the supervision session will be identified and documented; where the focus has been a task (e.g. a training session the supervisee is planning) the bridge addresses what the supervisee will do next. This can be construed as an action planning or goal setting phase – agreeing plans and discussing how these will be enacted. This step might also consider what outcomes might be expected and what to do if the anticipated outcomes do not occur. Where teaching has taken place in the supervision session this step would involve consolidation of what has been learned.

Often within a supervision session, the first item on the agenda might be worked on and a bridge to practice completed with time to spare. In such circumstances the supervisor and supervisee return to step 2 (as shown by the dotted line in Figure 4.2) and briefly review what remains on the agenda. It may be that the next item on the list is selected and supervision returns to step 3 or it may be that some further negotiation is needed to revise the agenda (further planning) before moving to step 3. This 'loop' can be gone around as many times as time allows. In O'Donoghue's (2014) research, the participants appeared to combine the elements of space and bridge into a step the authors referred to as 'working'. It may be that in order to cement the agreed actions and aid their translation into practice, approaches such as forming implementation intentions (e.g. Gollwitzer, 1999), might be used.

Step 5: Review

This step is designed to review the session. This might include mutual formative feedback such as what has worked or what was unhelpful; a summary of actions or decisions; identifying any items that need to be carried forward to the next session (e.g. unaddressed agenda items, actions to follow up next time); arrangements for future supervision (and any changes that need to be made to the supervision agreement) and occasionally, summative feedback – a formal review of how the (usually supervisee) has done. This step might also include time to complete necessary audit paperwork unless there is an agreement that one party does this afterwards.

Actions

This phase happens after the session has finished and is the means in which the content of supervision is brought into the 'real world'. This phase may well start with supervision notes/records being written up. Sometimes there will be definitive and concrete links between supervision and specific actions or decisions, whilst at other times they may be less obvious or cumulative (e.g. based on several supervision sessions) as might be enacted through shifts in the supervisee's focus, interactions or approach over time. The key evidence for this phase are the links that can be drawn between the supervisee's work to the supervision session. Typically, actions will be captured by the supervisee in their log or diary so that they can be considered when preparation and agenda setting is occurring for the next setting.

O'Donoghue (2014) suggests that a checklist could be developed for use by new supervisors to help plan and review sessions to ensure that steps are addressed. They provide an example which interested readers may wish to use as the basis to develop their own.

A developmental model for supervision

It is perhaps unsurprising given the view of supervision as a 'formative' and 'life-long' endeavour, that several developmental models have been constructed to understand supervision (see Bernard and Goodyear, 2014). These models are typically generic in that (a) any aspects of practice could be mapped into them, and (b) they can be used by practitioners alongside other models or approaches to supervision. As the name implies, developmental models consider practitioners to be at different stages (characterised by such things as their level of skill, knowledge, motivation, ability and autonomy) as a result of the extent of training and experience they have. However, this is a complex matrix, as a single practitioner is likely to vary with regard to stage of development according to the 'task in hand' and the competency area being considered including supervision itself (Davies et al., 2004). The developmental stage of the supervisee may inform the selection of the supervisor (Johnston and Milne, 2012), and awareness of the developmental level might enable supervisors to adapt their approach according to the needs and characteristics of the supervisee (Scaife,

2013). In addition to individual developmental levels, Shanley and Stevenson (2006) using nursing as an example, argue that professions themselves might be at different developmental stages with regard to their understanding and readiness for practice supervision. They suggest that this might be reflected in the model's that different professional groups selected to guide supervision, with the use and adoption of more 'complex' models increasing as levels of knowledge and skill develop.

One of the most widely used developmental frameworks is the Integrated Developmental Model (Stoltenberg and McNeill, 2010) developed for therapist supervision. In this model, functioning in any particular domain can be characterised into one of four levels. Each level is characterised by descriptions of the supervisee's needs and presentation with associated guidance for the supervisor as to the core functions they need to fulfil. This framework has been adapted for use in forensic settings (Davies et al., 2004) by broadening the concepts from therapist to forensic practitioner. In their study of staff working in a high security forensic mental health setting, Davies et al. (2004) described practice at four different levels (from foundation to 'integrated practice') across a number of domains (including interpersonal skills, teamship skills, formulation and treatment planning). The intention was to develop a framework which might offer useful information to the supervisor and supervisee in relation to practice strengths and areas for development. The authors demonstrated that using a developmental framework, practitioners generally rated their skills and competencies to a level predicted by their job description. A simple summary of the characteristics of functioning at each level along with supervisor guidance is presented in Box 4.1.

BOX 4.1: Developmental levels – examples of characteristics, supervisor approach and level (adapted from Stoltenberg and McNeill, 2010)

The examples given against each level show some of the characteristics of the supervisee when functioning at a particular level for a task. It is important to remember that for different aspects of practice the supervisee may be at different levels, although there may be a 'typical level' which indicates their general level of competence. At transition points, supervisees will start to take on the characteristics associated with the higher level of performance – supervisors should review their style where necessary and experiment with introducing elements of the approach associated with the next level.

Level 1

Supervisee characteristics: The supervisee is motivated although they will also be anxious about their lack of knowledge and skill. They will focus on tasks and 'learning how to . . .' and will be dependent on their supervisor.

Supervisor approach: The supervisor needs to provide structure for the supervisee both in supervision and in their practice. Within supervision teaching and 'prescribing' by the supervisor are usually evident. The supervisee needs support and encouragement which can be provided by adopting a facilitative stance. It is important that the supervisor directly observe work undertaken by the supervisee as their focus is often on themselves and their actions rather than appraising the whole event. In a forensic setting, careful support around risk and boundaries will be needed along with possible modelling and role play of ways to manage potential situations.

Minimum supervisor level: inexperienced supervisors who are at level 2 or above in other areas of their practice

Level 2

Supervisee characteristics: By now the supervisee has a range of skills and as a result becomes less focused on 'what to do' and more aware of the client. This can result in the supervisee feeling overwhelmed or over-identifying with the client (and loosing sight of the bigger picture). The supervisee may fluctuate between dependency (associated with level 1) and a desire for autonomy (level 3) which can lead to variable motivation. In a forensic setting, being overwhelmed, over-identification and apparent over-confidence in one's ability or skill can produce 'blind spots' or avoidance which may lead to risky practice. Some authors have likened this level to a 'period of adolescence'.

Supervisor approach: The supervisor needs to be able to balance guidance with fostering independence and encouraging supervisee decision making. This can be coupled with increased disclosure by the supervisor of their practice and the range of ways situations might be approached. Supervisors can introduce more challenge, however the supervisor needs to consider 'what is not presented' and wider issues of risk. Live supervision and practice observation remain useful.

Minimum supervisor level: an experienced supervisor is recommended due to the need to be sensitive and responsive to the varying needs and 'presentations' of the supervisee.

Level 3

Supervisee characteristics: At this level, the supervisee is typically proficient in a range of areas and is able to hold multiple perspectives (e.g. client, system). Their motivation is typically stable and they are generally aware of their strengths and needs thus they will typically take an active lead in directing their supervision. Their focus tends to be on integrating different areas of practice, addressing complex problems and on personal and professional development.

<u>Supervisor approach:</u> The main form of supervision may be group supervision although individual supervision remains appropriate. The focus is to support integration across domains of practice.

<u>Minimum supervisor level:</u> level 3 supervisor

Integrated/advanced practice

This level (now only touched upon by Stoltenberg and McNeill (2010) unlike in their previous work) is worthy of mention as it represents a level of general integration across domains of practice – thus such practitioners are likely to have experience of functioning at level 3 in most if not all domains. These different domains will themselves be integrated, and skills, knowledge and practice are highly transferable to novel situations. Such practitioners are likely to be acknowledged by others as advanced practitioners. Their general characteristics and supervision needs are similar to those at level 3 and they may seek to 'add new domains to their repertoire' (moving from level 1 through to 3 for these new competencies). Supervision is typically group or individual reciprocal supervision.

The ability of a supervisor to respond to individual needs at different levels of supervisee development requires further research. However, in one small but detailed study by Davies, Salmon and MacDonald (2000), the supervision sessions of a single supervisor working individually with three supervisees at different developmental stages were video recorded. These were analysed for observable behaviours which were considered characteristic of supervisor behaviour/tasks for different supervisee levels of development. The expected differences between the individuals at different stages and the supervisor's behaviour were seen. In contrast, a survey of trainee counsellors by Ladany, Mori and Mehr (2012) found that the supervisee's ratings of the skills and approach of the supervisor did not vary across trainees at developmental stage. This self-report study may not have been sufficiently sensitive to detect differences in 'how' the supervisor acts but instead may have captured 'what' was needed to foster a good relationship (e.g. a supervisor who is empowering, providing positive and challenging feedback).

Some have criticised developmental models because of their linear approach (i.e. the incremental move from stage to stage, see Beddoe and Davys, 2010) and more generally because development can be seen as an underlying assumption of all practice supervision (Bernard and Goodyear, 2014). However, there is growing acceptance that development may be much more subtle and complex than a simple 'growth over time'. For example, the developmental framework suggests that when you are new to something you are likely to need direction whilst when experienced you need more reflection and self-directed space. Whilst this is true it is important that even as a novice practitioner, supervision attends to how you feel alongside how you function.

Two final observations are worth noting. The first is the intuitive appeal of developmental approaches. The second is the observation that supervision as a competency itself, follows a developmental trajectory. Thus, supervisors themselves move from being overwhelmed, anxious and self-conscious to integrated, secure and competent (Russell and Petrie, 1995).

Process model

The seven-eyed supervision model, also referred to as the double matrix model (Hawkins and Shohet, 2006), was originally developed as a supervision model for use with counsellors, however according to its authors it has now been used with a range of other staff groups. As a process model, it is concerned with 'what happens in supervision' and attempts to explicitly draw together the different 'players', i.e. the client, the practitioner (who is also the supervisee) and the supervisor within their respective context(s). The strength of the process model is in recognising that, within supervision, attention can be given to each of these 'players' and the real or possible relationships between them as well as to the context. Hawkins and Shohet (2006) describe seven modes (or eyes/viewpoints) that can be used to explore issues. These modes are not sequential, and each should be used within supervision although not necessarily in every session. As part of describing the model, a brief vignette will be used to provide some concrete examples based on the particular presenting issue (in this case, problems of client engagement).

The vignette

Rhys, a newly qualified member of staff in a forensic mental health service, is working with Steffan to provide individual support as part of a drug treatment programme. Rhys is unsure what he should do to maintain Steffan's engagement so raises the issue with his supervisor, Angharad.

The seven modes

Mode 1: A focus on the client – attention in this mode is on the client, their needs and strengths and how they present in the session (e.g. what do they say, what does their body language and tone of voice suggest, what are their goals, why do they attend). Information relating to the client might be gained by the supervisor asking questions or through reviewing audio or video recordings. These latter two approaches are particularly useful as they also provide information that may be of use for other modes. In addition to providing information, however, supervision in this mode is also concerned with shedding new light on the client or the 'problem'. In our case, Angharad might ask Rhys to compare points in the session when Steffan seems engaged with those when he doesn't; how Steffan presents to others or in other settings and how the sessions are relevant to Steffan (why he might want to engage)

ANGHARAD: Why do you think Steffan keeps attending the sessions?
RHYS: I guess he thinks he has to.
ANGHARAD: Do you think he wants to attend or does he need to be cajoled?
RHYS: Well ... I think he just comes along.
ANGHARAD: What do you think he wants out of the meetings with you?
RHYS: I'm not sure.

From this brief exchange a number of possible areas for further work with the client are identified, for example why he attends and what his goals are.

Mode 2: A focus on what is being done (or attempted) – in this mode the focus moves to what is being done, the style and the approach, what has been tried and what have been the outcomes. Supervision in this mode is about generating new ideas and possibilities about what might be done, interventions to try or style to adopt. In our case, Angharad might ask Rhys to consider what else he might do, how he might engage with another client who presents 'like this', what he has seen others do that might work, what he has thought about doing but hasn't tried or what radically different approach he might take. Angharad might also offer some suggestions or observations from theory or from her own experience. In mode 2, Angharad also needs to attend to Rhys's skill and knowledge level, and how she might foster development through such actions as providing training or an opportunity for skills practice within supervision to address this.

ANGHARAD: What else could you do when Steffan says 'It's alright for you – you haven't had to put up with the things he has'?
RHYS: I guess I could try techniques from motivational interviewing such as 'rolling with resistance' but I'm not really sure how to.
ANGHARAD: Do you want to explore some ideas for rolling with resistance and then maybe practice your ideas?

In this discussion, possible skills development is identified which may offer new engagement options.

Mode 3: A focus on the client-practitioner relationship – attention in this mode is on the relationship within the session (or sessions) between the client and the practitioner. Supervision in this mode is concerned with understanding the relationship and, in particular, any features of the relationship itself which may be helpful or exacerbating the problem. Angharad might ask Rhys to describe the nature of their relationship; how Rhys thinks he is viewed by Steffan, and pose questions to explore this further such as 'if you were watching the session how would you characterise the relationship?', 'what roles do you think Steffan and you have been drawn into?'

RHYS: Sometimes he seems to get really angry with me even when I just ask about how his week has been.
ANGHARAD: Why do you think he gets so angry – anything in your tone, or what you say that might be relevant?
RHYS: I'm not sure – I suppose he thinks I'm here to tell him what to do.
ANGHARAD: Why might that get him so angry?
RHYS: He always gets cross when he tells me about his dad nagging him and feeling like he was always failing.
ANGHARAD: How do you react when he gets angry?
RHYS: I guess I try to make him feel okay or end up trying to explain again why we should meet.
ANGHARAD: How might you act or do things differently – could you raise your theory about a link to his dad?

This conversation identifies possible tensions in the relationship with ideas for how these might be understood and responded to.

Mode 4: A focus on the practitioner/supervisee – this moves attention from the client to the practitioner themselves. Focus here is on emotions aroused by the client and the motives and intentions of the practitioner. In this mode, supervision can be seen to attend more to the practitioner's experiences. This may be associated with a move to more attention to the restorative function of supervision in addition to developing self-awareness and ways of maintaining physical, psychological and emotional safety and resilience.

ANGHARAD: How do you feel when he gets angry with you?
RHYS: Sometimes I'm a bit scared but more frustration I think – I'm just here trying to help.
ANGHARAD: How do you deal with that feeling during your discussions?
RHYS: I just try to ignore it mostly … or move on.
ANGHARAD: Is there a way you might use this feeling differently or is there a way you might plan to respond the next time this happens?

There are a number of roles that have been described that practitioners can be drawn into – these are especially relevant to forensic settings. Probably the most commonly used description is that of the Drama Triangle (sometimes referred to as Karpman's Triangle; Karpman, 1968) which describes the roles of Rescuer (person trying to 'save'), Persecutor (person trying to punish) and Victim (person being victimised). In addition, Karpman describes 'drama' as taking place when a switch in roles takes place (e.g. the supervisee moving from Rescuer to Victim). It could be argued that there is a fourth position – that of being outside the triangle – with drama taking place when the triangle is entered (e.g. supervisor moving from supervisor role to Persecutor through criticism of the supervisee) or when it is exited.

As with the other modes, Angharad maintains their focus on linking supervision with practice.

Mode 5: A focus on the supervisory relationship – the focus at this level concerns how the supervisory relationship may be influenced by or share similarities with the practitioner-client relationship. This is often thought of as parallel process (see Box 4.2) and provides an opportunity for learning because the 'practice issue' is present in the supervisory relationship.

ANGHARAD: I noticed when we were discussing ideas for responding to Steffan you seemed reluctant to try out the ideas and I started to offer more and more – I've not noticed this happening before.
RHYS: Normally what we talk about seems useful, but this time I didn't think there would be much point, nothing seems to work.
ANGHARAD: That sounds like something Steffan might say.
RHYS: I guess it does really, I often feel I'm working hard and he just has to say 'good idea but it wouldn't work for me'.
ANGHARAD: Maybe working hard and generating loads of ideas isn't the way to go?

By noting the possible link between Rhys's response and those of Steffan, Angharad provides a new angle to consider the 'stuck pattern' that Steffan has experienced both with the client and echoed in supervision.

Mode 6: A focus on the supervisor – this concerns how the supervisor feels and thinks during the time with the supervisee. For example, the supervisor may feel challenged or upset or be reminded of experiences they have had with clients. They may also have thoughts about the client the supervisee is working with. As with the other modes, this might give rise to new ideas or observations which prompt a new or different way forward.

ANGHARAD: When you were talking about Steffan's family life I felt very sad – I wonder if that is something you've experienced with Steffan?
RHYS: Sometimes – I guess much of his life has been difficult and traumatic.
ANGHARAD: How do you think this impacts on his work with you and what he needs from you?

In this exchange, Angharad uses her emotional response to trigger an exploration of Rhys's work with Steffan.

Mode 7: A focus on the context – here the focus might be on the context of any of the 'players' or the systems in which they work. This might include a focus on the wider context of the client, the system/organisation, the profession of the practitioner or the setting where the client and practitioner meet. It is important to recognise that the wider community and societal factors are also aspects of the context which may need to be considered in order to understand their influence and impact on the supervisee, the client and the work being undertaken. The context might also include such factors as gender, age, race, cultural expectations, power, personal history and developmental stage.

ANGHARAD: How might Steffan's social context have impacted on his drug use and violence?
RHYS: From what he's said it was part of fitting in – normal I guess.
ANGHARAD: And how has that translated to being in here?

Here Angharad links two differing contexts, Steffan's life in the community and his life as an inpatient. This could be developed further by Rhys to consider issues relevant to engagement.

In the model, Hawkins and Shohet (2006) use the ideas of transference and counter-transference to describe aspects of the supervision process. It is beyond the scope and purpose of this text to discuss this in detail, however, in brief, transference can be described as a client experiencing and therefore acting within a current relationship 'as if' it were another relationship (usually from the past) – the 'here and now' gets affected by the 'then and there'. In the example above it may be that Steffan is acting towards Rhys 'as if' he was his nagging father with the longstanding anger towards his dad being 'unleashed' towards Rhys. In this same exchange, Rhys's counter-transference can be thought of as his unconscious response to Steffan. So when Steffan becomes angry, Rhys responds either by being drawn into re-rehearsing ('nagging') why they need to meet (acting in line with the transference) or by acting opposite ('avoiding nagging') to try to direct the conversation (acting to block the transference).

> **BOX 4.2: Parallel process**
>
> The idea of parallel process has its origins in psychotherapy and can be described as a process (e.g. set of emotions, behaviours or interactions) from one relationship being replayed in another. In the case of supervision the client-practitioner relationship is paralleled in the practitioner (supervisee) – supervisor relationship (Azar, 2000). Thus the practitioner's experiences (such as thoughts feelings and actions) from the client encounter may be acted out within supervision. This is sometimes described as a 'here and now' process mirroring a 'then and there' one (i.e. what is happening between the supervisor and supervisee in some important way(s) reflects the interaction or process between the practitioner (supervisee) and the client (Playle and Mullarkey, 1998)). Houston (1995) refers to this process as an 'echo'. It is important to note that this process is not intentional and therefore may be completely outside the

awareness of the supervisee, thus the supervisor needs to be able to identify the process in order to begin to address it.

By way of an example, Polly (the practitioner) was meeting with Beryl (the client) for an individual review of Beryl's treatment. During the discussion Beryl became very angry and began accusing Polly of being a bully and treating her unfairly. Polly responded by apologising and becoming quieter, reducing her eye contact and ultimately ended the session early. In supervision, Polly spoke about the session with her supervisor. During the supervision discussion, Polly became uncharacteristically cross with the supervisor and began challenging the supervisor's skill. Initially the supervisor responded by apologising and 'placating' Polly, however soon realised this was exacerbating the situation. The supervisor suggested that this might be a parallel process and suggested they try to refocus on how Polly felt in the session and how the trigger for Beryl's anger might be identified.

One key reason for understanding the idea of parallel process is to prepare the supervisor for the possibility of this occurring within supervision. A supervisor who is able to identify parallel process can assist the supervisee to recognise the process and they can then work together to determine how to respond to it. In the example above, a failure to recognise the process may have resulted in the supervisor spending time 'defending their position' or in focusing on Polly and possible reasons for her 'out of character' behaviour. As observed by Houston (1995) the critical aspect is not in noticing (although this is vital) it is in the response.

Giordano, Clarke and Borders (2013) identify a number of markers which may indicate the possibility of parallel process. These include the supervisor's emotional reactions; atypical behaviour by the supervisee; supervisor and supervisee feeling stuck and changes in the supervision relationship. They suggest that making the parallel process explicit in order to develop a plan is a helpful goal however the stage of development of the supervisee might be important in considering how explicitly to name and address parallel process. They note that identifying and addressing parallel process can result in defensiveness and resistance and therefore advocate the use of a 'motivational interviewing stance' when working with parallel process. Using this framework they suggest assessing how the supervisee responds to the supervisor's observation from which they should gauge the level of the supervisee awareness and readiness to address parallel process. They suggest that the supervisor convey empathic understanding through reflection, a shift in focus (where necessary), the use of change talk (e.g. describe future changes), and the use of options. They also describe the use of 'developing discrepancy' where contrasts are made between current behaviour and past behaviour or current experience and desired experience in relation to the client. By way of an example – you [supervisee] were confident, now you focus on your

> shortcomings; is there any connection between your experience and the client?
>
> Shanley and Stevenson (2006) suggest that parallel process could work in both directions – for example positive experiences in the supervisor-supervisee relationship might be replicated in the supervisee/practitioner relationship with the client. Johns (1993) makes the same argument in relation to empowerment; empowerment within supervision could be paralleled by the supervisee (practitioner) taking this experience out into their work with clients – acting in ways which empower their clients as they themselves have been empowered.

Approaches to supervision

Common factors approach

From their review of the literature, Morgan and Sprenkle (2007) present a descriptive model representing 'essential components of effective supervision' through the use of three dimensions, namely, emphasis, specificity and relationship. They suggest that it should be possible to characterise any given moment of supervision according to their place along these dimensions. The first two dimensions describe 'what' supervisors do:

(1) *emphasis* – i.e. what is being focused upon at any specific moment ranging from practice competence (e.g. skills and ability in relation to their job role) at the one end and professional competence (e.g. ethical and legal issues) at the other.
(2) *specificity* – i.e. the supervisor's level of individual detail or focus ranging from idiosyncratic/particular (e.g. the specific supervisee, client or task) at one end and nomothetic/general (e.g. the service or profession) at the other.

Using these two 'what' dimensions, Morgan and Sprenkle (2007) suggest that four supervisor roles can be mapped. These are briefly described in Box 4.3. Although these are presented as discrete roles, it will often be the case that there is overlap and that different roles will be needed at different times even in relation to a single supervision topic. These roles share similarity to the more widely known Discriminant Model of supervision (see Bernard and Goodyear, 2014) in which three roles (teacher, counsellor and consultant) and three possible foci for supervision (intervention, conceptualisation and personalisation) are presented. It also bears some similarity to Scaife's General Supervision Framework (Scaife, 2013) in which the supervisor's behaviour, the focus of the supervision and the way in which supervision takes place are mapped. The third dimension described by Morgan and Sprenkle (2007) addresses the nature of the supervisory *relationship* – 'how' the supervisor/supervisee are interacting. This is described as ranging from collaborative through to directive.

BOX 4.3: Supervisory roles (based on Morgan and Sprenkle, 2007)

		Specificity	
		Particular	General
Emphasis	Practice	**Coach:** Focus on direct practice with a specific instance in mind (*what to do in this case*). Aim to improve knowledge and skills application through activities such as offering advice, providing feedback, skills practice and trouble-shooting	**Teacher:** Focus on direct practice at a general level (*widely applicable learning*). Aim to support wider skills and knowledge acquisition through teaching, discussion, supplying reading and skills training
	Professional	**Mentor:** Focus on individual supervisee's professional development. Aim to facilitate identification of strengths and weaknesses, career development, role identity and professional identity	**Administrator:** Focus on broad professional, ethical and legal elements. Aim to ensure standards, resolve ethical practice dilemmas and undertake necessary evaluation of supervisee performance

In a number of ways this approach shares similarity with the detailed Systems Approach to Supervision (SAS) comprehensively described by Holloway (1995). In her model, the supervisory relationship is at the centre with six other dimensions surrounding it – each of which are comprised of several factors themselves. The six dimensions are:

(1) supervision functions (the 'how' of supervision, e.g. instructing, supporting, modelling);
(2) supervision tasks (what supervision is trying to achieve, e.g. specific skills, knowledge, professional identity);
(3) supervisor factors (these include professional experience and cultural characteristics);
(4) institution factors (including the organisational structure and climate);
(5) supervisee factors (referred to as trainee in the model; including learning needs and style); and
(6) client factors (including identified problems and relationship with staff).

Holloway advocates that supervision sessions can be analysed using the SAS framework to help be explicit about the ways supervision is being conducted and the factors leading this and perhaps to indicate other possibilities open to the supervisor and supervisee.

Solution-focused supervision

It is probably better to describe this as an approach or style of supervision rather than as a model per se; however, it provides a way to ensure that 'what works' and what is being done well form a routine part of supervision. In essence, solution-focused supervision (SFS) shifts the emphasis from deficits, limits, mistakes and weaknesses to competence, strengths and possibilities (Juhnke, 1996). The other factor in SFS is that it is very action orientated and easy to link directly to the client or task issue. Although developed for use with those providing solution-focused therapy, it offers a range of ideas and suggestions which could be incorporated by any supervisor. Effective supervision is seen to be a result of a solution-orientated approach and being client (task) focused. Focus on recognising and amplifying successes and competence with the intent of enhancing client outcome (Triantafillou, 1997) – building on what is working and what is already being done well. Based on Juhnke (1996) and Triantafillou (1997), the following techniques might be helpful:

Goal setting – distinguishing time specific goals (i.e. those that are written into the supervision agreement) and session specific goals (what needs to be achieved in relation to the specific clients and task brought to this supervision session).

The miracle question – the supervisor might ask, 'if a miracle happened tonight and your ability to do X increased as you expected what would be the first thing you would notice?' – this approach enables the supervisee to begin to identify the behaviours, skills, attitudes or knowledge they might use or shape to achieve the goal.

Fast-forwarding – 'if you fast-forward to [a time from now e.g. 10 weeks] what will you be doing in relation to [the client or task] that you are not doing now?' – this approach may help the supervisee identify new behaviours, skills etc. that can become goals.

Promoting and developing skills – there are many SFS techniques that can be drawn upon including questions that can be used to:

(a) further develop ideas that have been identified – 'where will you start?'; 'what can you begin to do now?';
(b) generate options – 'what else could you do?';
(c) use others to identify possibilities – 'how might [another skilled practitioner] or [expert A] approach this?';
(d) seek exceptions to concerns – ' ... on the occasion X didn't happen (or Y did happen) – what was different; what could you do to repeat that?';
(e) scale goals/skills to develop them – 'what score would you give yourself (from 0–10) in relation to [goal Z/skill Y]? How might you increase this/repeat this next time?'; and
(f) identify improvements – 'what improvements have you noticed in your [skills/abilities] since the last supervision session?'.

Triantafillou (1997) presents guidelines for solution-focused supervision:

(a) establish an atmosphere of competence;
(b) focus on strengths and resources, what has worked, knowledge of what is being done correctly;
(c) search for client-based solutions;
(d) clarify goals, look for exceptions, explore hypothetical solutions;
(e) provide feedback to the supervisee;
(f) organise around compliments, education and formalising goals and task follow up; and
(g) elicit, amplify, reinforce and start again.

In a small pragmatic study, Triantafillou (1997) found all participants rated the solution-focused supervision approach above average or clearly superior to other approaches with comments relating to the positive aspects of the approach. In addition, most considered that the supervision had improved their effectiveness. They also found differences in client outcomes relating to the use of medication and the number of serious incidents. However, as the study also included other training, it is possible that the positive impact on clients was not the result of supervision.

Evidence-based supervision

In something of a contrast to most of the models above, Milne (2009) has emphasised the importance of research evidence as the basis on which to found a definition and a model of supervision. Through examination of the evidence of 'what works' in supervision, he has compiled a model based on what is currently identified as important. However, perhaps more important are the 12 principles of evidence-based supervision that he identifies (see Box 4.4). His framework is explicit in enabling hypotheses and research questions to be developed in order to further advance the understanding of supervision. Milne's approach provides a synthesis based on the current status of a range of published knowledge, however, it requires constant review in the light of emerging literature. It is perhaps best thought of as both a consolidation of the literature and research and an approach for the supervisor themselves to provide supervision founded on available evidence – a 'what works' in supervision approach. Its possible limitations include the possibility that it might privilege research evidence over other forms of evidence and knowledge in deciding what works. Bernard and Goodyear (2014), also suggest that this approach may have a bias towards technique (i.e. what to do) rather than understanding (i.e. how and why to do) as implied by a model. Interested readers should consult Milne's text directly for a full understanding of his 'evidence-based' approach. Finding ways to unite 'theory-based models' with an 'evidence-based approach' would be a very worthwhile development.

> **BOX 4.4: The 12 principles of evidence-based supervision (Milne, 2009)**
>
> Milne proposes 12 principles which together underpin the evidence-based approach to supervision practice.
>
> 1. Take account of the context in which supervision takes place.
> 2. Adopt a problem-solving cycle.
> 3. Draw critically on what is known.
> 4. Clarify your model of practice.
> 5. Integrate theory with practice.
> 6. Verify assumptions.
> 7. Critically engage with ideas, theories, evidence etc.
> 8. Build and maintain the supervisory alliance.
> 9. Utilise the full supervision cycle (e.g. assessing need, agreeing goals, reflection or teaching, evaluation).
> 10. Engage the supervisee as a collaborator.
> 11. Ensure there is appropriate support for your supervisory efforts.
> 12. Evaluate supervision.

Conclusion

Although there is no single agreed model or theory of supervision, there are a wide set of conceptual frameworks and approaches which can provide a point of reference (Hyrkäs, Koivula and Paunonen, 1999). This chapter provides supervisors and supervisees with an introduction to some of these. For many, the models presented here will provide a sufficient foundation from which to engage in supervision, however, it is hoped that they will also serve as a catalyst for further exploration of the many supervision frameworks and models.

References

Atkins, S. and Murphy, K. (1993) 'Reflection: a review of the literature', *Journal of Advanced Nursing* 18(8): 1188–92.

Atkinson, C. and Woods, K. (2007) 'A model of effective fieldwork supervision for trainee educational psychologists', *Educational Psychology in Practice* 23(4): 299–316.

Ayer, S., Knight, S., Joyce, L. and Nightingale, V. (1997) 'Practice-led education and development project: developing styles in clinical supervision', *Nurse Education Today* 17 (5): 347–58.

Azar, S. T. (2000) 'Preventing burnout in professionals and paraprofessionals who work with child abuse and neglect cases: a cognitive behavioral approach to supervision', *Journal of Clinical Psychology* 56(5): 643–63.

Beddoe, L. and Davys, A. (2010) *Best Practice in Professional Supervision*, London: Jessica Kingsley Publishers.

Bernard, J. M. and Goodyear, R. K. (2014) *Fundamentals of Clinical Supervision* (5th edn), International Edition, London: Pearson.

Bordin, E. S. (1983) 'A working alliance based model of supervision', *The Counseling Psychologist* 11(1): 35–42.

Cutcliffe, J. R. (2005) 'From the guest editor – clinical supervision: a search for homogeneity or heterogeneity?', *Issues in Mental Health Nursing* 26(5): 471–3.

Cutcliffe, J. R., Butterworth, T. and Proctor, B. (eds) (2005) *Fundamental Themes in Clinical Supervision*, Abingdon: Routledge.

Davies, J., Salmon, A. and MacDonald, F. (2000) 'Supervision: what works for whom?', *Clinical Psychology Forum* 146: 17–20.

Davies, J., Tennant, A., Ferguson, E. and Jones, L. (2004) 'Developing models and a framework for multi-professional clinical supervision', *The British Journal of Forensic Practice* 6(3): 36–42.

Fowler, J. (1996) 'Clinical supervision: what do you do after saying hello?', *British Journal of Nursing* 5(6): 382–5.

Fowler, J. and Chevannes, M. (1998) 'Evaluating the efficacy of reflective practice within the context of clinical supervision', *Journal of Advanced Nursing* 27(2): 379–82.

Giordano, A., Clarke, P. and Borders, L. D. (2013) 'Using motivational interviewing techniques to address parallel process in supervision', *Counselor Education and Supervision* 52(1): 15–29.

Gollwitzer, P. M. (1999) 'Implementation intentions: strong effects of simple plans', *American Psychologist* 54(7): 493.

Hair, H. J. (2013) 'The purpose and duration of supervision, and the training and discipline of supervisors: what social workers say they need to provide effective services', *British Journal of Social Work* 43(8): 1562–88.

Hawkins, P. and Shohet, R. (2006) *Supervision in the Helping Professions* (3rd edn), Buckingham: Open University Press.

Holloway, E. L. (1995) *Clinical Supervision*, London: Sage Publications, Inc.

Houston, G. (1995) *Supervision and Counselling*, Gillingham: The Rochester Foundation.

Hyrkäs, K., Koivula, M. and Paunonen, M. (1999) 'Clinical supervision in nursing in the 1990s – current state of concepts, theory and research', *Journal of Nursing Management* 7(3): 177.

Jenkins, E. (2000) 'Clinical supervision: what is going on in West Wales? Results of a telephone survey', *Journal of Research in Nursing* 5(1): 21–36.

Johns, C. (1993) 'Professional supervision', *Journal of Nursing Management* 1(1): 9–18.

Johnston, L. H. and Milne, D. L. (2012) 'How do supervisee's learn during supervision? A grounded theory study of the perceived developmental process', *The Cognitive Behaviour Therapist* 5(1): 1–23.

Juhnke, G. A. (1996) 'Solution-focused supervision: promoting supervisee skills and confidence through successful solutions', *Counselor Education and Supervision* 36(1): 48–57.

Kadushin, A. (1976) *Supervision in Social Work*, New York: Columbia University Press.

Karpman, S. (1968) 'Fairy tales and script drama analysis', *Transactional Analysis Bulletin*.

Ladany, N., Mori, Y. and Mehr, K. E. (2012) 'Effective and ineffective supervision', *The Counseling Psychologist* 41(1): 28–47.

Milne, D. L. (2009) *Evidence-Based Clinical Supervision*, Oxford: John Wiley & Sons.

Mor Barak, M. E., Travis, D. J., Pyun, H. and Xie, B. (2009) 'The impact of supervision on worker outcomes: a meta-analysis', *Social Service Review* 83(1): 3–32.

Morgan, M. M. and Sprenkle, D. H. (2007) 'Toward a common-factors approach to supervision', *Journal of Marital and Family Therapy* 33(1): 1–17.

O'Donoghue, K. B. (2014) 'Towards an interactional map of the supervision session: an exploration of supervisees and supervisors experiences', *Practice: Social Work in Action* 26(1): 53–70.

Playle, J. F. and Mullarkey, K. (1998) 'Parallel process in clinical supervision: enhancing learning and providing support', *Nurse Education Today* 18(7): 558–66.

Proctor, B. (1986) 'Supervision: a co-operative exercise in accountability', in M. Marken and M. Payne (eds), *Enabling and Ensuring*, Leicester: National Youth Bureau for Education in Youth and Community Work.

Russell, R. K. and Petrie, T. (1995) 'Issues in training effective supervisors', *Applied and Preventive Psychology* 3(1): 27–42.

Scaife, J. (2013) *Supervision in Clinical Practice*, Abingdon: Routledge.

Schoenwald, S. K., Mehta, T. G., Frazier, S. L. and Shernoff, E. S. (2013) 'Clinical supervision in effectiveness and implementation research', *Clinical Psychology: Science and Practice* 20(1): 44–59.

Shanley, M. J. and Stevenson, C. (2006) 'Clinical supervision revisited', *Journal of Nursing Management* 14(8): 586–92.

Stoltenberg, C. D. and McNeill, B. W. (2010) *IDM Supervision* (3rd edn), Abingdon: Routledge.

Triantafillou, N. (1997) 'A solution-focused approach to mental health supervision', *Journal of Systemic Therapies* 16: 305–28.

Watkins, C. E. (1997) *Handbook of Psychotherapy Supervision*, Oxford: John Wiley & Sons.

Westergaard, J. (2013) 'Supervision in the helping professions: making the case for support and supervision for career counsellors', *Australian Journal of Career Development* 22(1): 21–8.

Whitehead, P. R., Ward, T. and Collie, R. M. (2007) 'Time for a change: applying the good lives model of rehabilitation to a high-risk violent offender', *International Journal of Offender Therapy and Comparative Criminology* 51(5): 578–98.

Wosket, V. and Page, S. (1994) *The Cyclical Model of Supervision*, Abingdon: Routledge.

Yegdich, T. (1998) 'How not to do clinical supervision in nursing', *Journal of Advanced Nursing* 28(1): 193–202.

Zeni, T. A., MacDougall, A. E., Chauhan, R. S., Brock, M. E. and Buckley, M. R. (2013) 'In search of those boundary conditions that might influence the effectiveness of supportive supervision', *Journal of Occupational and Organizational Psychology* 86(3): 317–23.

5 Approaches to learning in supervision

Understanding some of the many ideas and theories of learning can be helpful to the supervisor, especially as learning about oneself and one's work are core features of supervision. This chapter considers three related aspects of learning in supervision: theories of adult learning; what needs to be learned; and how supervisors can support learning. Consideration will be given to the ways in which past learning experience, preferred styles and the nature of what is to be learned might influence the approach taken to learning. The ways in which the supervisor might act as teacher and facilitator will also be explored. Readers may wish to reference the chapter on models and the special topics on reflective practice and creative approaches as they consider the information and ideas in this chapter. Before continuing, it is worth working through Box 5.1 which contains exercises and information to help explore your own approaches to learning and development and how you might investigate learning styles and preferences with supervisees.

Supervision as learning

It has been suggested that professional practice can only be mastered through supervised practice (Fowler, 1996) and that, within a forensic context, supervision provides a forum for learning, to ensure that skills are developed and utilised (Mothersole, 2000). Therefore, it could be argued that 'the aim of supervision is to engage practitioners in a learning process, helping them to integrate what they are doing, feeling and thinking' (Zorga, 2002, p. 267). In this way, supervision facilitates 'advanced integration' (Goodyear and Bernard, 1998), supporting the development of awareness of strengths and weaknesses, and facilitating both assimilation (i.e. incorporating experiences and learning into what is already known) and accommodation (i.e. adjusting, revising, unlearning, unfreezing and developing 'internal structures and models') (Zorga, 2002). Based on this, the supervisor's task is, at least in part, to be that of a 'facilitator of learning' (Knowles, Holton and Swanson, 1998, p. 199) and development. In order to achieve effective learning, the supervisor may also need to gain an understanding of a range of supervisee factors such as personality and learning style (Jones, 2006).

Supervision might also provide a learning opportunity for the supervisor (e.g. Carrington, 2004). Although this is unlikely to be the primary focus of providing supervision, professional development may occur not only with regard to supervision skill but also for wider practice and professional competencies (e.g. obtaining the latest knowledge from students/trainees).

> ### BOX 5.1: Taking stock
>
> Think of times when you have learned something such as a new skill, a piece of information or about yourself or your practice. Try to identify several examples and ask yourself 'how did I learn in that situation?'; 'what role (if any) did others play in my learning?' and 'what did I learn about my learning style or preferences from that episode of learning?'
>
> It is quite likely that your thoughts and reflections will contain a wide range of learning approaches, some emotional reactions (to the event or the learning) and some observations about preferences, dislikes or biases you might have when learning. You might also notice that the situation and the purpose of the learning had an influence along with some of the following:
>
> - What was being learned – was it knowledge or a skill, was it about your practice or your views and beliefs.
> - Your past experience of learning – you may have preferences for different types of learning approach based on your level of confidence and the fit between the method and what needs to be learned. For example, some individuals find didactic learning difficult whilst others thrive on this; some people enjoy reading whilst others find this boring. Past successes and difficulties with particular learning approaches may make them more or less comfortable to engage in.
> - Your style and the ways in which you visualise and think about things – some people find that they are able to learn through metaphors, others prefer logic, some like creating diagrams to connect ideas.
> - The current salience of the learning and the emotional 'charge' associated with it. Such factors can foster creativity, learning and motivation or may narrow available resources and restrict your ability to think, reflect and develop.
>
> It can be very helpful to explore learning and development styles both when developing the supervision agreement and periodically thereafter. In addition to reflective exercises such as the one above, supervisors should consider discussing their observations of learning styles shown by the supervisee, and experiment with different approaches and styles to

explore their effectiveness. As a supervisor, it is also valuable to share your own preferences and experience of learning and supervising with the supervisee.

Theories of adult learning

It has been suggested that adult learning differs from the learning engaged in by children in that adult learning 'is not preparatory, as with children, but life-long ... helping adults realise their potential and better carry out the roles and duties associated with work ... ' (Burns, 2002, p. 231). As discussed later, there are debates about the extent of the difference between adult and child learning, however it is clear that those supporting adult learning need to be able to draw upon a range of skills and approaches. There are many theories of learning as demonstrated by the list produced by Knowles, Holton and Swanson (1998) which contains almost 100 theorists in the period from 1885–1986. These have been grouped into clusters such as *elemental*, comprising behavioural theories in which 'learning takes place through association', and *holistic* approaches in which 'learning is functional and purposive' taking place to achieve something (Knowles, Holton and Swanson, 1998). Burns (2002) presents a slightly more elaborated framework using three clusters, namely: *behaviourist* in which knowledge is transmitted through shaping, reinforcing and providing feedback; *cognitive* in which discovery, problem solving and understanding is facilitated, and *humanist-phenomenological* where individual potential is developed through self-direction and support. These different theories, styles and methods give rise to different forms of teaching and learning such as didactic methods and coaching.

The adult learning model (andragogy) (Knowles, Holton and Swanson, 1998)

Knowles argues that adult learning differs from the ways in which children are taught and learn in several ways. He uses the term 'andragogy' to delineate adult learning and suggests that understanding the assumptions and principles underpinning this model enables the learning environment to be developed to better meet adult learners' needs. The principles underpinning his approach are that:

(1) Adults *need to know* why they need to learn something and thus play a collaborative role in determining their learning goals. Typically adults need to know how learning will take place, what learning will occur and why the learning is important.
(2) Adult learners have a self-concept of being responsible for their own decisions for their own lives and thus engage in *self-directed learning*. Self-directed learning refers to the goal or purpose of the learning not the method in which the learning takes place. Therefore, adult learners may

engage in traditional teaching situations as well as self-teaching. This will be informed by such factors as the individual's learning style(s), previous experience and the most efficient way to learn the specific skill or information.
(3) Adults enter learning situations with a range of prior *experience*. This may provide the source material for learning as is found in many approaches to reflective learning such as 'reflection on action' (see Special Topic 10). It may also influence future learning with prior experience creating models and 'schema' which influence new learning.
(4) Adults become *ready to learn* those things they need to know and/or be able to do in order to cope effectively with their real-life situations. Thus learning readiness will be influenced by learning relevance.
(5) Adults tend to be task or problem centred in their *orientation to learning* and typically prefer a real-life context to learning. This idea leads to the conclusion that much of adult learning is based on an experiential approach. Thus, models such as Kolb's experiential learning model (Kolb, 1984) are of particular relevance to adult learning.
(6) The dominant *motivation* is typically from internal pressures rather than external forces and thus adults typically learn when this has some personal value to them. Although this might include external gains (e.g. a promotion) learning is motivated by a belief they can learn, that the learning is relevant to the goal and that the learning is important.

However, as noted by Knowles, Holton and Swanson (1998), there is a great deal of variation between learners that may result from individual differences (e.g. cognitive ability, personality and prior knowledge), learning skills and styles (i.e. the ability to learn in a range of ways and from a range of sources), and life-span development (i.e. changes in individuals across the life course). Thus, the factors above are not necessary conditions but may be desirable for adult learning. Further, Knowles, Holton and Swanson (1998) argue for three dimensions in relation to adult learning, which influence how the learning might take place or the teaching might be provided to support this:

(1) the principles described above and how these need to be shaped and modified based on an analysis of individual characteristics;
(2) the subject matter and the learning situation; and
(3) the goals and purpose of the learning.

Critics of this model suggest that it contains internal tensions (as it is derived from different models and philosophies) and that the differences between the ways in which children and adults learn have been overemphasised (Burns, 2002). Its strength may be in the challenge it poses the trainer or supervisor – to consider the individual's needs and how these might be influenced, shaped and harnessed.

Stages of learning (e.g. Benner, 1982)

One widely cited stage approach to learning and development (especially within the nursing literature) is that of Benner (1982). She describes four stages of development from *novice* to *advanced beginner*, then *proficient* and finally *expert*. For her the 'novice' and 'advanced beginner' may have 'textbook knowledge' about what and how to do something or 'experiential knowledge', that is experience of doing something without the understanding of why. Therefore, if you were to ask the novice, 'why did you do that?' the response might be 'the book said or I've done it that way before'. The novice and advanced beginner have to focus on recalling what they have been taught, or are limited to an isolated set of actions at the expense of taking in and understanding the whole situation. In contrast, the 'expert' has both 'textbook' and 'experiential' knowledge and is able to view situations 'less as a compilation of equally relevant bits and more a complete whole in which only certain parts are relevant' (p. 403). However, experts also work with apparent 'unconscious competence' (e.g. Adams, n.d.) in which decision making and actions are automated and without conscious effort. Indeed, requiring such effort can interrupt the smooth operation of the task. Therefore, if you were to ask the expert, 'why did you do that?' the response might be 'I'm not sure, it just seemed right'. Rolfe (1997) argues that Benner's approach is limited in that her view of the expert as someone who can operate 'intuitively' and 'on autopilot', based on textbook and experiential knowledge, is not the endpoint. Using the ideas of Schön (1983), he suggests that there is a point 'beyond expertise' which he refers to as the 'reflexive practitioner'. Here, the practitioner is highly competent but also uses the ability to 'reflect in action' by undertaking conscious, mindful actions with real-time experimenting. This enables conscious modifications of action where needed – conscious problem solving. This has also been referred to as 'reflective competence', 'meta-conscious competence' and 'conscious competence of unconscious competence' ('Conscious competence learning model' – www.businessballs.com). At this level the individual is aware of what they are doing and able to make it explicit, either in real time or subsequently. These developmental stages give rise to different approaches to the teacher or supervisor from acquisition of knowledge or experience (novice/advanced beginner), consolidation (proficient) and finally to reflection (expert).

In a critique of stage models of professional skill development, such as that of Benner, Dall'Alba and Sandberg (2006) note that the evidence for a step-wise progression of learning as demonstrated by a linear accumulation of knowledge and skills is problematic. They describe how such models are based on snapshots of individuals at different levels of experience, and that the great variation that exists between individuals at each of the levels is down-played. Further, they argue that rather than learning by rote or simply following rules, even novices can benefit from active participation and problem-based learning. As an alternative, they suggest that learning and development are a combination of skill development and professional 'knowing, acting and being' (referred to as 'professional ways of being'). Thus, development comprises of being able to carry out the skill *and* understanding 'when it is appropriate to use such knowledge and skills, how to use them, and to what purpose' (p. 403); 'understanding *of* practice must be integrated with understanding *in* practice' (p. 402, italics in original). Dall'Alba and Sandberg (2006) also note that there is an 'unfolding circularity' present in learning and development in that understanding develops over time and elaborates what is already in place or understood. However, they observe that such comprehensive understanding can be limited by one's existing knowledge and experience which they suggest might explain why not everyone becomes an expert in their chosen field. Using the example of the architect, they describe how learning rules and being proficient in each part of the task is not sufficient for being an expert architect – this requires an 'embodied understanding of practice'. Thus, their stance would suggest that supervision needs to support development, integration and reflection with all levels of worker.

Direction and support in adult learning (Pratt, 1988)

Pratt argues that Knowles' model described earlier, is overly simplistic and in some ways creates an unrealistic picture of the adult learner as self-directed and capable. Whilst many adults may conform to the principles in Knowles' model, Pratt asserts that some adults learn in more traditional forums with the 'teacher' providing the direction and lots of support to the learner. He suggests that factors such as the situation and 'learner variables', impact on the style and approach needed on the part of the teacher (or supervisor). He argues that the learner's *support needs*, based on their level of motivation and confidence to achieve the goal, and *need for direction* based on the level of knowledge and skill they have in relation to the specific topic will effect the most appropriate learning approach in the given circumstance. He suggests that adult learners may have dependencies on the teacher (in our case the supervisor) either in terms of direction and/or support. From this he describes four types of learner:

(1) *The learner needing direction and support*: such individuals lack relevant knowledge, skills and experience and motivation or self-confidence to achieve the learning goal. The supervisor needs to provide sufficient support and direction to enable the supervisee to achieve the goal. However, the goal needs to be sufficiently challenging in order to ensure that the learning is meaningful. The supervisor will need to ensure that there are clear goals, that the learning is appropriately structured, that the reason for the learning is clear and the ways in which achievement and progress will be monitored are described. Such supervisee's are likely to be dependent on the supervisor.
(2) *The learner who needs direction*: where learners are motivated and confident but lack relevant skills and knowledge, the supervisor will need to

provide direction with less need for support. The supervisor may need to help structure the learning and define the goal. They will also still need to provide feedback and guidance and monitor support needs. Such supervisees are also likely to be dependent on the supervisor.

(3) *The learner who needs support*: some learners have sufficient experience and information and can play an active role in determining the direction of the learning. However, learners may still need support if their confidence or motivation are low. In such situations, the supervisor may need to provide encouragement, help the supervisee to recognise progress and foster confidence in their development. However, according to Pratt, this type of learner has moved into andragogy as signalled by their engagement in decisions about their learning (self-direction).

(4) *The learner who can provide their own direction and support*: in many ways this type of learner is the one described in the adult learning model (Knowles, Holton and Swanson, 1998). The learner takes responsibility for learning and the supervisor's role is one of helping the supervisee to take a step back, aiding reflection, both in relation to learning goals and how learning is taking place.

Assisted learning and the Zone of Proximal Development (Tharp and Gallimore, 1988)

The Zone of Proximal Development (ZPD) first described by Vygotsky (see Tharp and Gallimore, 1988) has been discussed by several authors in relation to learning within supervision (James *et al.*, 2006; Wilson and Lizzio, 2009; Zorga, 2002). The ZPD describes the difference between what an individual can achieve with support and they are able to achieve alone. This process involves increasing autonomy over time, moving from 'other regulation to self-regulation' of the task through four stages:

(1) assistance from more capable others;
(2) assistance from self (through self-talk/self-directed speech);
(3) performance 'developed, autonomised and fossilised'; and
(4) de-autonomisation and recursion.

Supporting the learner to achieve and develop relies upon the supervisor providing 'assisted performance' – giving assistance where and when it is needed. This support enables the learner to achieve, with assistance, what they would not achieve alone. Inappropriate assistance (too much, too little or the wrong kind) might disrupt or interfere with learning, thus assistance must be responsive and tailored. The term 'scaffolding' has been used to describe the process in which, rather than simplify the task, the level and type of support is varied to help the learner achieve. The process is said to be recursive as the learner may re-learn, modify or revise prior learning and ways of doing or understanding over time.

Unhelpful learning roles and styles (Ekstein and Wallerstein, 1958)

A number of approaches to learning which may block or hamper learning have been noted. Although not exhaustive, problems can include:

(1) *vigorous denying* in which the supervisee reduces all new ideas to the familiar, subsuming them into existing ideas, models and concepts;
(2) *submission* in which the supervisee engages in apparent learning through submission to the supervisor, however this is accompanied by occasional stubbornness and hostility;
(3) *'mea culpa'* in which the supervisee adopts a self-critical stance to their performance. This may be borne out of an expectation of critical responses from the supervisor; and
(4) *'the problem of finding a problem'* in which the supervisee does not recognise any learning or development needs or opportunities, instead relying on the supervisor to identify learning needs for them.

The above highlights the importance of attention to patterns within learning, as these styles would be revealed through different learning opportunities and events. The supervision therefore needs to attend to learning processes across time, situations and domains/topics to help respond to both style and role patterns.

It is important to acknowledge that the above theories and models are examples from the vast array of approaches to learning. A number of widely used theories such as that of Transformational Learning (Mezirow and Associates, 2000) and humanistic theory (Rogers, 1983) have not been described here, however those interested in developing their understanding of adult learning further may wish to consult such texts or texts, on adult learning such as Burns (2002).

Domains of learning

The work of Alf Lizzio and colleagues provides a very helpful framework to outline the areas of practice and learning contained within supervision. Lizzio and Wilson (2002) conceptualise six specific goal areas grouped into four broad domains, namely, professional identity and purpose; personal integrity; responsive stance to clients; and professional competence. These are framed around the core learning purpose – for the supervisee to achieve self-regulated learning. This is conceptualised as the 'ability to make "quality choices" in response to environmental demands' (p. 29). Table 5.1 describes the six goal areas for supervision and outlines supervision tasks and supervisee outcomes associated with these. This table is intended as a basis from which the individual supervisor/supervisee can construct personalised learning shaped by the setting, the client group and the supervisee. For those working within the National Health Service within the UK, for example, it may be possible to map these

Table 5.1 Domains of learning goals

Goal area	Brief description/supervisee outcome	Supervision task examples
Systemic competence	Ability to understand and manage the organisational context of the activity taking place	Understanding the power relationships and 'politics' of the context
		Establishing and maintaining effective relationships with others and ability to understand and manage interpersonal conflict
		Understanding the ways in which the context can be influenced and ability to do so
		Managing own well-being and understand and influence how you are seen by others (personal and professional identity)
Role efficacy	Clear and agreed understanding of job purpose, expectations from and interface with others	Understanding of (unique) skill and knowledge
		Clarity re work standards, responsibilities and lines of accountability
		Understanding of who the supervisee needs to 'relate to' (e.g. who they need to influence; what will be gained or lost through maintaining certain relationships; how this might be done)
		Understanding possible areas of role 'ambiguity' such as a lack of clarity about role and conflict caused by competing but incompatible expectations of the individual or, overlap in role with/encroaching upon the work of others and how to manage these
Conceptual competence	Ability to theorise about practice to achieve 'wise practice' more so than just 'clever practice' (p. 34)	Integrate knowledge and practice – knowing what, how, when and why to do things
		Personalise knowledge and practice – own understanding of what, how, when and why to do things based on own experience
		Make explicit implicit theories by scrutinising actual practice
		Plan 'what to do' and why this would be appropriate, what outcomes are expected
Ethical judgement	Issues of personal and collective responsibility and accountability concerning moral and ethical issues and dilemmas	Recognise the ethical and moral issue(s) and dilemma(s) present
		Identify what might inform decision making in relation to this matter (e.g. legal frameworks; codes of conduct; service ethos; others' views)
		Awareness of own 'core values' and principles and understanding the importance

Table 5.1 (continued)

Goal area	Brief description/supervisee outcome	Supervision task examples
		of personal integrity – 'am I doing what is "best", "right", "fair" or "just"'
		Identify how the issue will be worked through (c.f. problem solving approach)
Personal awareness and development	The interaction between the personal and the professional	Recognise personal and professional issues through attention to own feelings, thoughts and behaviour
		Understand how personal processes (e.g. feelings, experiences, thoughts, history) might impact on practice
		Understand how to manage/address/productively use the personal/professional interface
		Awareness of own strengths and limitations
Technical competence/proficiency	Sufficient skills and proficiency in order to undertake job at the level required	Supervisor and supervisee awareness of the 'skill set' required. This might include interpersonal, therapy, report writing, planning and organisation skills for example
		Ability to identify areas of competence, transferable learning and gaps in technical competence
		Knowledge of ways to acquire and maintain skills and competence (learning modes and styles)
		Ability to monitor technical competence and integrate 'new methods and approaches' that are presented

Source: adapted from Lizzio and Wilson, 2002.

goals and specific task examples onto existing frameworks such as the Knowledge and Skills Framework which is used as the foundation for all job descriptions.

Drawing on the work of Lizzio and Wilson (2004), Day (2012) presents a supervision framework for forensic psychologists in which he 'translates' a general framework for supervision into a forensic context. Day suggests that forensic-specific practice can be mapped onto their framework, thus:

(a) professional competence might include current knowledge of legal systems, risk assessment and psychological tools;
(b) professional identity and purpose may address the interface between the profession and the organisation;

(c) personal integrity contends with trustworthiness, responsibility and acting in best interest; and
(d) responsive stance to clients requires being supportive, empathic, neutral and objective.

Day also highlights specific skills and competencies such as understanding the legal system, skills in formulation, managing and defending professional integrity, providing evidence in legal processes and recognising and managing bias within reports. Such aspects could easily be introduced as specific task examples when personalising Table 5.1.

Promoting learning

Having considered some theories of learning and supervisory domains in which learning is likely to be needed, how learning might be supported must be considered. In a broad sense, in order to enable any form of learning and development, the supervisor needs to foster a facilitative approach within supervision (Wilson and Lizzio, 2009). As discussed by Zorga (2002), this might include the supervisor holding a number of core values and skills, namely, the pursuit of common goals; the belief in growth and development; a willingness to use different tools and approaches; and an ability to help foster mastery. This will form the foundation upon which learning can be based.

Once the supervisory alliance is formed (and actively maintained) and key conditions met, it may be possible to summarise learning within supervision using a simple five-step learning process (James *et al.*, 2006):

Step 1: assess learning needs.
Step 2: establish a baseline level of competence for each need.
Step 3: work within the zone of proximal development.
Step 4: use effective supervision techniques.
Step 5: evaluate progress.

There are many ideas and strategies that might be thought of as fitting into step 4 in the process above. These include problem solving, skill building and action planning (Schoenwald *et al.*, 2013), the use of case studies, observations and role play/skills rehearsal (Wilson and Lizzio, 2009), teaching and role modelling. A number of techniques are briefly explored below.

Explicit teaching

There may well be times where a more formal teaching role is warranted – where being a 'content transmitter' (Knowles, Holton and Swanson, 1998, p. 200) is required. This is most likely to be the case where the supervisee is learning specific knowledge or skills and may be more common when the supervisee is a novice, lacks confidence and direction and is therefore more dependent on the supervisor. Such an instructional approach should be based on ensuring that the material is delivered clearly and in a non-patronising and informative way. The 'whole-part-whole' approach may be useful for this (see below). It may also be that the supervisor's role is to support the supervisee to access appropriate training and learning provided by others to meet the identified needs.

The 'whole-part-whole' approach (Knowles, Holton and Swanson, 1998)

This is a systematic approach that provides a template for adult learning. The premise is that the first 'whole' provides an introduction to help the learner cue into the meaning and relevance of the learning for the individual and to provide a common framework or 'scaffolding' for the more detailed content to follow. The 'part' phase provides detailed knowledge and skills relating to specific elements of the topic using whatever learning approaches are best suited to the learner and the content. Each part (which themselves may have sub-parts) should be fully understood and mastered before moving on. The second 'whole' brings the elements together to consider their inter-relationships and sequencing. This is likely to be followed by implementation, review and troubleshooting or refinements over time.

Learning from experience

The use of experience has been widely acknowledged as an important source of raw material for learning to take place. Special Topic 10 on reflective practice provides a range of ideas in relation to this. However, one widely used approach is that of Kolb.

Experiential learning cycle (Kolb, 1984)

Kolb's experiential learning cycle (Kolb, 1984) is used as the foundation for many problem solving and experiential learning approaches. In this model, learning takes place in a cycle that takes an experience as the starting point. This is then considered from multiple viewpoints and concepts and ideas are derived. Finally, through experimentation of these ideas in new situations they might be revised or consolidated. This cycle can be summarised as:

(a) concrete experience;
(b) reflection and observation;
(c) conceptualisation and generalisation; and
(d) experimentation and testing.

Assisted learning approaches

Based on the idea of assisted learning, Tharp and Gallimore (1988) suggest that there are a number of approaches open to the teacher (or in our case supervisor):

(a) Modelling – where behaviours are offered for imitation. However, it is important to note that modelling is more than simple mimicry. Modelling may be used for a range of learning including cognitive and behavioural.
(b) Contingency management (CM) – is a well-developed behavioural concept in which the use of reward (e.g. praise) and punishment (e.g. reprimand) are used to strengthen actions and ideas. CM is not suited to generating new ideas but for shaping those already available to the learner.
(c) Feedback – is based on performance in relation to some form of 'standard' against which the individual is compared or assessed. Feedback often includes information to inform future performance.
(d) Instruction – providing directions for approaching a problem or new skill and should be informed by questions designed to determine the instruction type and level required.
(e) Questioning – Socratic or dialectic questions are designed to assist development through guided discovery or exploration.
(f) Cognitive structures – these help to organise information and functions both for this example and also 'like instances'.
(g) Direct coaching.

Interpersonal Process Recall

Using recordings of client-practitioner interactions within supervision can be a rich source of information and learning. Whenever recordings are made with clients it is important that issues of consent are addressed and relevant local or professional policy and guidance adhered to. One structured method for making use of audio-visual material is Interpersonal Process Recall (IPR). This is a 'sensitive and non-invasive method for prompting a person to help them retrieve many of the passing thoughts, hopes, fears, risks, images, feelings, decisions and perceptions that had run through their minds too fast to be dealt with at the time of the original interaction' (Clarke, 1997, p. 93). It was developed by Kegan and colleagues and has been used in a number of settings (see H. Kagan and Kagan, 1997) and as a research method (Larsen, Flesaker and Stege, 2008). However, its use in forensic settings is not known. In the method, the audio-visual material is reviewed and the inquirer (a role the supervisor may take on) asks questions to help prompt recall and explore the experience at the time of the encounter. This can be done individually (i.e. with just the practitioner) or through mutual recall in which the client also participates in the process.

Learning specific skills

When learning specific skills it may be helpful to adopt an approach such as that outlined in the 'Model of Practical Skill Performance' (Nielsen *et al.*, 2013). This model suggests that some skills can be built up and developed in a staged way starting with what needs to be done and in what order (substance and sequence); then accuracy (ensuring the action is exact); fluency (undertaken in a smooth fashion); and finally integration (harmonising all aspects). Where the skill relates to a task involving clients (as in the nursing example used by Nielsen et al., 2013), the ability to show caring to the client spans across all these elements of performance.

Live supervision

It must be remembered that much of supervision relies on the report of the supervisee and the ability of the supervisor to be able to reconstruct what occurred (Jones, 2006). Therefore the supervisor 'seeing the supervisee in action' can provide important information for supervision. Further, it has been argued that live supervision is especially important with those new to practice as their ability to monitor and report their performance is yet to be developed.

Live supervision typically takes one of two formats: (1) the supervisor physically present when the supervisee is undertaking the task being supervised (e.g. an assessment interview); or (2) the supervisor watching the supervisee performing the task via a screen or video link and entering the situation periodically to provide supervision (e.g. via a phone link or by the supervisor and supervisee periodically meeting during the 'session'). In both instances it is also usual for the supervisee and supervisor to meet immediately after the session/situation to discuss what took place and in some cases to review recordings. In a small study set within a university setting, counselling students received either live supervision or supervision (within 24 hours of the counselling session) based on reviewing a video recording of the session. Live supervision was found to enhance or accelerate performance in some areas and lead to a stronger working alliance as reported by the client (Kivlighan, Angelone and Swafford, 1991). Bernard and Goodyear (2014) and Scaife (2013) provide useful discussions on the approaches, methods and advantages and disadvantages of live supervision.

Problem-based learning (see Burns, 2002)

Although problem-based learning (PBL) is a specific approach to learning in which the 'teacher' sets problems and difficulties for the learner to work through and thereby learn, much of the learning in supervision will be triggered by naturally occurring difficulties, challenges or impasses. In PBL, addressing or overcoming the problem is the principle objective with knowledge acquisition as a secondary gain. PBL is increasingly used in university-based courses including foundation training in medicine. Techniques such as facilitating access to resources might be important as might working alongside the supervisee to solve a problem (collaboration in problem solving).

Apprenticeship learning

Being an apprentice requires the opportunity to see others practice in order to build templates and experiences by proxy. The medical training maxim widely stated, 'see one, do one, teach one' contains a summary of one form of apprentice development which places equal weight upon modelling and vicarious experience; active engagement in practice and the opportunity to consolidate learning and demonstrate development (for appraisal by the supervisor) through passing the knowledge and skills onto someone else.

Learning to learn

For many supervisees there is a period of learning to use supervision (Hyrkäs, Appelqvist-Schmidlechner and Haataja, 2006) and (re)learning to learn (e.g. Burns, 2002). This might include experiencing new forms and approaches to learning, experimenting with, revisiting and revising 'known forms' of learning and (re)appraising one's relationship with learning. The supervisor's role in supporting this exploration, experimentation and discovery is an important aspect of the supervisee's engaging in learning and development.

The supervisor as assessor

The final aspect to consider here in relation to learning is the role of the supervisor as an assessor of learning as shown through the development of new competence, skills, abilities or knowledge. As discussed in other chapters (e.g. Chapter 7) feedback, both as a formative method (i.e. providing information, critique and advice) and as a summative technique (i.e. appraising the performance level) are important. The assessment of learning should be an explicit part of the supervision agreement (including what is to be assessed and how). Evaluation places particular requirements on both the supervisee and supervisor such as seeking and testing evidence of performance. It is important that both parties are clear about the formal requirements associated with practice (and learning) which will often be developed and stated by a professional body. Where skills are being assessed it is important that the supervisor has seen direct evidence of practice.

Conclusion

Learning within supervision needs to cover a range of domains and can be supported and facilitated with reference to a number of models of adult learning. Adult learners control their learning through a process whereby they identify the learning *need*, *create* a strategy to achieve this goal, *implement* a learning strategy and *evaluate* the attainment of the desired learning. However, it is acknowledged that the adult learner may need assistance to determine their needs and to address them. Thus the supervisor needs to find a balance in which they 'must not do for learners what they can do for themselves and, conversely, must do for learners what they cannot do for themselves' (Pratt, 1988, p. 170). The supervisor must be able to use a range of techniques to support learning and should help all supervisees, regardless of level of skill and experience, to experiment and explore different ways of learning and developing (Dall'Alba and Sandberg, 2006).

References

Adams, L. (n.d.) 'Learning a new skill is easier said than done', *Gordontraining.com*. Retrieved 3 May 2014, from www.gordontraining.com/free-workplace-articles/learning-a-new-skill-is-easier-said-than-done/.

Benner, P. (1982) 'From novice to expert', *AJN the American Journal of Nursing* 82(3): 402–7.

Bernard, J. M. and Goodyear, R. K. (2014) *Fundamentals of Clinical Supervision* (5th edn), International Edition, London: Pearson.

Burns, R. (2002) *The Adult Learner at Work* (2nd edn), London: Allen & Unwin.

Carrington, G. (2004) 'Supervision as a reciprocal learning process', *Educational Psychology in Practice* 20(1): 31–42.

Clarke, P. (1997) 'Interpersonal process recall in supervision', in G. Shipton, *Supervision of Psychotherapy and Counselling: Making a Place to Think*, Buckingham: Open University Press, pp. 93–104.

Conscious competence learning model (n.d.) 'Conscious competence learning model', *Businessballs.com*. Retrieved 3 May 2014, from www.businessballs.com/consciouscompetencelearningmodel.htm.

Dall'Alba, G. and Sandberg, J. (2006) 'Unveiling professional development: a critical review of stage models', *Review of Educational Research* 76(3): 383–412.

Day, A. (2012) 'The nature of supervision in forensic psychology: some observations and recommendations', *The British Journal of Forensic Practice* 14(2): 116–23.

Ekstein, R. and Wallerstein, R. S. (1958) *The Teaching and Learning of Psychotherapy*, New York: Basic Books, Inc.

Fowler, J. (1996) 'The organization of clinical supervision within the nursing profession: a review of the literature', *Journal of Advanced Nursing* 23(3): 471–8.

Goodyear, R. K. and Bernard, J. M. (1998) 'Clinical supervision: lessons from the literature', *Counselor Education and Supervision* 38(1): 6–22.

Hyrkäs, K., Appelqvist-Schmidlechner, K. and Haataja, R. (2006) 'Efficacy of clinical supervision: influence on job satisfaction, burnout and quality of care', *Journal of Advanced Nursing* 55(4): 521–35.

James, I. A., Milne, D., Marie-Blackburn, I. and Armstrong, P. (2006) 'Conducting successful supervision: novel elements towards an integrative approach', *Behavioural and Cognitive Psychotherapy* 35(2): 191.

Jones, A. (2006) 'Clinical supervision: what do we know and what do we need to know? A review and commentary', *Journal of Nursing Management* 14(8): 577–85.

Kagan, H. and Kagan, N. I. (1997) 'Interpersonal process recall: influencing human interaction', in *Handbook of Psychotherapy Supervision*, New York: John Wiley & Sons, pp. 296–309.

Kivlighan, D. M., Angelone, E. O. and Swafford, K. G. (1991) 'Live supervision in individual psychotherapy: effects on therapist's intention use and client's evaluation of session effect and working alliance', *Professional Psychology: Research and Practice* 22(6): 489.

Knowles, M. S., Holton III, E. F. and Swanson, R. A. (1998) *The Adult Learner* (5th edn), Woburn, MA: Butterworth-Heinemann.

Kolb, D. A. (1984) *Experiential Learning: Experience as the Source of Learning and Development*, Upper Saddle River, NJ: Prentice Hall Inc.

Larsen, D., Flesaker, K. and Stege, R. (2008) 'Qualitative interviewing using interpersonal process recall: investigating internal experiences during professional-client conversations', *International Journal of Qualitative Methods* 7(1): 18–36.

Lizzio, A. J. and Wilson, K. L. (2002) 'The domain of learning goals in professional supervision', in M. Patton and W. McMahon, *Supervision in the Helping Professions: A Practical Approach*, Frenchs Forest: Pearson Education Australia pp. 27–41.

Mezirow, J. and Associates (2000) *Learning as Transformation*, San Francisco, CA: Jossey-Bass Inc. Publishers.

Mothersole, G. (2000) 'Clinical supervision and forensic work', *Journal of Sexual Aggression* 5(1): 45–58.

Nielsen, C., Sommer, I., Larsen, K. and Bjørk, I. T. (2013) 'Model of practical skill performance as an instrument for supervision and formative assessment', *Nurse Education in Practice* 13(3): 176–80.

Pratt, D. D. (1988) 'Andragogy as a relational construct', *Adult Education Quarterly* 38(3): 160–72.

Rogers, C. (1983) *Freedom to Learn for the 80's* (2nd revised edn), London: Merrill.

Rolfe, G. (1997) 'Beyond expertise: theory, practice and the reflexive practitioner', *Journal of Clinical Nursing* 6(2): 93–7.

Scaife, J. (2013) *Supervision in Clinical Practice*, Abingdon: Routledge.

Schoenwald, S. K., Mehta, T. G., Frazier, S. L. and Shernoff, E. S. (2013) 'Clinical supervision in effectiveness and implementation research', *Clinical Psychology: Science and Practice* 20(1): 44–59.

Schön, D. A. (1983) *The Reflective Practitioner*, New York: Basic Books.

Tharp, R. G. and Gallimore, R. (1988) *Rousing Minds to Life*, Cambridge: Cambridge University Press.

Wilson, K. L. and Lizzio, A. J. (2009) 'Processes and interventions to facilitate supervisees' learning', in N. Pelling, J. Barletta and P. Armstrong, *The Practice of Clinical Supervision*, Samford Valley: Australian Academic Press, pp. 138–64.

Zorga, S. (2002) 'Supervision: the process of life-long learning in social and educational professions', *Journal of Interprofessional Care* 16(3): 265–76.

6 Being supervised

Taking an active role as a supervisee requires planning, skill and some knowledge and understanding of the processes involved. This is true for those experienced in supervision but is especially the case for those new to the supervisee role and the experience of supervision. This chapter focuses explicitly on issues relating to being supervised, answers some of the most common questions asked by supervisees, and provides information that will help with the task of taking an active role in supervision. Further, it aims to take away some of the mystery and confusion that often accompanies supervision. Throughout this chapter, reference will be made to information contained elsewhere in this book that might be of particular interest or use.

Being a supervisee requires the ability to effectively use supervision time. Whilst learning to use supervision is often acquired 'on the job', this leaves the development of knowledge and skills as a supervisee to the 'luck of the draw' with respect to who provides supervision. This chapter outlines some of the expectations a supervisor might have of the supervisee, the expectations the supervisee should have for their supervision and some of the ways in which a supervisee can shape their supervision experience. The ways in which supervisee's can prepare for supervision and use models themselves are also outlined along with a glossary of terms.

Understanding supervision

In order to prepare for your first supervision session, it is helpful to consider some of the background to and knowledge of supervision. This is done here through considering the answers to some commonly asked questions.

Why bother with supervision?

Supervision has been used by some professional groups and in some settings for many years. In this time, evidence has been gathered that shows supervision can have a positive impact in a number of ways including increasing how effective individual practitioners are (i.e. the positive impact on clients); improving how practitioners feel (e.g. reduced stress and burnout); and improving learning and skill development (e.g. a skilled workforce). The evidence for practice supervision is discussed in more detail in Chapter 2.

What is discussed in supervision?

Supervision is concerned with all aspects of work and is therefore task and client focused. For those very new to supervision the entire process may appear mysterious as it is not formal teaching or management, nor is it therapy (see below) yet it has some overlaps with each. Supervision includes thinking, reflecting, learning, developing and 're-energising' amongst other things. It can also provide an opportunity for rehearsing how something might be done and trying out ideas in a safe forum where immediate feedback can be obtained. All of these are used with the intentions of supporting learning, facilitating development and fostering reflection, with the ultimate goal of helping the practitioner/supervisee to provide safe and effective services. A definition of supervision and what it entails is presented in Chapter 1.

I've been around a while and I'm good at my job – why do I need supervision?

Supervision should be provided to all staff not just those who are facing problems in their practice or who are new to their job. Supervision is a way of accessing career-long support and training to continue to develop and remain 'fresh' and able to perform at your best – in the same way as the highly successful sportsperson continues to have a professional coach. This metaphor also serves well to characterise the relationship between supervisee and supervisor – a meeting of equals who have different skills and knowledge and perhaps different roles and positions in the system. That said, there is often a power imbalance between the supervisee and supervisor based on their responsibilities (see later) or the formal hierarchy that cannot be avoided. However, where this is the case it is important to discuss this openly to ensure that it doesn't become a block to accessing or using supervision.

I already have support and informal supervision ...

Many people will have informal arrangements for workplace support and 'debriefing' or seeking advice. What these arrangements typically share, however, is that they are reactive, ad hoc/unplanned, unstructured and don't capture or support learning, reflection and development in a systematic way. Although they may, at least in part, address the supportive or normative aspects of supervision, other functions of supervision are typically not met. Supervision provides a planned and organised forum for these activities to take place. This is discussed further in Chapter 10.

How does supervision differ from line management?

Sometimes your supervisor will be your line manager, however supervision has a different focus. Line management could be represented by the questions 'are you doing what you are supposed to, when you are supposed to and in the way you are supposed to?' whilst supervision might be captured by 'how can I develop my practice and do things better; what am I already doing well; where are my weaknesses and blind spots (and how might I address these)?'.

How is supervision organised?

To some extent this will be guided by local service decision and policy, however there are a number of common factors typically found in the way supervision is provided. Supervision meetings generally take place at least monthly, for around an hour at a time and should form part of your core hours. These factors have been found to be associated with the most effective supervision. Your service may have a supervision policy (as might your professional body if you have one) which you might wish to read. The topics and ideas that are likely to be included are described in Chapter 9.

What can I expect in my first supervision session?

To a large extent this will depend on your supervisor and whether or not you already know them. If you don't know them, then the first supervision session is likely to involve a bit of 'getting to know one another' e.g. work history, professional and job-related training; discussion about previous experience of supervision (where relevant). This first session may also include discussions about learning styles and the expectations you might have of one another. During this first session it is likely that you will draw up a supervision agreement with your supervisor which will contain basic information such as when and where you will meet and what aspects of your work will be discussed in supervision. An example of an agreement can be found in Chapter 3.

In thinking about the first supervision session it can be helpful to consider your position in relation to supervision. This can be done in many ways but a simple approach is to complete the following sentences – 'My image of successful supervision is ... ?'; 'What I fear happening in supervision is ... ?'; 'What I think I need from supervision is ... '. If you have no prior experience of supervision it can still be useful to respond to these and to discuss your thoughts in your first supervision session.

How much personal information will my supervisor ask?

There is often concern about what is and is not appropriate within the context of supervision. As described in Chapter 1, some have been concerned that supervision can 'morph' into therapy. As noted above, supervision is *not* therapy and is based around the broad idea of the adult learner and maintaining appropriate standards in your work. Therefore, supervision is generally not a place for discussing your personal life or making personal or life changes. Lizzio and Wilson (2002), offer two conditions to help ensure that any discussions of the 'personal' that take place in supervision are appropriate. First, they suggest that the personal is legitimate and appropriate if the content has clear relevance to the effectiveness of the practitioner (e.g. if the issue might affect client or task outcomes) and second such issues can only be discussed where the supervisor and supervisee have explicitly agreed that this is the case and that such discussion is appropriate within supervision. Therefore, if the personal is impacting on your ability to do your job, your supervisor may seek to discuss the issue in enough detail to allow them to point you in the right direction of the support or assistance you might need or, where appropriate, for you to resolve it.

How does supervision 'work'?

Supervision uses a range of methods and approaches, but at its core is a conversation between the supervisor and the supervisee. There are supervision models and frameworks which your supervisor might use to help them structure the supervision session or to guide the questions they ask or the way in which they provide supervision. It can be helpful to ask your supervisor about the models they generally use and why they think they are useful. For example, many supervisors make use of the 'functions of supervision' described by Kadushin (1976) and Proctor (1986), namely: restorative/supportive (concerned with emotions, stresses and personal challenges); formative/developmental (concerned with enhancing practice through skills and knowledge development); and normative/administrative (concerned with workload and the ethical and professional aspects of practice). Further, it can be helpful to ask your supervisor what guided their thinking/which model(s) they were using when they asked a particular question or focused on a particular aspect of your work. You might agree other ways of making explicit any use of models and frameworks in supervision such as discussing when you experience new insights, new learning, personal development or new ideas. Supervision might be one-to-one or in a group, however, in general, the skills used in supervision is broadly similar in both these formats – supervision works by revealing new ideas, skills, theories, knowledge, insights and awareness. Chapters 3 and 4 review types and models of supervision, Chapter 5 learning and Special Topic 10 reflection styles and models which can be consulted to further understand how supervision 'works'.

I'm not sure I want supervision

The idea of supervision can be daunting, especially for those new to this role. However, supervision should be seen as a partnership in which your supervisor is charged with aiding your development (through learning and reflection), providing you with support (fostering your workplace emotional wellbeing) and maintaining your practice standards (through fostering boundaries, ethical and principled practice). To work most effectively both supervisee and supervisor need to be active and responsible to meet the challenge and demands and to develop useful and responsive supervision.

Practice supervision and the trainee/new practitioner

In many ways, initial practitioner development can be seen as an apprenticeship where skills are developed and honed under the guidance of more senior practitioners. Thus supervision can be viewed as a process of translating theory into practice and shaping reflective-scientist-practitioners. In addition to the moulding and shaping of skills, knowledge and competence, supervision also provides structures (e.g. to contain anxiety and allow planning and rehearsal) and role modelling. This description of supervision is not specific to working in the forensic field, but is also in evidence within mental health settings and therapies for example.

Practice supervision and the experienced practitioner

Those who have 'seen it' and 'done it' before, face challenges brought by such experience and seniority. Here the need is not around what to do (or how to do it) but more on opportunities to develop, reflect and explore practice, to avoid stagnation and to remain mindful of one's own strengths, limitations and assumptions. In this way, supervision for the experienced professional serves to make explicit those ideas and actions that are embedded and taken for granted; reflect on decision making (both the process and the outcomes); consider personal strengths and weaknesses; 'calibrate' themselves against practitioners at a similar level; explore complex issues for which multiple perspectives might hold true; and to be challenged in a safe and supportive setting.

Getting the most out of supervision

Some useful things to remember about supervision

(1) Supervision is your time for your development.
(2) Be willing to make clear what you need from a supervision session.
(3) Negotiate to ensure that supervision works for you.
(4) With your supervisor develop clear expectations for supervision and of one another.
(5) Supervisors want to do a good job.
(6) Supervisors can worry about providing good enough supervision.
(7) Supervisors need feedback to be as effective as possible.
(8) Supervisors cannot read minds!
(9) Seek regular feedback from your supervisor about your strengths and weaknesses.
(10) Formally review supervision on a regular basis.

What will be expected of me?

To some extent this will depend on your supervisor and the focus of your supervision, however expectations should be discussed from the very first supervision session and revisited from time to time. For example, if you are a student or a trainee, your supervisor may have a list of specific expectations that form part of your placement or internship. It is important to remember that supervision is your time to develop your skills and knowledge, process your experiences and benchmark your practice. Therefore, as with all situations in which we need to 'get something out' we also need to be able to 'put things in'. In general there are four expectations that a supervisor may have and that you should have of yourself, namely:

Be prepared: It is important to arrive at supervision having given some time and thought to what you might need from the session. This skill will be developed over time, however it can be helpful to keep a supervision list, diary or log between sessions into which you record possible topics and needs for supervision. There is more on preparing for supervision later in this chapter.

Be actively involved: As a supervisee you share responsibility for maximising the effectiveness of supervision to you and your practice and for ensuring that you are able to extract as much as possible from the limited supervision time available. Take an active role in your supervision through discussion, questioning and developing skills. Make use of your supervisor's knowledge and skill to help with your own personal and professional development and knowledge.

Be open: In order to facilitate learning, reflection and development it is important to be willing to explore and try new ideas and think through how and why you work in the way that you do. Supervision should provide a chance to see the 'warts and all' version of your work in order to help you become even more skilled at what you do. This can only be achieved if you are open to looking, investigating and hearing another's view.

Be willing to learn and reflect: A willingness and enthusiasm for 'borrowing what works from others' and adapting and embedding comments, suggestions, teaching and experience into the way you work is critical if supervision is to be of value. Supervision may involve learning new ways to do things but is also likely to help you review and reflect on what you have done to allow learning from successes and mistakes and to enable you to consider something extra/different to the way you approached it. The chapter on learning (Chapter 5) and the special topic on reflection (Special Topic 10) provide more on this.

What do I need from supervision?

Supervision provides an important forum within which practice can be reviewed and critiqued and the impact and personal challenge of practice can be considered. Supervision is a unique space which meets a wide range of practitioner needs including:

(a) a place to reflect on work openly;
(b) opportunities to consider the way in which the personal and the professional interact;
(c) validation of one's viewpoint and emotional experiences;
(d) time to identify areas of good practice, resources and strengths;
(e) space to seek advice and gain another person's perspective;
(f) a place to generate ideas and explore new ways of working; and
(g) a forum in which confidence, knowledge and skills in dealing with challenges and difficulties is enhanced.

It is helpful to monitor your supervision over time to see which of these feature most and if there are any which you have not experienced in supervision. You might want to discuss your findings with your supervisor as part of your regular review and decide how you might ensure each of these is met.

What are the goals of forensic practice supervision?

In addition to the needs listed above, there will be specific supervision goals which will, to a large degree, be determined through discussions with your supervisor and documented in your supervision agreement. However, a number of general goals for supervision have been identified which may well be of relevance. These are detailed in Box 6.1. It is important to identify which goals from the list, or that you/your supervisor have added, are most important or relevant at this point in time and will form the basis for your supervision agreement. Revisit this as part of your regular review of supervision with your supervisor, re-negotiating and revising or adding goals as necessary.

BOX 6.1: General goals for supervision

The following list shows common supervisee goals for supervision. The first six in the list are taken from Bordin (1983), who identified 10 goals for those supervisees who work as therapists. The remainder (goals 7–12) have been added as likely additional goals in a forensic context.

1. Mastery of specific skills – becoming highly competent and proficient at certain tasks.
2. Enlarging one's understanding of clients – developing knowledge about different clients in forensic settings, their needs and presentation.
3. Deepening one's understanding of concepts and theory – extending knowledge and ability to use ideas, models and theories relevant to the setting/clients.
4. Provide a stimulus for research – identifying questions and ideas that need to be researched in order to develop a better understanding or way forward.

5. Maintenance of standards of service – ensuring practice is of the expected standard.
6. Overcoming personal and intellectual obstacles towards learning and mastery – identifying what gets in the way of learning and developing.
7. Increasing one's awareness of the impact of the context on client's and practitioner's behaviour and presentation – understanding how the setting (e.g. prison) might lead to the presence of absence of behaviours, attitudes etc.
8. Increasing awareness of own reactions and feelings and how these impact on work – understanding what triggers particular emotional responses and how these affect how you do your job.
9. Increasing awareness of boundaries – building knowledge and skill in relation to boundary setting, monitoring and breaches (recognising and responding).
10. Deepening ones understanding of legal processes and duties – understanding the requirements associated with these and how they are relevant to your work.
11. Enhancing competence in risk assessment and management – being skilled in relation to risk both immediate and longer term.
12. Enhanced understanding of team roles and functioning – have a working knowledge of the roles of different team members and associated responsibilities and own place within this.

What do I take to supervision?

As outlined in Chapter 3, what is taken to supervision will be influenced by the type and form of supervision arrangement you have. Assuming that supervision is with a more senior/experienced staff member and focuses on all your work (as described in professional, training or support practitioner supervision in Chapter 3), then what you take should reflect the range of work that you do as part of your job. This could include:

(1) *general client issues* – such as common themes and patterns in the types of need or presentation or how to deal with a recurrent problem. Comparing and contrasting different clients – what their needs are; how you work with them; how the team responds to them etc.;
(2) *one-to-one time spent with clients* – for example where you support a particular client or undertake a specific task with them (such as an assessment, counselling or support);
(3) *group time with clients* – for example as the facilitator of a therapeutic group, as the member of a community meeting, through overseeing a group activity or monitoring group association time;
(4) *indirect work with clients* – for example where your role involves developing (or helping to develop) care and treatment plans for others to deliver;

(5) *family and carer contact* – such as roles involving contact with family and carers (either face to face, via telephone or through writing). This may be overseeing visits, providing information or answering complaints;
(6) *successes* – this should include anything that is working well but is also an important mind-set throughout supervision. Therefore, looking for 'what am I doing that works (did work)?' should be part of any topic for supervision;
(7) *general team issues* – this might include difficulties between staff members, new tasks or assignments, how to share new ideas and encourage others to adopt them;
(8) *tasks* – such as teaching or training, project work, research, audit and evaluation;
(9) *critical incidents* – these may be one off or recurrent events that are identified by the service or yourself as a critical incidents. This can include rule breaking, medical emergencies or intentional harm caused by a client or staff member. Where such events arise you should take the action required of you at the time (based on your local policies) and use supervision for reflection on 'what went well and lessons learned'. It may be that the organisation will also arrange other forms of review in certain circumstances;
(10) *near misses* – this includes those events which do not become a critical incident but could have. Often, such events provide a wealth of information and learning and are therefore important to review;
(11) *supervision of others* – if you provide supervision to other staff this should be one of the tasks taken to your own supervision; and
(12) *providing reports or testimony* – some roles will include providing written reports or evidence to meetings, tribunals, courts or other formal settings. Supervision can be used to clarify points, seek advice and test out arguments being made.

It is helpful to discuss what your role involves with your supervisor in the early sessions to identify what you do and how you might bring it to supervision (see also the next point).

How do I prepare for supervision?

There are many ways to prepare and plan for supervision and it may take some 'trial and error' to find an approach that works well for you. Typically these are written, however you can prepare in any way that works for you. Written examples include keeping a diary or developing a supervision log or list. Regardless of how you keep a record of possible topics and events for supervision, you should review this list and the actions from previous supervision prior to the supervision session to determine what might need to be discussed. Box 6.2 provides a simple six-point plan to offer some structure for preparing for supervision. You might want to develop a personalised template from this or in discussion with your supervisor. You could also ask your supervisor how they plan for their supervision and if there are any structures they think you should try. You might want to develop a structure for presenting certain kinds of work, e.g. individual cases, assessment reports. Thinking about what you want from the supervision session might help guide and shape what and how you present the material. It is usually most helpful to 'have information available' rather than to go through in detail – time spent describing and presenting background is time out of skills building, thinking, reflecting and action planning. Therefore, it can be as useful to hold the simple question 'what must my supervisor know in order for us to begin supervision in this case?' in mind when preparing case material to present. Often the answer to this question can be reduced to the success or difficulty being brought and some basic contextual information – far less material than you might otherwise detail. If more is needed, your supervisor will be sure to ask!

> **BOX 6.2: Preparing for supervision**
>
> There are many ways to prepare for supervision and you will develop your own approach over time. Here's a starter:
>
> 1. Keep a supervision log/diary/notes to review before supervision. From the list
>   a. What do I need to take?
>   b. How will I present it?
>
> 2. Review any actions that were agreed in the previous supervision - did I do them?
>   i. If yes
>   - What did I do?
>   - What did I decide not to do (and why)?
>   - What was the outcome?
>   ii. If not
>   - What got in the way?
>   - What did I do instead?
>
> 3. Ask yourself . . . since my last supervision:
>   a. What has worked well?
>   b. What am I proud of?
>   c. What have I found difficult?
>   d. What hasn't gone to plan?
>   e. What has surprised me in my work?
>   f. When have I felt angry/sad/content/scared/embarrassed etc.?

4. Which individual clients/job tasks do I want to talk about?
    a. Why?
    b. What do I want to achieve by taking them to supervision?
    c. How will I present them/the issues?
5. What team issues do I want to discuss?
    a. Why?
    b. What do I want to achieve by taking them to supervision?
    c. How will I present them/the issues?
6. What am I not (or avoiding) taking to supervision?
    a. Why?
    b. How can I ensure I'm not overlooking this issue?
    c. How would I know if I need to take it to supervision?

Achieving balance

It is important that through supervision you are able to reflect, learn from and consider a wide range of practice. To this end it is worth bearing in mind the following observations from others. First, Johns (1993) found that when using a reflective diary, staff were more likely to notice and record negative incidents. It is important, even if it is difficult, to focus on successes as well as mistakes or gaps in your knowledge or understanding. Second, in a survey of newly qualified social practitioners, Manthorpe et al., (2013) found that discussion of individual cases dominated supervision (e.g. seeking advice) along with discussion of training needs. It is worth holding in mind the three broad functions of supervision, namely, formative, normative and restorative. Third, it is important that supervision uses different strategies and techniques such as teaching and reflection, to match your need and the topic or issue. This balance allows different forms of development to take place and ethical, technical and practical aspects to be considered. Finally, it can be easy to omit whole areas of practice (and individual clients) from supervision. It is a good idea to periodically review what you do in your role by going through your past week or month in order to identify any areas which are neglected in supervision.

Developing the supervision relationship

The relationship between the supervisor and the supervisee is a critical component of successful supervision. As with all relationships, making the supervision relationship effective requires input from both sides. Being prepared, having clear goals and expectations, and negotiating (some) control (e.g. sole or co-responsibility for the agenda) are important as are being responsive through providing feedback, seeking clarification where needed and developing ideas.

Responsibilities

Responsibilities for practice are complex, however they are important to understand in the context of supervision (and may need to form a clear part of your supervision agreement). Responsibilities and accountability will vary according to your role and position. For example, if you are a registered practitioner psychologist, you are responsible for your practice – supervision is an opportunity for reflection and development but the supervisor does not become responsible for your work. The exception to this is where your practice is in breach of a code of conduct, is unethical or where you appear unfit to practice. In such circumstances your supervisor would have a duty to raise these according to service or professional protocols. In contrast, if you are a trainee practitioner psychologist, your supervisor is likely to be responsible for your practice. In this case, being the supervisor will carry with it both the support, learning and development components but also regular checking of fitness and ability ... in some ways the work of a trainee is undertaken 'on behalf' of the supervisor with the supervisor retaining those associated responsibilities. It is therefore essential that both supervisor and supervisee are clear about their responsibilities from the outset of supervision – and consequently whether the supervisor can direct your work or simply advise. This can be thought of as a simple question, 'who has the final decision about what to do?' Readers may wish to review Chapter 8 on boundaries and the ideas in Special Topic 2 and should also consult local or professional guidance on this.

Reviewing supervision

From the first supervision session, it is important to think through goals and outcomes (see above). A start to this discussion can be had by considering questions such as 'How will we know if supervision is effective?' and 'How will we reassess my supervisory needs?' As you become more experienced and skilled in the role of supervisee, what you want from supervision and the way you wish to use it may change. It is important that you and your supervisor regularly review what's working, what needs are neglected, what needs to be added etc. Although reviewing supervision is generally a feature of all supervision sessions, periodically (at least six monthly) you and your supervisor should take time to undertake a more detailed review of supervision including your needs and development. This should also identify what you do that aids the supervision process and what your supervisor does that helps or hinders your development and practice. Helpful and good practice should be highlighted to ensure 'more of the same' for the future. Reviews should be planned from the start and be captured in your supervision agreement. This review will help you develop your understanding of your style as a person, practitioner, learner and professional, your current needs and goals and what you might need from future supervision all of which will inform the development of a new agreement. Part of any review should be an exploration of what needs might be better met elsewhere and what pros and cons there might be in changing supervisor. There are no rules about how long you should have the same supervisor but if you find yourself able to predict what the supervisor might say or how they might respond to a range of issues you raise in supervision you may be running the risk of the supervision no longer being able to meet all your needs. This may be a good time to seek someone new and add your existing supervisor to the list of people you can consult with about specific issues if you need to in the future.

Finding a supervisor

Identifying a supervisor is a difficult task. In an ideal world, your supervisor will have a wide range of qualities such as being approachable, challenging, supportive, reflective and skilful. If you are new to a service or role it may be easiest to have a supervisor allocated to you for your first 4–6 months. In some services all supervisor–supervisee dyads are allocated. If you have the opportunity to choose you should select someone that you will be able to work with but usually you will not want a relationship that is too cosy and safe. For example, in a study of prison healthcare in the UK, Freshwater, Walsh and Storey (2002) found that for those individuals who worked closely together, supervision could be hampered by being too close and too friendly. This was especially the case where supervisor and supervisee socialised together and were close friends – in such circumstances they suggest that such people either can't provide supervision or shouldn't! Thus choosing a supervisor and how you do this is important and may require you to try out or discuss possibilities with others. Information on a supervisor's approach, your learning style and your goals for supervision might be used to influence this decision.

Dealing with problems in supervision

Problems sometimes occur in supervision that mean that supervision is not able to meet your needs. If you are facing a problem in supervision it will be necessary to speak with your supervisor and/or your line manager about it. However, you might also want to consider the ideas in Special Topic 6 to help with this.

It is important to ensure that the supervision you receive is useful and productive. In a study of supervisee experiences, Ellis and colleagues (Ellis *et al.*, 2014) developed a taxonomy of inadequate and harmful supervision and found that a large proportion of supervisees were (or had been) receiving supervision that would be classed in one of these ways. Ellis *et al.* (2014) provide a method for supervisees to check their supervision and identify areas of shortcoming using a set of questions rated on a seven-point scale. The authors also define *minimally adequate supervision* which they argue might represent the bare minimum necessary for supervision. These form the basis for the Minimally Adequate Forensic Supervision list presented in Box 6.3.

BOX 6.3 Minimally adequate forensic supervision (based on Ellis *et al.*, 2014)

The figure below presents suggested minimum supervision 'standards' which can be supplemented by profession specific requirements as appropriate.

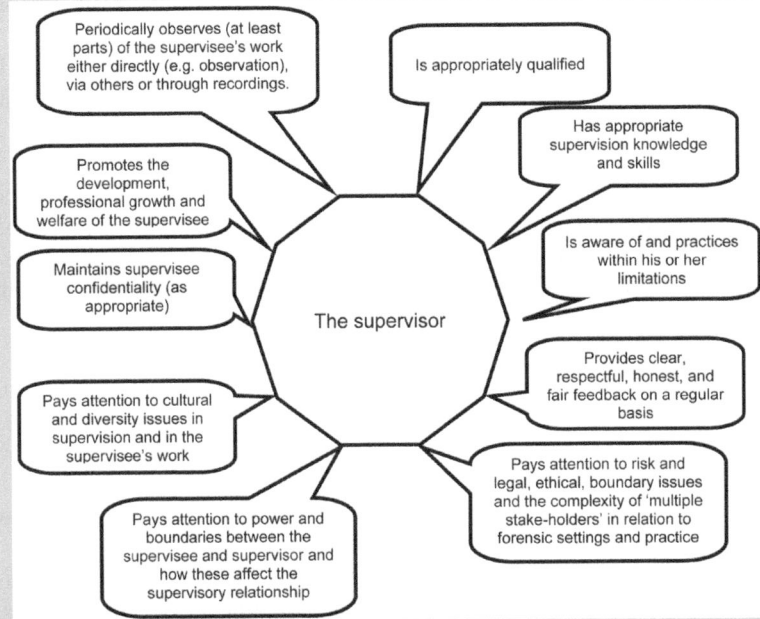

Figure 6.1 Minimally adequate forensic supervision

Supervision components in addition to the above:

1. I have an up-to-date supervision agreement with my supervisor (see Chapter 3).
2. I receive at least the amount of supervision as laid out by my professional body or service (whichever is the greater; at minimum one hour per month).

Supervision glossary

Supervision practice has a number of terms that are used and which you need to become familiar with. Listed below (in alphabetical order) is a brief description of some of the most common terms – this is intended as a start from which you can develop your own personalised glossary if this is useful. As a general principle for supervision – if you don't understand something or something doesn't make sense – discuss it with your supervisor.

Action planning – the phase, usually following discussion, in which the steps that will be taken as a result of supervision are detailed. Actions should be clear, should detail how they will be carried out and should identify the expected outcome or consequence of the action.

Agenda – this contains the list of possible topics (i.e. clients, issues or tasks) that might be discussed during the supervision session. Details on compiling and using an agenda can be found in Chapter 3.

Agreement – the 'contract' between the supervisor and supervisee that outlines the goals and practical arrangements for supervision. There is more detail on this in Chapter 3.

Alliance – based on Bordin (1983) and Burke, Goodyear and Guzzard (1998) the supervisory alliance can be viewed as a collaboration or relationship based on three components: (1) a mutual agreement (of what supervision is being used for); (2) clear tasks (what each person will do and is responsible for); and (3) a bond between the supervisor and supervisee (the trust and respect each has for the other).

Line manager – this is the person who is responsible for your employment and work practices. They will usually be the person you report to (e.g. if you are sick or wish to take leave) and are accountable to (e.g. are you doing what you are supposed to in a timely fashion to the expected standard). There are some overlaps between the roles of supervisor and line manager and sometimes the same person will undertake both roles. Where this is the case, it is wise to have separate time with them for each of these functions.

Models – these are the 'maps' and 'frameworks' used to guide the supervision process. Some of the models and approaches to supervision are described in more detail in Chapter 4.

Process – is a general term to describe what takes place in the supervision session. This is likely to be guided by the tasks and models as described in Chapters 3 and 4.

Reflection – is the process of active review and (re)consideration of what has or is being done, why it is being done, the alternatives and the effect(s). There are a number of models that can be used to aid reflection as discussed in Special Topic 10.

Supervisor – is the person who facilitates supervision and is often a more senior and/or more experienced practitioner. Their role is to aid the supervisee in the tasks of supervision (see Chapter 3). The supervisor may also undertake the role of assessor where the supervisee is a student or trainee.

Supervisee – the person whose work and practice is the focus of supervision.

Conclusions

Acclimatising or becoming familiar with the ways in which supervision 'works', what your role is and what is and isn't expected may take time before the process of learning, development and reflection can take place (Johns, 1993). However, being an active participant, as opposed to a passive recipient, is essential if supervision is to meet your goals and enhance the work you do. Having explored being a supervisee in this chapter all you need to do is meet with your supervisor and start using supervision. Carpenter, Webb and Bostock (2013) suggest that supervision works best when attention is paid to the supervisor–supervisee relationship, the task and providing support; and argue that practitioners should insist on receiving good quality supervision.

References

Bordin, E. S. (1983) 'A working alliance based model of supervision', *The Counseling Psychologist* 11(1): 35–42.

Burke, W. R., Goodyear, R. K. and Guzzard, C. R. (1998) 'Weakenings and repairs in supervisory alliances', *American Journal of Psychotherapy* 52: 450–62.

Carpenter, J., Webb, C. M. and Bostock, L. (2013) 'The surprisingly weak evidence base for supervision: findings from a systematic review of research in child welfare practice (2000–2012)', *Children and Youth Services Review* 35(11): 1843–53.

Ellis, M. V., Berger, L., Hanus, A. E., Ayala, E. E., Swords, B. A. and Siembor, M. (2014) 'Inadequate and harmful clinical supervision: testing a revised framework and assessing occurrence', *The Counseling Psychologist* 42(4): 434–72.

Freshwater, D., Walsh, L. and Storey, L. (2002) 'Prison health care: developing leadership through clinical supervision', *Nursing Management* 8(9): 16–20.

Johns, C. (1993) 'Professional supervision', *Journal of Nursing Management* 1(1): 9–18.

Kadushin, A. (1976) *Supervision in Social Work*, Columbia University Press.

Lizzio, A. J. and Wilson, K. L. (2002) 'The domain of learning goals in professional supervision', in M. Patton and W. McMahon, *Supervision in the Helping Professions: A Practical Approach*, Frenchs Forest, NSW: Pearson Education Australia, pp. 27–41.

Manthorpe, J., Moriarty, J., Hussein, S., Stevens, M. and Sharpe, E. (2013) 'Content and purpose of supervision in social work practice in England: views of newly qualified social workers, managers and directors', *British Journal of Social Work*.

Proctor, B. (1986) 'Supervision: a co-operative exercise in accountability', in M. Marken and M. Payne, *Enabling and Ensuring*, Leicester: National Youth Bureau for Education in Youth and Community Work.

7 Core skills and knowledge for supervisors

It is reasonable to expect that anyone who undertakes the role of supervisor wants to be effective, however all too often individuals take on this task without adequate training or preparation. Although this chapter is aimed particularly at the first-time supervisor, the intention is also to provide information that will be of use for the seasoned supervisor. This chapter is structured to parallel the process of being a supervisor – beginning with taking 'stock' of oneself, followed by preparation, then focusing on establishing supervision and finally undertaking the task itself. In doing this we will consider again the four functions of supervision (described in Chapter 4) as they relate to the supervisor, i.e. (a) the supervisory relationship and the ability to (b) foster development (reflection, training etc.), (c) provide support, and (d) undertake the normative and administrative elements. The headings used throughout this chapter can be used as a simple aide memoire to help structure, develop and deliver supervision. To supplement this you may wish to develop a more detailed checklist for some aspects of supervision such as getting supervision established.

Before considering the 'what's' and the 'how's', it is important to think through why you are going to take on this role. On the one hand, it may be that becoming a supervisor is a natural progression that you have sought out and feel ready for whilst, on the other, it may be something that you feel is demanded of you despite your own uncertainties and misgivings. In either case, it is worth taking some time now, and again after reading this chapter, to ask yourself – 'why am I considering being a supervisor?'. Whatever your personal position and your reasons for taking this on, it is worth noting the findings from a study reported by White and Winstanley (2010). They found that, on average, individuals who trained to be a supervisor showed higher scores on the Manchester Clinical Supervision Scale, and importantly that high scores were associated with lower scores on the Maslach Burnout Inventory. Further, the participants in Landmark *et al.*'s (2003) study reported that supervising students was both challenging and stimulating. So, regardless of other reasons, it may be that supervising others could be good for you!

Having gathered your thoughts about why, the next task is to review your own experiences of supervision to date – either as a supervisee and/or as a supervisor. Supervisors often have a role model from their own experiences of being supervised (Severinsson and Hallberg, 1996). Think of your own experiences of supervision ... what do you consider good supervision to be? In answering this you may find yourself drawn to factors such as the personal qualities of the supervisor (e.g. approachable, supportive); the role being undertaken (e.g. being an evaluator, a facilitator of reflection or a role model); or how supervision is conducted (e.g. creating a space to think of the supervisor as a 'critical friend'). Make a note of your views and ideas of good supervision and again return to this at the end of the chapter and periodically thereafter. You might also invite supervisees to let you know their views on good supervision.

A final exercise at this point is to review your current position in regard to supervision through four simple questions:

As a (would be) supervisor:

(1) What do you feel confident in doing?
(2) What are you nervous about?
(3) What do you need to learn?
(4) What support do you need?

As with the other exercises above, you should make a note of your answers and return to them at the end of the chapter and from time to time.

Supervisor qualities

There are many supervisor qualities that have been identified as contributing positively to the effectiveness of supervision. In its most general, as stated by one of the participants in Hair's (2013) study, 'the best supervisors I have had encouraged self directed practice with clarity around accountability issues' (p. 1576). Cushway and Knibbs (2004) suggested that supervisory behaviours could be rated across two dimensions, namely: *competence*, ranging from incompetent to competent and skilled, and *alliance*, from disinterested and remote to establishes a good rapport. However, it is necessary to unpick the qualities, competencies and approach embedded within them. For example, *supervisor social skills* have been found to predict supervisee's ratings of both the supervisory alliance and the supervisee evaluation of supervision (Bambling and King, 2013). This chapter will consider the broad spectrum of factors in two clusters – personal qualities and supervisor behaviours. These are described below and key elements are summarised in Box 7.1.

BOX 7.1: Qualities of 'good' supervisors

An excellent 'recipe' for supervisor qualities and approach is given by Nelson and colleagues (Nelson *et al.*, 2008) from their study of 'wise supervisors'. They found that 'wise supervisors' had a 'remarkable sense of humility' (p. 177) and were aware of their limits and shortcomings as a supervisor (of which they conveyed a sense of acceptance). They enjoyed being supervisors and learning from supervisees; had a willingness to set clear boundaries, to undertake supervisee evaluation and to provide difficult feedback where necessary. Wise supervisors were able to be flexible and to adapt to the supervisee's need, and demonstrated an awareness and sensitivity to difference. They also showed a clear ability to empathise with and express support to the supervisee, and importantly they recognised and accepted that mistakes would be made and that these were important for learning to take place. Further, they attended to process and made use of contracting, appropriate self-disclosure (to close the power difference gap), attended to successes and sought feedback from the supervisee on the supervision being provided. As might be expected from the above, wise supervisors worked to establish positive and collaborative supervisory relationships.

Additional qualities of good supervisors that have been identified by others and through personal experience include being someone who is encouraging, inspiring, validating, possesses relevant knowledge, is curious and open-minded, and is able to provide balance (can remain focused on both the supervisee and the purpose or task of supervision). They also provide the conditions of equality, safety and challenge.

However, it is essential to note two things. First, that many of these features coalesce and second, that it is possible to create an unachievable and off-putting ideal for a supervisor that becomes disabling rather than inspiring. Therefore, it is worth holding in mind that what is needed is a supervisor who can provide 'good enough supervision' (Hawkins and Shohet, 2006).

Personal qualities

A range of personal supervisor attributes have been noted by researchers as having a positive impact on the effectiveness of supervision. For example, supervisor interpersonal qualities such as empathy, congruence and unconditionality were identified as having the biggest impact on the supervisees' effectiveness (as therapists) (Schacht, Howe and Berman, 1989). Russell and Petrie (1995) provide a fairly comprehensive list of supervisor qualities that includes support, tolerance, inner security, being non-judgemental and nurturing, genuineness, empathy, clarity, self-disclosure, attentiveness, honesty, sensitivity, openness, praise and the ability to match style to learning (level and need). Echoing many of these attributes, Worthen and McNeill (1996) also noted the ability to focus on both the alliance and the task, validate supervisee experiences and engage in appropriate disclosure of the supervisor's experience (e.g. emotional reactions, past mistakes) were important.

The reader should be cautious about using this as a crude 'personality test' to see if they (or perhaps their own supervisor) possesses all the features listed, however it may be helpful to be aware of what qualities can positively impact on supervision.

How supervisors behave

As noted by Worthen and McNeill (1996), the 'safe foundation' of supervision is created through the relationship, style and approach of the supervisor. Supervisors who have the greatest reported impact on supervisees engage in a number of behaviours which appear to characterise their approach. A study by Schacht et al., (1989) found that the most effective supervisors of therapists took a facilitative approach and shared the same theoretical orientation as the supervisee. It may be that this latter factor is important to ensure a common language and understanding between the supervisor and supervisee. In addition, those supervisors who are identified as helpful are able to normalise the anxiety felt by the supervisee in relation to their practice (and their competence); show their own vulnerabilities and anxieties; assist supervisees to manage and accept uncertainty and facilitate positive risk taking (Nelson et al., 2008). Positive risk taking is discussed in more detail in Chapter 8.

Good supervision has been associated with encouraging supervisees to explore and experiment with ideas and options, and aiding the supervisee to 'free' themselves from self-imposed restrictions such as assumptions about themselves or their ability. 'Good' supervisors facilitated non-defensive analysis of experiences and aided the supervisee to adopt meta-perspectives (i.e. develop coherence from complex situations). Such elements led to increased skill and confidence on the part of the supervisee (Worthen and McNeill, 1996). Johnston and Milne (2012) suggest that important supervisor qualities include having personal and professional credibility, establishing clear roles and boundaries, engaging in mutuality and undertaking explicit contracting. They may also need to take on different roles such as instructor, role model, teacher and consultant (Russell and Petrie, 1995).

As well as the behaviours and approaches associated with helpful and effective supervision, a number of harmful and problematic factors have been identified. Amongst the unhelpful factors are a lack of autonomy given to the supervisee, a lack of clarity and direction within supervision, being unsupportive (engaging in a cold, aloof or hostile way) and the supervisor taking on the role of (or acting as) therapist to the supervisee (Russell and Petrie, 1995).

A novel approach to understanding the features and qualities of good supervision was taken by Magnuson and colleagues who investigated 'lousy supervision' (Magnuson, Wilcoxon and Norem, 2000). Using a qualitative method, they identified features associated with 'lousy supervision' through which they were able to reveal possible traps and errors for the would-be successful supervisor to avoid! Their findings suggested that poor supervisors provided supervision that contained a number of features or 'overarching principles'. Lousy supervision was found to be:

(a) *unbalanced* in that it failed to focus on the specific *and* consider wider issues;
(b) *developmentally inappropriate* and unresponsive to the changing needs of the supervisee; and

(c) provided by supervisors who were:

    (i) *intolerant of differences* shown through being rigid, impatient, inflexible and resistant to innovation;
    (ii) *poor professional/personal role models*; they violated boundaries and were intrusive and/or exploitative;
    (iii) *untrained* and were providing supervision without adequate preparation and professional maturity; and
    (iv) *professionally apathetic* shown through laziness and a lack of commitment to the profession.

Magnuson et al. (2000) further suggested that lousy supervisors could display these failings across three broad domains, namely: organisation (e.g. failing to clarify expectations, not paying attention to continuity over time, failing to prepare); technical (e.g. vague and abstract feedback, being an unreliable professional resource); and relational (e.g. failing to provide a safe environment, being overly critical, viewing supervision as a chore). Thus, in theory a matrix could be created plotting overarching principles against spheres in order to show where the problems lay.

Research by Ladany, Mori and Mehr (2012) indicated that the differences between 'best' and 'worst' supervisors was based on the presence of ineffective (rather than effective) supervisor behaviours. Specifically, they identified that an emphasis on evaluation and limitations, weakening in the supervisory relationship, and ineffective client conceptualisation and treatment contributed to making supervisors less effective. Importantly, supervisees rated having a stronger emotional bond, greater agreement on tasks and more effective goal setting and feedback processes with 'best' supervisors who they reported as having a supervisory style that was 'more attractive', interpersonally sensitive, task orientated and involving more supervisor disclosure. This reinforces the importance of the supervisory relationship.

Through an analysis of successful and negative critical incidents experienced by nurse supervisors, Arvidsson and Fridlund (2005) reported a number of supervisor features which they grouped into two categories. First, 'exhibiting a professional stance' contained 'creating a secure learning environment'; 'facilitating reflection'; 'underlining the importance of structure', and awareness of fundamental [nursing] values. Second, 'exhibiting a personal stance' contained two juxtaposed elements: 'doubt about performance as a supervisor' and 'security regarding supervisory performance'. They highlight the need for supervisors to ensure they take their supervisory work to supervision (see supervision of supervision in Chapter 10). Therefore, 'being yourself' as a supervisor requires personal integrity and strong self-esteem especially when asking questions and providing feedback and challenge may lead to being unpopular, at least for a while.

Within occupational psychology, analysis has shown that supportive supervisors (this role being different to the one defined in Chapter 1) show characteristics such as humility and personal warmth, good communication skills, trustworthiness and a 'non-competitive' social identity (Paustian-Underdahl et al., 2013). This would suggest that in other facilitative relationships in forensic settings (e.g. mentoring) the personal qualities listed in this section may be relevant.

Preparing for supervision

Supervisor competence

Good supervision might be thought of as a safe, secure and productive encounter between supervisor and supervisee. However, in preparing for supervision it is necessary to distil some of the competencies which need to be evidenced within supervision and are required of the supervisor. According to Falender (2014; Falender et al., 2004), there are a number of aspects of effective 'competency based supervision' which have been identified. They produced a list of over 30 interrelated competencies under four headings: knowledge, skills, values and overarching social context issues. Competencies included:

(a) formation of a strong supervisory alliance;
(b) the presence of a supervision agreement;
(c) supporting supervisee self-assessment of competence;
(d) agreeing goals and tasks for supervision;
(e) monitoring supervisee progress;
(f) provision of constructive feedback;
(g) transparent formative and summative feedback;
(h) recognition and repair of 'ruptures' in the therapeutic alliance;
(i) attention to diversity;
(j) attention to ethical practice;
(k) managing supervisee emotional reactions;
(l) managing supervisees who fall below expected performance standards;
(m) assessment of client outcomes;
(n) assessment of the effectiveness of supervision; and
(o) attention to self-care.

They also identified two training competencies (e.g. has received supervision of supervision) and seven assessment related competencies (e.g. successful completion of a supervision course).

Whilst this list is helpful especially to the 'assessment' and review of supervision itself, there are a number of additional components worthy of consideration. For example, in a review study by Berggren and Severinsson (2006), they identified the:

(a) use of structure and a structured model;
(b) integration of theory and practice;
(c) focus on the range of factors which could impact care;

(d) space to share feelings;
(e) use of challenge in order to promote development of competence;
(f) use of reflection; and
(g) treating the supervisee with justice and respecting their integrity.

In some ways aspects of this latter list could be viewed as the 'how to address' the 'what needs to be done' of the first one. Other chapters in this book provide some approaches for achieving these.

Increasingly within therapy supervision, tools and checklists are used to examine the 'fidelity' of the practitioner and the supervision process to the model and approach. For example, Milne et al. (2011) has developed 'SAGE' (Supervision: Adherence and Guidance Evaluation) to measure the 'formative' element within CBT supervision. In this approach, 23 items are rated on a three-point scale with the assumption that a competent supervisor will use various strategies such as listening and problem solving to foster learning within the session.

Student and trainee supervision: Although most of the areas of supervisor competence are generic, there are a number which are particular to supervising students or trainees. For example, Landmark et al. (2003) identified three areas of supervisory competence in student supervision:

(1) didactics – such as the ability to support the integration of theory and practice using up-to-date knowledge, ability to facilitate student reflection and competence in student evaluation;
(2) role functions – this includes the ability to support the student to become responsible for their own learning and development and to be a self-aware role model; and
(3) organisational framework – for example supervisors need to know the expectations that the training programme has of the supervisor and supervisee and they need to be clear what expectations they as a supervisor have of the trainee.

In many ways this supports a slightly earlier review by Kilminster and Jolly (2000) who identified that those who are supervising trainees/students needed to be clinically competent; have good interpersonal skills; be a good teacher and role model; give direct and clear guidance and feedback and link theory with practice. They also identified features associated with ineffective behaviours such as rigidity, low empathy and being indirect. More recently, Johnston and Milne (2012) reported that structured, collaborative and experiential work within supervision was important to learning, along with being able to provide the supervisee with a framework for understanding (scaffolding) and making use of a Socratic approach within supervision (use of questioning, testing and scrutiny).

When supervising trainees and students, it is important to know and understand your responsibilities and to be mindful that in many instances the trainee or student is practising under 'your' registration or licence to practice. In supervision this means that the supervisor must be clear whether they are providing advice and/or suggestion that the trainee/student is free to use or ignore, or whether the information is an instruction that you (the supervisor) expects to be carried out. In this way, supervision of trainees and students can be distinguished from other forms of supervision because of the power, responsibility and liability the supervisor holds (Falender, 2014).

Training

Being an effective supervisor is onerous and complex, and ideally requires specialist training in supervision in addition to relevant forensic knowledge and experience (Mothersole, 2000). Supervisor training is covered in more detail in Chapter 10.

Establishing supervision

In order to get supervision 'up and running' it is usually necessary for the supervisor to undertake a number of important tasks. These typically include clarifying the purpose of supervision (goals), establishing the ground rules, determining responsibility and accountability, agreeing boundaries, exploring available resources and developing a supervision agreement. Supervisors should also be familiar with and consider which models and approaches to supervision might be used or be most helpful. It is important that in the initial supervision meeting(s) the supervisor and supervisee share their experiences of supervision, discuss what is expected, explore styles, agree specific learning and development needs, and discuss disciplinary procedures and assessment criteria (e.g. see Bordin, 1983; James *et al.*, 2006). Additional material on these 'tasks' of the first supervision session(s) can be found in Chapters 3 and 6.

Role clarity

Having clarity around the nature and purpose of your role is essential. For example, in a study of clinical placement facilitation within nurse training, four levels of supervisor were identified, each with a distinct role and set of responsibilities (Hall-Lord, Theander and Athlin, 2013). Providing students or trainees with multiple contacts and supports such as mentors and buddies, as well as multiple supervisors for clinical placement and research can also be found in UK clinical psychology training. Thus in all situations, but especially where there are multiple supervision mechanisms in place, it is essential that the supervisor understands what their function is and what responsibilities they carry, as it is important that supervision provided to students and trainees is more than simple oversight of their work (Nelson *et al.*, 2008). This should be captured through the means of an agreement between the supervisor, supervisee and, where appropriate, the training provider such as the university or college. Similar clarity should be sought between supervision and line management where different people undertake these tasks. What should be borne in mind is that enabling practitioners to take control of and responsibility for supervision may also have an effect on these aspects of their work outside supervision (Johns, 1993).

Understanding the supervisee

Assumptions about the supervisee: In his description of solution-focused supervision, Wheeler (2007) provides a list of helpful assumptions about supervisees in relation to work with clients. His assumptions are: *supervisees want the best for their clients; supervisees are likely to be already doing something that clients find valuable; supervisees are likely to have hidden talents; most supervisees underestimate the value of their work*, and a more generally useful idea – *there is always more to learn*. In a similar vein Azar (2000), discussing supervising those who work with child abuse cases, lists a number of assumptions about the supervisee and the people they are working with:

(a) they are doing the best they can;
(b) they need to feel a sense of mastery in their role;
(c) they have difficulty being easy on themselves;
(d) they are ambivalent about wanting help; and
(e) they expect you to tell them 'you're doing a bad job'.

They also stress that there is no right way to do things, and in relation to clients, they may well carry the assumption that:

(a) help is dangerous; and
(b) change is dangerous and slow.

These assumptions may be helpful to both hold in mind and to share as appropriate with supervisees. However, it is also worth being mindful of the finding that supervisors are more likely to believe in the value of supervision than practitioners themselves (Bober and Regehr, 2006).

Supervisee non-disclosure. In the context of supervision, it is assumed that supervisees will share with the supervisor any concerns, limitations, mistakes and problems relating to their work. Indeed, the supervisor can only work with the supervisee on those aspects of performance and practice that are shared. However, the possibility of non-disclosure (i.e. the intentional withholding of information which may be relevant) has been subject to some research which is worthy of consideration. In a study of over 100 psychotherapy trainees, Ladany *et al.* (1996) discovered that almost all (97 per cent) had withheld information from their supervisors, and that on average there were eight non-disclosures reported per supervisee. Some of these were described as 'personal issues that were not directly relevant to supervision' and therefore were likely to be appropriate non-disclosures. However, the most common relevant information being withheld were negative reactions to the supervisor (90 per cent of supervisees reported this kind of non-disclosure) and clinical mistakes (44 per cent reported this form of non-disclosure). Supervisees reported a number of reasons for non-disclosure including not thinking the matter was important, and impression management. Also of high relevance to a forensic setting was the finding that 36 per cent of the supervisees withheld information about negative reactions to the client and 9 per cent where there was some form of attraction between the client and the supervisee (in one direction or the other). Clearly such non-disclosures may have a consequential impact on risk (and safety), client outcomes, the maintenance of appropriate boundaries and service functioning (see Chapter 8 for more on this). Most non-disclosures (83 per cent) were described as passive (i.e. the supervisee didn't offer information and the supervisor didn't ask relevant questions) whilst the supervisee used a diversionary approach in 10 per cent of incidences. Three other factors are particularly important in the context of supervision. First, over half of the non-disclosures were discussed with a peer or colleague. This may have implications for the training of peer supervisors and colleagues in forensic settings – for example how they might redirect the individual to discuss the matter with their supervisor. Second, supervisee non-disclosures were influenced by their perception of supervision quality based on their reactions to their supervisor ... a good alliance (e.g. being open and collaborative) being important for revealing significant information. Finally, the use of live supervision or forms of recording of practice may be useful to discover what actually happens in practice.

Bias. There are a number of sources of bias (e.g. Bazerman, 1990), each of which can lead to significant problems in supervision. Some of these stem from lack of awareness or an inability to recognise and report information whilst others are the result of cognitive biases to which all can be susceptible. In 'novice' practitioners, difficulties in providing an account of specific issues might be expected (for further discussion see the developmental model section in Chapter 4), however missing key issues and overlooking problems may be 'blind spots' experienced by all practitioners from time to time – how can you take to supervision things that are outside your awareness? In addition, the process of recalling events to discuss in supervision is likely to be susceptible to hindsight bias (Jones, 1995). In this form of bias, what is reported is influenced by knowledge of the 'outcome'. This might lead to reappraisal of ideas and modification of opinions, intentions and causal explanations. Thus supervisors need to be attentive to managing forms of bias using methods such as understanding what was planned, periodically seeing the practitioner in action and reviewing all areas of work. It might also be helpful to discuss possible sources of bias periodically within supervision.

Supervisee burnout. It is possible that practitioners in forensic settings will experience workplace stress and burnout. If this occurs, it is important to be able to recognise and respond in order to minimise the negative impact on the practitioner, and others. Azar (2000) suggests that the presence of burnout may be identified in supervision through a number of supervisee attitudes and actions. These include:

(a) avoiding responsibility;
(b) focusing on detail;
(c) remaining silent;
(d) being overly compliant with or resistant to the supervisor and their observations and suggestions;
(e) frustration, rage, anger or emotional numbing;
(f) blame towards the supervisor (e.g. seeing the supervisor as uncaring, distant or cut-off);
(g) greater risk taking in their practice;
(h) complacency in practice; and
(i) a sense of invincibility.

Within supervision sessions, burnout might lead to the supervisee being less able to describe their practice and the accuracy and quality of the information they provide may decrease. In response, Azar (2000) describes an approach to provide support to individuals who might be experiencing burnout or the precursors to it. She conceptualises the difficulties using a CBT framework and suggests that the approach in supervision needs to support cognitive flexibility and help test assumptions using four steps:

(a) addressing emotional dis-regulation;
(b) counteracting feelings of inconsequentiality;
(c) reframing differences between supervisee and client goals/expectations; and
(d) addressing risk issues.

It may also be important to directly discuss the idea of burnout or stress with the practitioner (supervisee) and redirect them to appropriate sources of workplace support.

The supervisory relationship

The supervisory relationship can be thought of as the crucible within which the activity of supervision takes place. In order for this relationship to be secure and functional it needs to have certain qualities. Wilson and Lizzio (2009) identified three supervisory relationship factors, namely: that supervision needs to be *open* and non-defensive; it needs to provide sufficient *challenge* to foster supervisee development; and needs to offer 'enough *support* to enable the supervisee to adequately respond to the learning opportunity without retreating' (p. 143; my italics). In addition, Johns (1993) states that it is important for the supervisee not to feel judged.

At times it may be necessary for the supervisor to take on a 'leadership' role. However, as observed by Severinsson and Hallberg (1996), leadership in this context can be complex – the supervisor needs to have techniques in order to provide supervision, be able to accept responsibility for facilitating the process of supervision and be responsible for creating a conducive climate.

Managing strains and ruptures: It is important that the supervisor is able to notice and address difficulties, disagreements or conflict within the supervisory relationship in order to be able to repair it. Although the individual situation will need to be responded to, key steps have been described by Falender (2014), namely: identifying and discussing the difficulty including identifying the supervisor and supervisee roles/contributions, acknowledging and addressing the emotional elements associated with the difficulty, and developing a strategy to continue/restore the alliance. Wilson and Lizzio (2009) suggest that openness is particularly helpful for conflict resolution.

In an interesting study of university counselling and mental health services in California, Burke, Goodyear and Guzzard (1998) investigated 10 'supervision dyads' across 10 consecutive sessions. They found that generally the supervisor rated the working alliance more consistently and as more stable than did the supervisee. Further, they found that 'weakening and repair' varied across the dyads. For example, in one supervisory relationship there were multiple weakening events – these centred around differences in approach (to the case and to therapy) – few of which were resolved. However, in a number of the dyads there were no weakening events recorded. The authors identified a number of important factors in the process. 'Causes' of the weakening events were found to differ according to the supervisee's experience level. With inexperienced supervisees the causes were often in relation to issues with basic practice. In such instances, the supervisor initiated the repair by changing their comments or style. In contrast, those with more experience were more likely to encounter weakening due to differences in style, therapeutic orientation and strategies for treatment. 'Power' and 'being evaluated' were also found to be factors. The supervisors tended to use exploration to try to overcome weakening events and rarely used confrontation. Perhaps surprisingly, ratings of the supervision session and overall outcomes were positive regardless of the number of weakenings – this may mean that there were sufficient benefits of supervision regardless of the issues that arose in the alliance.

Providing supervision

Promoting learning and development

There are many approaches to 'delivering' supervision that the supervisor needs to be able to use. These might include, problem solving, skill building and action planning (Schoenwald *et al.*, 2013), the use of case studies, observations and role play/skills rehearsal (Wilson and Lizzio, 2009), teaching and role modelling. These may be agreed formally within the supervision agreement or within an individual supervision session. Where role play is to be used, Wilson and Lizzio (2009) provides a seven-step guide for this process. This consists of

(1) being clear about the focus for the role play;
(2) identifying tentative goals for the role play;
(3) the supervisee enacting the present behaviour;
(4) the supervisor and supervisee analysing the situation;
(5) reassessing goals;
(6) developing a preferred strategy; and
(7) planning for action.

In addition, it is useful to have a range of questions and ideas to use in supervision when appropriate. Supervisors should also consider how they might make the frameworks and models they use explicit during supervision in order to foster both learning and empowerment of the supervisee. It is useful to develop your own resource of questions, however some examples can be found in Box 7.2.

BOX 7.2: Some useful questions for supervisors

As a supervisor one of the main skills is that of facilitating exploration, learning and reflection. It is worthwhile developing your own repertoire of questions that can be used for these purposes however the following provide some to start you on your way.

WHAT . . . . .

- else could be tried (based on the literature or other cases/staff)?
- do others notice or do?
- are you trying to achieve?
- works/do you do well?

WHY . . . . .

- have you noticed this now?
- has this happened now?
- has this happened to you?
- do you feel like this?

WHERE . . . . .

- are the exceptions?
- are the aspects of good practice?
- are there opportunities to do things differently?
- would you normally go from here?

WHO . . . . .

- does things differently?
- else shares your view?

- do you think could do things better and why?
- might give you some new ideas/directions?

HOW . . . . .

- do you feel when you are with XX; does XX feel when they are with you?
- do others experience X?
- did you expect things to be at this point?
- would you notice if things were changing?

Supervising case work

Supervising individual client work in forensic settings requires the supervisor to attend to a number of elements such as the supervisee, the client and the work being done. Two very important issues relate to expectations and experience. For example, Azar (2000) points out that interventions and our efforts may have a limited impact on the client; clients may be resistant to our help (no matter how genuinely we offer it); clients may not be able or not wish to engage; expectations may be set too high; small achievements may be missed or there may be a failure to recognise the link between the supervisee's work and the change taking place. As a result, these authors suggest that, in some situations, engagement itself might be an outcome and that models such as the Stages of Change, which has also been used in other areas of forensic practice (e.g. Williamson *et al.*, 2003; Wong, Gordon and Gu, 2007) may be helpful in framing expectations and understanding. It is important to remember that supervision should also consider cases where there are successes and where things are already working well (Ingram, 2013).

Where case work is the focus within supervision, a framework is needed to help structure the presentation and consideration of the information. Although there are many approaches available for this, the one by Gordon (2012), developed as a guide for new Cognitive Behaviour Therapy supervisors, is useful as a basis from which to develop a system of your own.

Identification of the question being asked – this provides the focus of the supervision with questions falling into one of three types:

(1) information questions, e.g. which risk assessment tool should I use?
(2) feedback questions, e.g. were my report conclusions okay?
(3) learning questions, e.g. how might I manage this boundary?

He suggests that learning questions are characterised by open enquiry, and that information questions can often be developed into learning questions by the supervisor. Once the question is determined, the remaining steps can be worked through.

Gather relevant background and contextual information – this should be focused and brief to ensure that this doesn't take up the supervision time. It is important that supervision avoids the 'drift towards case description and inefficient use of supervision time' (p. 79).

Identify an example of the problem – Gordon advocates using recordings of case work so that this can be precise, however it may need to be based solely on supervisee report – what's working also needs to be noted.

Check supervisee's current understanding – this might be based on a case formulation/conceptualisation and current ideas and thinking.

Decide on a focus – this identifies what 'direction' to address the problem from. For example a boundary issue might be considered from a number of angles such as professional guidance, ethical issues raised, interpersonal functioning, risk assessment, emotional impacts or team responses and standpoints.

Active supervision methods – this identifies how supervision will be used to address the problem (e.g. role play; information sharing; skills building).

Determine if the original question has been addressed – return to the trigger question and identify what's changed, been learned or new options/ideas.

Develop a client-related action plan – identify what will be taken from the supervision session to the case work. This needs to be specific in order to be useable.

Set 'homework' – although a typical CBT process, this step builds on the 'what' in the action plan to ask 'what else', e.g. reading, discussions to have with the team, things to observe with other clients.

Elicit feedback on supervision – checking the usefulness and identifying helpful (and unhelpful) practice on the part of the supervisor so appropriate actions can be taken (e.g. more of what works and less of what doesn't) in future supervision sessions.

As can be seen, this framework also fits very well with the Supervision Hour model described in Chapter 4. Where formulation or case conceptualisation is the focus, supervisors may also wish to consider the practical, theoretical and ethical issues associated with this aspect of forensic work (Davies *et al.*, 2013).

Harkness and Hensley (1991) describe a 'client focused' approach to supervision based on 10 questions and found that this approach was associated with changes in outcomes. The questions in Box 7.3 are taken from their framework but have been modified to incorporate some of the additional factors associated with being in forensic services.

BOX 7.3: Client-focused supervision questions

The following questions are drawn from Harkness and Hensley (1991). Four additional questions have been added to reflect the forensic context (marked with an ★).

1. What does the client want help with?
2. ★What does the client need to achieve while they are in the service (e.g. treatment conditions, discharge or release goals)?
3. ★What does the client think about these 'imposed goals'?

4. How will you and the client know you are helping?
5. How does the client describe a successful outcome?
6. Does the client say there has been a successful outcome?
7. *What do others say about the client's progress?
8. *How has the client's risk changed over time?
9. What are you doing to help the client?
10. Is it working?
11. Does the client say you are helping?
12. What else can you do to help the client?
13. How will that work?
14. Does the client say that will help?

Providing 'remote' supervision

Sometimes it is necessary to undertake supervision via phone or video link. This is often the case when there is a large distance between supervisor and supervisee. Indeed, a study by Marrow *et al.* (2002) based on a small number of nurses who had engaged in supervision via video-conference (VC) it was found that VC could be of 'immense value', reducing travelling time and stress, and promoting active communication. However, they noted that the technology itself posed problems because of access, support and training. Therefore, where this arrangement is to be used, there are a number of factors to consider as part of the planning process:

(a) time differences (e.g. where more than one time zone is involved);
(b) practicalities (e.g. back up if the preferred technology fails, note keeping);
(c) preparation (e.g. how will materials for consideration in supervision be shared);
(d) etiquette (e.g. how will discussion and turn taking be facilitated); and
(e) training in using the equipment.

Providing feedback

Feedback is an essential element of learning and development and can lead to changes in skills, practice and self-awareness (Hoffman *et al.*, 2005), however providing good quality feedback can be enhanced through a number of means. Feedback in supervision can be thought of as being 'information that supervisors communicate to their supervisees about aspects of their skills, attitudes, behaviour, and appearance that may influence their performance with clients or affect the supervisory relationship' (Hoffman *et al.*, 2005, p. 3). Falender (2014) argues that feedback should take place in each supervision session and should be balanced (strengths and development needs); respectful; timely (i.e. as close to the event in question as possible); and contain formative information covering what and how the individual might address their weaknesses. It is also important that in giving feedback the supervisor makes clear distinctions between the person and the actions being discussed (Chur Hansen and McLean, 2006; Rolfe and Gardner, 2006).

Feedback should be given to improve practice, develop personal and professional issues or improve the supervisory relationship (Hoffman et al., 2005). Their research suggested that direct feedback tended to be given in relation to practice and where the issue was clear cut or where the supervisor had been able to directly observe (or review via video) the event. Things that made giving feedback easier were: supervisees being open; supervisor had expertise to share; strong supervisory relationship; clear need; supervisor had support.

Heckman-Stone (2004) notes that systematic feedback is objective, accurate and consistent whilst subjective feedback can be helpful but must be acknowledged as such. It should also be clear, specific, credible, collaborative and take place in a supportive relationship. They provide a feedback plan for student/trainee work, namely:

(a) describe the process of evaluation;
(b) agree clear performance criteria;
(c) undertake observation;
(d) compare observed performance with goals and objectives (see (b) above);
(e) allow time for self-evaluation before supervisor feedback;
(f) start with positive elements before negative ones;
(g) provide feedback based on the above characteristics;
(h) identify what the feedback is based upon (evidence);
(i) be explicit as to the skill being assessed;
(j) give control to the trainee re agenda, clarifying the feedback and setting new goals based on this;
(k) the above should be in the context of regular feedback; and
(l) monitor the student's use of feedback/evaluation.

When feedback has been given it is important for the supervisor to invite the supervisee to comment on how the feedback matches their perception, provide opportunity to discuss the feedback and review the supervision goals to identify any adjustments needed in light of the feedback (Chur Hansen and McLean, 2006). When supervisees are worried about feedback or it is delivered poorly, it is quite possible that the supervisee will attend more to themselves than the task and that they may censor what they take to supervision to avoid criticism (Wilson and Lizzio, 2009). Supervisors can provide helpful modelling by inviting regular feedback themselves and by requesting feedback 'of their feedback' and how it was delivered (Chur Hansen and McLean, 2006). Scaife (2013) makes a number of important observations about feedback in relation to learning, including that 'unless the recipient is open to feedback it will have little impact on learning'; 'feedback on issues that the recipient feels vulnerable about may produce a defensive response rather than a learning opportunity'; that 'feedback statements beginning with "You ... " are more likely to be perceived as addressing personal qualities rather than practice' and 'feedback needs to be perceived as genuine'.

Some areas of feedback can be particularly challenging but should not be avoided. For example, in a study of supervisor experience of providing 'cross racial' feedback, Burkard et al. (2014) reported differences depending on the background of the supervisor. For 'European American Supervisors' (EAS) cultural concerns typically arose when supervisees were struggling to engage clients, whereas for 'Supervisors of Colour' (SOC) cultural concerns emerged in a variety of ways. Both groups of supervisor had clear goals to promote self-awareness and engage in a discussion concerning multicultural awareness and knowledge. Both groups provided feedback that was specific and based on clear examples from the supervisee's work. However, the approaches and outcomes of the supervisor groups differed:

(a) SOC focused on the cultural/racial issues whereas EAS focused on the skills needed to address the issue;
(b) EAS feedback often led to enhanced supervision engagement whereas this was not the case for most SOC; and
(c) SOC reported often feeling uncomfortable with their supervisees' response to the issue, whereas this was only sometimes present in the EAS group.

They suggest that providing cultural feedback may positively affect the supervision relationship, rather than an existing positive relationship promoting it and suggest that the supervisor and the supervisee should have explicit goals relating to cultural competence within the supervision agreement.

'Disciplinary supervision'

On rare occasions, a supervisory relationship might be established as part of a disciplinary process a supervisee is subject to, most commonly in relation to competence. In such situations the supervisor should ensure that they are clear about their roles and responsibilities and ensure that an agreement is in place that is signed up to by the supervisee and the service or body responsible.

Differences of view/conflict

'Disruption in the usual' provides many possible opportunities for learning and may also produce a positive supervisory experience (Worthen and McNeill, 1996). Therefore, it is important that the supervisor is open to the likelihood of conflict and is able to recognise that it is natural, beneficial and necessary. Conflicts can arise for many reasons, however Nelson et al. (2008) identified a number of factors that may increase the likelihood of conflict. These included lack of clarity about the supervisee and supervisor's responsibilities; absence of people for the supervisor to consult with; supervisor gatekeeping anxieties (i.e. their role with regard to a student/trainee's entry into a profession); supervisor expectations that were too high and not being able to address supervisee resistance. As discussed earlier, supervisees may withhold information that may place them or their practice in a negative light, however 'the only way to manage conflict is to approach it' Nelson et al., (2008). They use the phrase 'tear and repair' (p. 173) to describe the process of recovering and learning from conflict, misunderstanding and disagreement which is not dissimilar to the idea of alliance ruptures and repair.

In a study of supervisors and trainees, Ratliff (2004) found that supervisors used ten different strategies to manage 'a lack of consensus' within supervision. These ranged in their degree of confrontation from low to high. They used the notion of 'constrained talk' to describe episodes where there was a lack of consensus and found that this occurred relatively frequently. At the low end of confrontation was the use of questioning or checking used to imply that a different view could be taken, whilst at the high end, explicit direction and reprimand was evident, for example an instruction for action is given or 'adverse utterances' are used. They noted that supervisors generally attempted to influence the supervisee through offering suggestions to the supervisee to consider – 'supervisors do not really tell trainees what to do, and trainees do not promise to do what supervisors say' (p. 381). On the other side they identified supervisees trying to present themselves as competent practitioners and cooperative supervisees. They identified eight supervisee responses which corresponded to different levels of resistance, namely 'Yes' (I will do that or I've tried that); 'Yes, but' (supervisee seeks clarification; asks for help to do it, some agreement – maybe); 'Not really' (general agreement but not in this instance). They found supervisors moved from lower to higher confrontation as resistance was presented. However, rather than be direct, both parties were viewed as using 'considerable subtlety in their interactions' (p. 383).

So what can be done to address conflict? Using the notion of 'dependable strategies' (i.e. ones that have been found to work), (Nelson et al., 2008) report that supervisors should engage in *reflective preparation* – careful planning, use of empathy, 'self coaching'; take an *interpersonal stance* – not shaming through the process of difficult feedback, not using power, empathising; and take a *technical approach* – in which they provide skills and theory training during supervision, engage in modelling and provide early and timely feedback. Further, it is important for the supervisor to learn through exploring one's own performance and any personal changes needed as a result. They noted that 'Most supervisors were remarkably willing to engage in questioning their present mode of working with a supervisee and try something else' (Nelson et al., 2008, p. 181). Additionally, Falender (2014) suggests that any issues of (a lack of) competence should be highlighted as soon as they occur in order to enable corrective feedback to be given and an opportunity for the supervisee to develop. Where there are on-going competence problems, they recommend that the supervisor seeks views from others and carefully documents and discusses with the supervisee what remedial action is being taken. Where the supervisee is a trainee or student, this should involve those who are 'academically responsible'.

Ethical, legal and diversity issues

It is important that the supervisor pay attention to diversity, legal and ethical issues (Falender *et al.*, 2004). These are discussed in more detail in Chapter 8 and Special Topic 2.

Conclusions

Being a good supervisor requires some key personal qualities, a range of competencies in supervision and a willingness to learn and develop. However acquiring skills and competence as a supervisor is a 'life-long, cumulative, developmental process' (Falender *et al.*, 2004). The key task is to provide supervisees with a safe and responsive place to learn, develop and reflect and a space where they can be empowered to influence the supervision they receive.

References

Arvidsson, B. and Fridlund, B. (2005) 'Factors influencing nurse supervisor competence: a critical incident analysis study', *Journal of Nursing Management* 13(3): 231–37.

Azar, S. T. (2000) 'Preventing burnout in professionals and paraprofessionals who work with child abuse and neglect cases: a cognitive behavioral approach to supervision', *Journal of Clinical Psychology* 56(5): 643–63.

Bambling, M. and King, R. (2013) 'Supervisor social skill and supervision outcome', *Counselling and Psychotherapy Research* (ahead-of-print): 1–7.

Bazerman, M. H. (1990) *Judgment in Managerial Decision Making* (2nd edn), Oxford: John Wiley & Sons.

Berggren, I. and Severinsson, E. (2006) 'The significance of nurse supervisors' different ethical decision-making styles', *Journal of Nursing Management* 14(8): 637–43.

Bober, T. and Regehr, C. (2006) 'Strategies for reducing secondary or vicarious trauma: do they work?', *Brief Treatment and Crisis Intervention* 6(1): 1–9.

Bordin, E. S. (1983) 'A working alliance based model of supervision', *The Counseling Psychologist* 11(1): 35–42.

Burkard, A. W., Knox, S., Clarke, R. D., Phelps, D. L. and Inman, A. G. (2014) 'Supervisors' experiences of providing difficult feedback in cross-ethnic/racial supervision', *The Counseling Psychologist* 42(3): 314–44.

Burke, W. R., Goodyear, R. K. and Guzzard, C. R. (1998) 'Weakenings and repairs in supervisory alliances', *American Journal of Psychotherapy* 52: 450–62.

Chur Hansen, A. and McLean, S. (2006) 'On being a supervisor: the importance of feedback and how to give it', *Australasian Psychiatry* 14(1): 67–71.

Cushway, D. and Knibbs, J. (2004) 'Trainees' and supervisors' perceptions of supervision', in I. Fleming and L. Steen (eds), *Supervision and Clinical Psychology: Theory, Practice and Perspectives*, Abingdon: Routledge, pp. 162–85.

Davies, J., Black, S., Bentley, N. and Nagi, C. (2013) 'Forensic case formulation: theoretical, ethical and practical issues', *Criminal Behaviour and Mental Health* 23(4): 304–14.

Falender, C. A. (2014) 'Clinical supervision in a competency-based era', *South African Journal of Psychology* 44(1): 6–17.

Falender, C. A., Cornish, J. A. E., Goodyear, R., Hatcher, R., Kaslow, N. J., Leventhal, G., et al. (2004) 'Defining competencies in psychology supervision: a consensus statement', *Journal of Clinical Psychology* 60(7): 771–85.

Gordon, P. K. (2012) 'Ten steps to cognitive behavioural supervision', *The Cognitive Behaviour Therapist* 5(4): 71–82.

Hair, H. J. (2013) 'The purpose and duration of supervision, and the training and discipline of supervisors: what social workers say they need to provide effective services', *British Journal of Social Work* 43(8): 1562–88.

Hall-Lord, M. L., Theander, K. and Athlin, E. (2013) 'A clinical supervision model in bachelor nursing education – purpose, content and evaluation', *Nurse Education in Practice* 13(6): 506–11.

Harkness, D. and Hensley, H. (1991) 'Changing the focus of social work supervision: effects on client satisfaction and generalized contentment', *Social Work* 36(6): 506–12.

Hawkins, P. and Shohet, R. (2006) *Supervision in the Helping Professions* (3rd edn), Buckingham: Open University Press.

Heckman-Stone, C. (2004) 'Trainee preferences for feedback and evaluation in clinical supervision', *The Clinical Supervisor* 22(1): 21–33.

Hoffman, M. A., Hill, C. E., Holmes, S. E. and Freitas, G. F. (2005) 'Supervisor perspective on the process and outcome of giving easy, difficult, or no feedback to supervisees', *Journal of Counseling Psychology* 52(1): 3–13.

Ingram, R. (2013) 'Emotions, social work practice and supervision: an uneasy alliance?', *Journal of Social Work Practice* 27(1): 5–19.

James, I. A., Milne, D., Marie-Blackburn, I. and Armstrong, P. (2006) 'Conducting successful supervision: novel elements towards an integrative approach', *Behavioural and Cognitive Psychotherapy* 35(2): 191.

Johns, C. (1993) 'Professional supervision', *Journal of Nursing Management* 1(1): 9–18.

Johnston, L. H. and Milne, D. L. (2012) 'How do supervisees learn during supervision? A Grounded Theory study of the perceived developmental process', *The Cognitive Behaviour Therapist* 5(1): 1–23.

Jones, P. R. (1995) 'Hindsight bias in reflective practice: an empirical investigation', *Journal of Advanced Nursing* 21(4): 783–88.

Kilminster, S. M. and Jolly, B. C. (2000) 'Effective supervision in clinical practice settings: a literature review', *Medical Education* 34(10): 827–40.

Ladany, N., Hill, C. E., Corbett, M. M. and Nutt, E. A. (1996) 'Nature, extent, and importance of what psychotherapy trainees do not disclose to their supervisors', *Journal of Counseling Psychology* 43(1): 10.

Ladany, N., Mori, Y. and Mehr, K. E. (2012) 'Effective and ineffective supervision', *The Counseling Psychologist* 41(1): 28–47.

Landmark, B. T., Hansen, G. S., Bjones, I. and Bøhler, A. (2003) 'Clinical supervision – factors defined by nurses as influential upon the development of competence and skills in supervision', *Journal of Clinical Nursing* 12(6): 834–41.

Magnuson, S., Wilcoxon, S. A. and Norem, K. (2000) 'A profile of lousy supervision: experienced counselors' perspectives', *Counselor Education and Supervision* 39(3): 189–202.

Marrow, C. E., Hollyoake, K., Hamer, D. and Kenrick, C. (2002) 'Clinical supervision using video-conferencing technology: a reflective account', *Journal of Nursing Management* 10(5): 275–82.

Milne, D. L., Reiser, R. P., Cliffe, T. and Raine, R. (2011) 'SAGE: preliminary evaluation of an instrument for observing competence in CBT supervision', *The Cognitive Behaviour Therapist* 4(4): 123–38.

Mothersole, G. (2000) 'Clinical supervision and forensic work', *Journal of Sexual Aggression* 5(1): 45–58.

Nelson, M. L., Barnes, K. L., Evans, A. L. and Triggiano, P. J. (2008) 'Working with conflict in clinical supervision: wise supervisors' perspectives', *Journal of Counseling Psychology* 55(2): 172–84.

Paustian-Underdahl, S. C., Shanock, L. R., Rogelberg, S. G., Scott, C. W., Justice, L. and Altman, D. G. (2013) 'Antecedents to supportive supervision: an examination of biographical data', *Journal of Occupational and Organizational Psychology* 86(3): 288–309.

Ratliff, D. A., Wampler, K. S. and Morris, G. H. (2000) 'Lack of Consensus in Supervison', *Journal of Marital and Family Therapy* 26(3): 373–84.

Rolfe, G. and Gardner, L. (2006) '"Do not ask who I am ... ": confession, emancipation and (self)-management through reflection', *Journal of Nursing Management* 14(8): 593–600.

Russell, R. K. and Petrie, T. (1995) 'Issues in training effective supervisors', *Applied and Preventive Psychology* 3(1): 27–42.

Scaife, J. (2013) *Supervision in Clinical Practice*, Abingdon: Routledge.

Schacht, A. J., Howe, H. E. and Berman, J. J. (1989) 'Supervisor facilitative conditions and effectiveness as perceived by thinking- and feeling-type supervisees', *Psychotherapy: Theory, Research, Practice, Training* 26(4): 475.

Schoenwald, S. K., Mehta, T. G., Frazier, S. L. and Shernoff, E. S. (2013) 'Clinical supervision in effectiveness and implementation research', *Clinical Psychology: Science and Practice* 20(1): 44–59.

Severinsson, E. I. and Hallberg, I. R. (1996) 'Clinical supervisors' views of their leadership role in the clinical supervision process within nursing care', *Journal of Advanced Nursing* 24(1): 151–61.

Wheeler, J. (2007) 'Solution-focused supervision', in T. S. Nelson and F. N. Thomas (eds), *Handbook of Solution-focused Brief Therapy: Clinical Applications*, Binghamton, NY: Haworth Press, pp. 343–70.

White, E. and Winstanley, J. (2010) 'A randomised controlled trial of clinical supervision: selected findings from a novel Australian attempt to establish the evidence base for causal relationships with quality of care and patient outcomes, as an informed contribution to mental health nursing practice development', *Journal of Research in Nursing* 15(2): 151–67.

Williamson, P., Day, A., Howells, K., Bubner, S. and Jauncey, S. (2003) 'Assessing offender readiness to change problems with anger', *Psychology, Crime & Law* 9(4): 295–307.

Wilson, K. L. and Lizzio, A. J. (2009) 'Processes and interventions to facilitate supervisees' learning', in N. Pelling, J. Barletta and P. Armstrong (eds), *The Practice of Clinical Supervision*, Samford Valley: Australian Academic Press, pp. 138–64.

Wong, S. C. P., Gordon, A. and Gu, D. (2007) 'Assessment and treatment of violence-prone forensic clients: an integrated approach', *The British Journal of Psychiatry* 190(49): s66–s74.

Worthen, V. and McNeill, B. W. (1996) 'A phenomenological investigation of "good" supervision events', *Journal of Counseling Psychology* 43(1): 25.

8 Managing risk and boundaries through supervision

Risk is a central feature in forensic work, and therefore needs attention within supervision. Risks can relate to the clients (and their behaviours either now or in the future), practitioner skills, ability and competence, practitioner safety and wellbeing and positive risk taking. A major factor within the overarching domain of risk are boundary factors, and in particular boundary crossing and violation. This chapter will provide an introduction to common risks and consider how they might be addressed before a more thorough examination of boundary problems is presented to enable an exploration of how supervision may aid with maintaining safe and effective boundaries.

Managing risk through supervision

Risk assessment, formulation and management, along with the maintenance of security are core aspects of practice within forensic settings. The notions of physical (e.g. the structure), procedural (e.g. the policies) and relational (e.g. the people) security (Collins and Davies, 2005) are used to convey the importance of all these elements in creating safe, secure and functional settings. These three features provide supervision with different viewpoints from which to inspect risk. Therefore, throughout this chapter it may be beneficial to ask: 'what physical, procedural and relational elements are present and what might be changed or added to address the risk presented?'

Client risks and supervision

Client risks can present in several ways either directly or indirectly. Direct risks include the behaviour of the client towards themselves (e.g. self-harm), the practitioner (e.g. threats or actual violence) or to others, whilst indirect risks include the practitioner trying to meet the expectations of society (i.e. that forensic practitioners should be able to predict and thus prevent all risky behaviour from occurring).

Azar (2000) discusses a number of dilemmas in relation to client risk. These include 'double binds' where two very significant but opposing factors need to be considered (e.g. in child protection work balancing the safety of the child with maintaining family cohesion) and the 'victim's dilemma' where there are significant consequences associated with acting or with remaining silent (e.g. a prisoner confides that he has heard others are planning to attempt an escape but says he will be attacked if the practitioner tells anyone). Azar (2000) suggests that such issues are difficult to address because the consequences cannot be fully known at the time of the decision – this can lead to practitioner ambivalence or ambiguity. Although there can be no easy answers, supervision can provide a forum through which the practitioner can consider the risks and tensions in order to make an informed decision. Azar (2000) also notes that managing client risk can be an intervention. For example, in some situations it may be possible for the practitioner to offer to assist the individual to report and manage the risks themselves: 'what you have told me needs to be acted upon – do you want me to report it to XX or shall I support you to do it'.

Managing risks associated with sub-optimal performance

Although supervision is typically associated with creating a reflective and learning environment in which the practitioner is supported and can develop, it also has a role in identifying and addressing poor or sub-optimal performance. Supervision is frequently the only context in which a practitioner's actions will be reviewed and discussed (based on self-report, direct observation or reviewing recorded material). Managing individual performance should be a matter for the line manager, however it may be through supervision that problems or difficulties will be identified. In the context of regular feedback from both supervisor and supervisee, difficulties should be identified early. This can provide the supervisee with an opportunity to develop and to take remedial action where this is appropriate. Where there are concerns about a supervisee's practice, it is important that the supervisor discuss with the supervisee any course of action they plan to take. The aspects of performance that are reviewed in supervision should be contained within the supervision agreement.

Within therapy practice, some attempts have been made to use regular session feedback from the client along with routine outcome measures of some type. This can be helpful in obtaining information about performance which the supervisee can use within supervision. However, within a forensic context, consideration needs to be given to how different clients might engage in such feedback and what, if any, motives they might have for giving anything other than honest feedback (e.g. anger at a report they have received from the practitioner or being attracted to the practitioner). The work by Overholser and Fine (1990) on 'worker incompetence' discussed in Special Topic 2 (Ethical Issues) is also relevant here.

Supervisee safety and wellbeing through supervision

There are many risks which need to be considered within supervision in order to maintain the safety of the supervisee both physically and psychologically. For example, it is possible that the supervisee may have been victim to a similar crime to that committed by a client they are working with or may have some other relevant experience which is triggered through work with a particular client (e.g. Azar, 2000). In forensic work, the behaviours and actions of those who the practitioner is working with are often highly destructive and at the extreme of human experience. Although practitioners can become skilled at managing these, Mothersole (2000) suggests that problematic responses can be encountered which he describes as 'repulsion' (trying to distance from the client either physically or psychologically); 'helplessness' (feelings of futility) and 'voyeuristic motivation' (focusing on the 'gory details'). Each of these can be highly problematic both for the practitioner and for the client, however supervision is one important mechanism for identifying and managing this. Supervisors need to be alert to such situations and provide appropriate support and opportunity to reflect, where appropriate. It may also be necessary for the supervisor to support the supervisee to obtain assistance from elsewhere (e.g. workforce well-being services).

Positive Risk Taking

Positive Risk Taking (PRT) is 'a deliberate and planned strategy designed to enhance health, welfare and educational outcomes' (Titterton, 2010, p. 1). It fosters finding a balance between rights and responsibilities at an individual level and is based upon the careful consideration of potential harms and benefits within clear boundaries. It is reported that PRT can promote 'risk literacy', collaboration and resilience (Titterton, 2010) and the underpinning philosophy appears to overlap with the Good Lives approach to offender rehabilitation (Ward and Maruna, 2007). Through a Person-centred Risk Assessment and Risk Management System (PRAMS) comprising of 10 steps, practitioners and clients can construct, undertake and review specific plans and actions (Titterton, 2005; 2010). Supervision provides an ideal forum for exploring PRT and seeking advice, opinion and support for this where needed. Indeed, Titterton (2005) suggests that reflective practice is an important feature in practitioners learning and developing risk assessment and risk management skills.

Addressing risk issues in supervision

In forensic contexts, risk is an ever present feature because of both the setting and societal expectations. This necessitates that the supervisor is able to strike a balance between supervision as a tool for monitoring staff (part of the normative function) and for supporting and developing staff (the formative and restorative functions). In contrast to the ideas of PRT above, Beddoe (2010) suggests that the focus on risk within society can constrict practitioner's actions leading to defensive practice and a reliance on procedures, rules and checklists in order to minimise the risk of missing something or acting 'incorrectly'. However, although policies and rules typically provide parameters within which to work (and usually a clear 'bottom line') and checklists may provide seemingly simple solutions (with the associated sense of relief), all can be severely limited without the addition of reflective and creative thought and application. The irony of such a reductionist approach is that (a) the all-important 'bigger picture' of context and interactions can be overlooked or missed, and (b) important issues may not be covered by the policy or checklist (see also Special Topic 2 – Ethical Issues). Such an approach can also negatively impact on staff (e.g. by leading to feelings of disempowerment) which can have an impact on how clients feel and respond. Thus inquiry reports (examples of which were discussed in Chapter 1), may unintentionally promote a culture of surveillance and 'doing it by the book' in order for services to create a defensible or auditable position rather than their intention to promote best practice, ethical behaviour and 'doing the right thing'. To move beyond this 'safe' yet constricted position requires the practitioner to be able to strike a balance between risk aversion and positive risk taking. Supervision can be a tool to provide a context within which practice can be both risk sensitive and progressive. Adopting such a stance is important for a number of reasons as outlined by Beddoe (2010):

(a) a constrictive risk focus impedes professional growth – anxieties about risk lead to micro-management and practice being limited or overly directed and supervisees fearing being judged. This might change how they report problems and concerns (see Chapter 7). Supervision therefore needs to support client focused practice whilst acknowledging and addressing issues of risk;
(b) good supervision concerns the process not just the content – supervisors need to invest in supervisee learning and development and be mindful of the distorting potential of rules and procedures;
(c) supervision functions need to be balanced – surveillance and support/ development; and
(d) supervision and management may be best separated – otherwise these may become blurred with management dominating.

The other danger created by the literal application of rules and policies is that risk can become routine and unthinking with practitioners no longer scrutinising their practice, interactions and behaviours. This can lead to 'risk silence' where difficulties or risk issues are not raised for fear of criticism or blame.

Thus supervision needs to promote a thoughtful approach to risk through maintaining a focus on practitioner development. Supervision offers an important 'one step removed' position to help review decision making and professional judgement. For example, discrepancies between a practitioner's opinion and the 'actuarial' position from the research base can be explored to ensure that all relevant information has been considered and the decision making process upon which the practitioner's actions are based has been 'tested' (Mothersole, 2000).

Managing boundaries through supervision

This section will consider two sets of boundaries, the boundary between the supervisor and supervisee and the boundary between the supervisee (practitioner) and the clients. It is important to be aware that boundary problems can also arise between staff members and colleagues (e.g. arguments and disagreements being 'played out in public', staff who are or have been in an intimate relationship working together), however staff-staff boundary issues are not included directly. Rather, it is hoped that the principles outlined in this chapter can be adapted and adopted for such situations by the reader.

Why a focus on boundaries? For the forensic practitioner (as with practitioners in other settings) boundaries are used to create a safe and predictable context to allow the tasks associated with the service to take place. Boundaries, are, as the word implies 'the "edge" of appropriate behaviour' (Gutheil and Gabbard, 1998, p. 410) and thus are subject to the potential to be 'crossed' (a benign breach) or 'violated' (a harmful transgression) (Gutheil and Gabbard, 1998). By way of example, the boundary of 'no touching' between practitioner and client may be *crossed* if a practitioner places their hand on a patient's shoulder to comfort them when giving some bad news. In this scenario, the boundary crossing has the important quality of being 'a human response' that can be discussed openly between the practitioner and client and the practitioner and others, including their supervisor. In comparison, the same boundary of 'no touching' may be violated if a practitioner strokes the patient's shoulder. Therefore, boundary violation has the important quality of harm through exerting power or misusing status or privilege. Further, such behaviour may be secretive, repetitive and progressive (i.e. moving from one form of boundary violation to another).

Boundaries between supervisor and supervisee

The supervisory relationship is founded upon establishing a trusting, respectful and collaborative alliance between the supervisor and supervisee. The supervision agreement can assist with this (see Chapter 3), and should contain boundaries concerning the relationship, content, time, space and confidentiality (Power, 2007). However, issues can arise when boundaries are not respected, are crossed or are violated. This can occur when supervision focuses on the personal rather than the professional, or when dual roles are entered into. A personal focus can have its place, however this should be limited to those situations where the personal might impact on the practitioner's performance or where work is impacting on the personal (White *et al.*, 1998).

Dual role relationships have been described as those in which 'one individual is simultaneously or sequentially participating in two role categories that conflict or compete' which results in difficulty deciding which behaviour is appropriate (Kitchener, 1988, p. 218). Such relationships may cause harm either to one of the parties involved or because they can be perceived as problematic by others. Although writing about therapeutic relationships, Kitchener's (1988) description is very useful for application to the supervision context. She describes three identifying features of dual role relationships:

(1) incompatibility of expectations (e.g. engaging in therapy and supervision with the same person);
(2) divergent obligations (e.g. supervising your spouse); and
(3) power and prestige differentials (e.g. a sexual relationship with a student or trainee).

Within the supervision context it is the duty of the supervisor to manage possible dual role relationships. Kitchener (1988) states that the ethical principle of 'doing no harm' includes being aware of potential for harm in dual relationships and suggests that relationships which have a high risk of harm (i.e. the presence of all three features above) should automatically be considered unethical. However, she also argues that the potential for harm is likely to be low when there is no conflict of interests, the power differential is small and role expectations are compatible. Nonetheless, when dual roles may be present, Kitchener (1988) suggests that informed consent be gained, and states that even though the principle of autonomy should be respected (i.e. each person having the right to choose), one party (in the case of supervision – the supervisor) carries more responsibility than the other (i.e. just because a junior staff member or supervisee 'consents' to a dual role relationship, the supervisor/senior staff member still has a primary obligation to that individual not themselves).

Boundaries between the client and the practitioner

Boundaries between the client and the practitioner are highly complex especially within a forensic setting. For example, Marquart, Barnhill and Balshaw-Biddle (2001) refer to the 'norm of reciprocity' in prison settings which can easily be extended to inpatient forensic mental health contexts. They suggest that the safe functioning of such services relies, to some extent, on an exchange between the staff and the clients – freedoms and privileges in exchange for co-operation and good behaviour. However, pressures to 'get along' can blur boundaries; there is a fine balance between any form of reciprocal relationship used as a form of relational security and collusion in which boundaries are compromised or lost. It is also important to remember that as interpersonal interactions and relationships are not static, boundaries will need to be constantly monitored and adjustments made. Such boundary adjustments may be advantageous whilst others may be problematic.

Although absolute boundaries may be appealing, with the exception of romantic and sexual boundary transgressions, most boundaries provide a 'normally' line (i.e. this is what is appropriate in most instances). As noted by Peternelj-Taylor and Yonge (2003), 'Apart from sexual exploitation, however, defining treatment boundaries is not always a clear phenomenon' (p. 56). Despite this, many services and professional groups seek to create a list of do's and don't's. This can be problematic as it is not possible to cover every possible situation and removes the practitioner's need to think and take responsibility for their conduct. Supervision therefore needs to provide a forum in which boundaries can be discussed and considered in an open and frank manner.

There have been different ways of representing the forms of boundary breach. In addition to the boundary crossing and boundary violation ideas (e.g. Gutheil and Gabbard, 1998), Love and Heber (2001) present a continuum from *boundary inattention* (ignoring the forensic setting) as indicated in practitioner behaviour such as carelessness with keys, excessive social interaction, avoiding knowing a client's history; *boundary crossing* ('on the verge') as revealed by sharing personal information, non-sexual touching, spending excessive time with a client; *boundary violation* (breaking policy and ethical code) in which gift giving, sending letters to a client, providing contraband may be present, and *dual relationships* (relationships for personal gratification) in which the practitioner engages in behaviour such as sexual or business relationships with a client. Evershed (2010) notes that boundary crossing may be subtle, e.g. allowing a clinical session to run over time; failing to confront a client over their behaviour when the practitioner normally would, and engaging in punitive responses. Faulkner and Regehr (2011) also gives examples including practitioners being 'protected' by clients or clients being permitted to take on staff roles (e.g. night checks). In addition, Evershed (2010) reports that some boundary breaches may be borne out of benign intent (trying to meet client needs) whilst others arise from the practitioner seeking to meet their own needs (either intentionally or unconsciously).

In a study undertaken in the US during the mid-1990s, Marquart *et al.* (2001) analysed information relating to 508 prison security staff who were disciplined for boundary violations. They found rates of around 2.5 per cent, with men in women's prisons at slightly more risk than women in male prisons. Further analysis revealed that boundary violations often occurred within the first year of employment. They clustered violations into three groups (based on other work, i.e. Strom-Gottfried, 1999 cited in Marquart *et al.*, 2001):

(1) *general boundary violations* – these were described as 'unserious' and consisted of accepting or exchanging items (e.g. food, craft-work) or writing letters to prisoners whom they had known prior to them becoming an inmate. This group accounted for 8 per cent of the violations (38 cases).
(2) *dual relationships* – these concern a blurring of the boundaries between the practitioner and inmate and were comprised of all those relationships 'up to but not including, sexual contact' (p. 894) (e.g. practitioner discussing their personal life in detail; exchanging letters; relaying information to the prisoner's family). Many staff in this group were classed as 'lovesick' (i.e. the practitioner was infatuated with the inmate). This group accounted for 84 per cent of the violations (428 cases).

(3) *sexual contact* – these constitute the most serious boundary violations and included any form of sexual contact (e.g. intercourse, fondling) that could be substantiated by a third party and/or were admitted to by the practitioner. This group accounted for 8 per cent of the violations (42 cases).

Analysis of the case files enabled the researchers to identify four situations in which violations took place:

(1) *rescue situations* – where the practitioner assisted the prisoner because they felt sorry for them. There were only five violations of this type;
(2) *naïveté/accident* – where the practitioner was unaware of the rules and showed regret, remorse and self-reproach. One hundred violations occurred of this type and those working in newer prisons were much more likely to engage in violations of this type;
(3) *lovesickness* – where the practitioner reported love for the inmate and a life together after release. These were often associated with a personal vulnerability (e.g. children leaving home, domestic violence). This type accounted for 356 violations and female employees were much more likely to be in this group;
(4) *predators* – where the practitioner manipulated the prisoner for personal gain (e.g. money, property, sex). There were 47 violations of this type with men more likely to be in this group.

A number of conclusions can be drawn from these violations – most occurred early in the period of employment, they often involved an incremental pattern, and they typically involved personal and institutional vulnerability (e.g. specific 'hot spot' locations that were isolated). They found that those who had engaged in violations had lower pre-employment evaluation scores and that they tended to view the client as someone 'who just happened to be in prison' (p. 906). In addition, Marquart *et al.* (2001) outlined that organisations (and line managers) need to ensure that they don't become 'wilfully blind' to such matters.

Some of the factors identified above, were echoed in a small-scale survey within a high secure hospital in the UK. Evershed (2010) reported that boundary violations were more common with female staff and those who were 'unqualified' despite the overall staffing demographics.

Why might boundaries be relevant to supervision? Practitioners in forensic settings are required to maintain boundaries in order to:

(a) keep themselves and others safe;
(b) deliver their input and intervention; and
(c) effectively monitor risk.

However, when staff feel isolated, overwhelmed, bullied, seduced or special, these may increase the risk of boundary crossing or violation. At the same time, the practitioner may be less able to monitor their own performance and

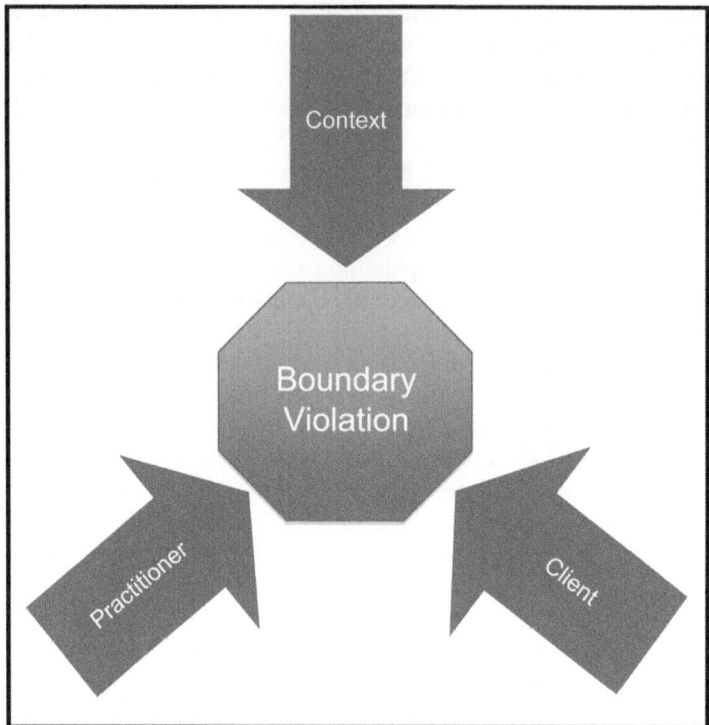

Figure 8.1 Factors associated with boundary violations

recognise potential difficulties. These might be thought of as deaf, dumb, blind and numb spots – things that are not (or once were but are no longer) heard, spoken about, noticed or felt by the supervisee. It would seem that violations are the result of three factors coming together: factors and characteristics associated with the practitioner; the client; and the context. Each of these provides a point at which an intervention could take place to prevent or manage a breach or potential breach (see Figure 8.1). This trio of factors (i.e. staff, clients and context/environment) have also been emphasised by Love (2001a) who focused on eroticised dual relationship. Love (2001a) observed that staff can often be seen as the victim in such situations, however she emphasises the need to see clients' behaviour as one of their treatment targets. This is underscored by her observation that the therapeutic relationship is designed to meet the needs of the client only – dual relationships indicate that staff needs are also being served.

Staff factors

Within forensic settings, the intensity and duration of client contact varies by profession, with those with the least training often having the greatest contact with clients (Moore, 2012). There are many opportunities for informal and spontaneous interactions between the practitioner and the client with every interaction bringing with it possible boundary dilemmas. This can be exacerbated by the multiple roles practitioners often engage in such as carer, companion, security and hospitality (Evershed, 2010). Others have noted that those in a therapeutic relationship may be vulnerable to violations because of their need to be compassionate and feel they are making a difference (i.e. a wish to be liked) (Peternelj-Taylor and Yonge, 2003) whilst those in more of a security role may be vulnerable to violations based on the need to manage and control situations. Love (2001a) also points out that boundary problems may occur when a client reminds the practitioner of someone else they know resulting in the practitioner acting towards the client 'as if' it were the other person (transference). As seen earlier, staff risk factors might include low education, less job experience and being 'underpaid' (Worley, Marquart and Mullings, 2003). However, Love (2001a) cautions against creating profiles of 'at risk' practitioners but instead concludes that 'being human is the best predictor' (p. 7) of possible boundary problems. Relying on the notion of a vulnerable type may lead to a misguided focus on some individuals whilst simultaneously neglecting others. However, the supervisor should pay attention to any factors which may increase the practitioner's vulnerability.

Engaging with, and establishing an appropriate boundary with clients is difficult. A balance needs to be found between being 'too involved' and detachment (Austin, 2001). Although much of this chapter deals with boundary crossing associated with over-involvement, it is important to note that detaching, i.e. the practitioner retreating into an expert position or using procedures and routines as a way of avoiding difficult contact, is also problematic. Indeed, Moore (2012) identifies two broad clusters of problematic staff responses: first, rejection or over control responses shown through belittling a client, pessimism about a particular client and 'switching off' from a client's needs, and second, over-involvement as demonstrated by over-friendliness, criticising colleagues with a client and flirtation in response to hostility.

Recognition – Being able to recognise possible boundary problems early is critical for the safety of the practitioner, the client and the service. Some of this responsibility rests with the practitioner – 'forensic practitioners should be self-aware regarding emotional vulnerability and, when vulnerable, more cautious regarding the risk of committing a boundary violation … the slippery-slope effect may be diminished by increased job training, understanding of duties, and supervision, thus decreasing the risk for both the practitioner and the prisoner' (Faulkner and Regehr, 2011, p. 157). There are also ways that the supervisee and supervisor can work together to recognise possible problems. Self-assessment checklists, such as the one presented by Love (2001a), can be used in conjunction with training and supervision. This checklist includes items such as 'spending a lot of time with a particular client', 'bending the rules for a client', 'feeling overly protective of a client', 'relying on clients to protect you at work', 'overly invested in the success or failure of a specific client' and 'referring to a client as your favourite client'. Practitioner behaviour within supervision may also indicate the potential for problems, e.g. practitioners may behave differently when they feel at risk.

Client factors

Some clients may be more likely to engage in a boundary violation with a practitioner than others. Reasons for this may include that they themselves are vulnerable and unable to avoid or stop a boundary violation taking place; that they are a willing participant in the boundary violation once it is instigated by the practitioner or because they attempt to engage practitioners in boundary violations. Clients may also be confused about the nature of the practitioner-client relationship and may test the boundaries to move the practitioner into more familiar roles (e.g. friend) (Peternelj-Taylor and Yonge, 2003). Elliott (2006) argues that some prison inmates seek power and control through 'exploiting and manipulating' staff. He presents a case study to highlight 12 tactics used by some prisoners, many of which may lead to boundary crossing and possible boundary violation (e.g. extortion, ingratiation, boundary intrusion). In many forensic settings, some of these (e.g. solidarity and negotiation) may be particularly likely because of the intense interpersonal relationships developed between practitioners and clients. It is for this very reason that an 'objective outsider' in the form of a supervisor might be helpful to raise these interactions into awareness from which they can be explored and addressed.

In an interesting study, Worley et al. (2003) interviewed prison inmates who had engaged in inappropriate relationships with prison officers. Based on a 'typology' developed by Allen and Bosta (1981), they interviewed 'turners' (inmates who befriend employees to engage in some form of boundary breach). They identified three types which they termed:

(1) "heart-breakers" who were motivated by wanting to establish a long-term romantic relationship with a specific staff member and as a result these individuals wanted to keep the relationship private. Such relationships often started with 'accidental touching' by the inmate to 'test the staff member's response'.
(2) 'exploiters' who aggressively forged relationships for the primary purpose of financial gain although they also claimed to have had sexual relationships with staff. They use intimidation, exploitation and 'entrapment', often starting with the exchange of small items. They suggest that prison staff may be vulnerable to such individuals because of low pay and the 'easy money' that could be made to supplement wages.
(3) 'hell-raisers' were motivated by causing trouble to the establishment, indicating that relationships with staff were the ultimate way to challenge the system. This group often had long histories of such relationships and focused on 'staff members' not security officers. They reported

engaging in behaviours such as masturbation to gauge how a staff member might respond. In these cases the relationships were terminated by the employee.

Love (2001b) notes that clients may have severely limited social support, may be relatively isolated and, for those in custody or in a hospital setting, unlikely to have a current intimate relationship. Love (2001b) suggests that some client groups may be at more risk such as those diagnosed with a personality disorder; the importance of personality has also been highlighted by others (e.g. Faulkner and Regehr, 2011). However, as with the identification of staff factors above, Love (2001b) cautions about being overly guided by definitive client features.

Addressing client factors – It should come as no surprise that those in forensic settings, who are by definition 'rule-breakers', can engage in problematic relationships with staff (e.g. Evershed, 2010). It therefore behoves staff to find ways to manage and respond to this. Indeed, Love (2001b) suggests that 'If we permit the patient with psychopathy to reoffend or engage in an exploitative dual relationship with staff, we have failed him' (p. 6). Therefore, supervisors need to help supervisees to interrupt problematic relationship patterns, not to engage in bending the rules and to establish cultures of 'caring watchfulness' where staff monitor the relationships of themselves and others through open questioning and support. Supervisors may also consider the use of approaches such as Offence Paralleling Behaviour (Daffern, Jones and Shine, 2010) to explore possible boundary issues. In this technique, a 'functional analysis' approach is taken to identify patterns in behaviour to allow future risks to be considered.

Despite the importance of noticing and responding to client factors where they present, it is important to remember that although client factors are relevant they cannot be used to excuse the practitioner's responsibility.

Environment factors (context)

The context within which the practitioner and the client are placed can itself facilitate safety or increase the likelihood of boundaries being compromised. These may be unintentional acts on the part of the organisation which result in cultural blind spots (Mothersole, 2000) (e.g. the organisation not acknowledging the need to consider practitioner-client interactions and relationships, or ignoring or sweeping away of problems and difficulties). Conflicting roles are embodied within most forensic practice settings where there is a need to engage with the client (e.g. to foster change and reduce risk) whilst attempting to protect society from potential harm. Love and Heber (2001) describe five environmental factor problems which may contribute to boundary problems. The first issue they raise is the availability of quality supervision for practitioners. They state that having 'large numbers of staff with little formal education and minimal clinical supervision exposed to complex patients for extended periods is a set-up for disaster' (Love and Heber, 2001, p. 12). It is therefore the responsibility of the organisation to ensure all staff have regular supervision and that this focuses on boundaries amongst other things (Evershed, 2010). They also describe four other issues, namely (a) role confusion (i.e. staff taking on multiple roles – see also Evershed above) which can create tensions between custody and care; (b) avoiding patient's criminal history and therefore not knowing or understanding past offending and behaviour that may be relevant for successful boundary maintenance; (c) unstructured time where workers may be 'socialising' with clients and where boundaries may be 'inadvertently' crossed; (d) lack of clinical guidelines and an absence of management or treatment plans which are communicated to all staff. Boundary problems occur in context which enables them to happen, therefore, organisations should provide staff with supervision, knowledge about the clients they work with and approaches to managing difficult interpersonal situations. They note that staff should be supported to recognise that maintaining boundaries is a form of intervention and therefore is important for clients (Love and Heber, 2001). In addition, there may be physical factors in the environment that need to be considered. For example, Faulkner and Regehr (2011) identify isolation as a 'facilitating condition' for boundary crossing and violations to occur.

Organisational responses – the most essential factor in relation to the environmental aspects of managing boundary problems is the recognition and ownership of such issues as an occupational hazard within forensic organisations (Love and Heber, 2001). This stance will legitimise boundaries and any associated problems being acknowledged and discussed especially through supervision. It may also help foster a culture of safe working through safe relationships. Love and Heber (2001) also suggest that recognition and 'early intervention' should be rewarded and, where appropriate, client monitoring should be formally designed and used. Profession specific codes of conduct can be helpful, however many practitioners are not covered (Evershed, 2010). Therefore, she argues that organisations have a responsibility to provide training in ethical and safe practice and to break down the barrier of silence.

Maintaining appropriate boundaries – the role of supervision

Supervision can aid in supporting effective boundary management and offers a forum to notice and recognise problems in order to identify ways to manage them. As discussed above, 'Isolation, potential confusion regarding the therapeutic relationship, and clientele with a history of poor interpersonal relationships' can all contribute to potential boundary problems (Schafer, 1997, p. 204). Further, being sceptical of clients and their motives, along with staff vigilance can be 'features' of the setting (Austin, 2001). Unfortunately, this is often accompanied by defensive practice and a culture of blame. Various factors can lead to the practitioner becoming 'out of balance' – either too focused on control, management and even punishment or overly invested in an alliance with the client.

This has been described as the boundary see-saw (Hamilton, 2010), with 'security guard' at one extreme and 'pacifier' at the other. As both of these ways of managing boundaries or responding to boundary challenge can lead to boundary violations, Hamilton (2010) describes the 'negotiator' as someone who is able to retain balance and thus maintain appropriate boundaries. Supervision can be considered to be a primary tool for managing risks such as those relating to boundaries (Peternelj-Taylor and Yonge, 2003). They state that 'Without regular proactive supervision, nurses and other clinicians can easily lapse into boundary problems' (p. 63) and further, that supervision 'can anticipate and head off possible boundary violations by intervening when signs of boundary erosion appear' (p. 64). Supervision can therefore help ensure that 'seemingly insignificant acts' do not become 'a progression of unethical patterns of behavior' (Peternelj-Taylor and Yonge, 2003, p. 64). Creating and sustaining effective boundaries can be thought of as a 'Triangle of Boundary Maintenance' (see Box 8.1) which requires attention to the physical environment (e.g. staff isolation); the procedural context (professional codes, local policy and the culture of the setting) and relational factors (e.g. training, supervision). The first two provide the firm base of the triangle on which relational factors rest. This parallels the broader maintenance of safety and security within forensic settings as described by Collins and Davies (2005). Although here we focus on supervision the other elements cannot be ignored.

Pre-emptive action – As a general strategy, supervisees should be encouraged to adopt a stance of 'explore before action' (Moore, 2012) and to engage in early detection and response. For example, it may be helpful for the supervisor and supervisee to describe how both safe and problem boundaries might show themselves in a particular setting or with a particular client. This could describe how boundary adjustments might be spotted and crossings or violations recognised (c.f. Hamilton, 2010). Alternatively, Evershed (2010) outlines a boundary traffic light system where green is used to detail the behaviours, emotions and interactions associated with appropriate boundaries; amber, boundary crossing, and red, boundary violations. Such approaches could be very helpful both to the individual supervisee and to the team.

BOX 8.1: Triangle of boundary maintenance

Maintaining effective boundaries rests on attention to three mechanisms – the procedural elements (e.g. the policies, codes of conduct and the culture of the service), the physical (e.g. the layout of the unit) and the relational (e.g. the ways interactions take place between people such as the staff and clients) (see Figure 8.2). Procedural and physical elements tend to be relatively static, however relational factors can change frequently. Supervision should attend to relational aspects of boundary maintenance on a regular basis and the organisation should create mechanisms to enable procedural and physical changes that are identified in supervision can be considered.

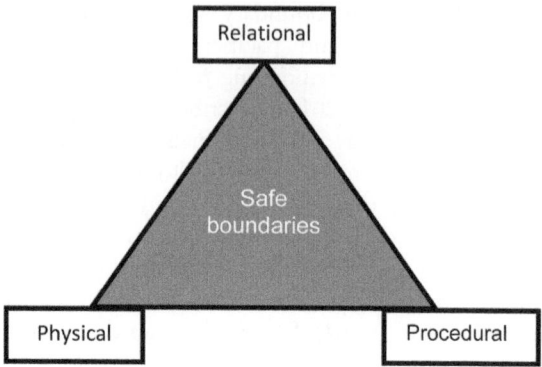

Figure 8.2 Triangle of boundary maintenance

Establishing and maintaining appropriate personal and professional boundaries also requires the supervisor to act as a role model. The supervisor needs to demonstrate that they can provide a safe place to check and explore personal reactions and responses (including those of attraction or repulsion); model an open and reflective stance and remain focused on the supervisees whilst avoiding abusing the authority that is bestowed on them.

Using policy to set the tone – Policies play an important role in setting the organisational boundaries, the acceptable parameters of working and stating the expectations and responsibilities of staff. However, policy and professional codes should be seen for what they are – a description of the limits, how going outside these must be reported and the possible consequences of such actions. In this way policies and codes, along with workplace culture, are the 'procedural security' element of boundary maintenance. However, Evershed (2010) warns of the false sense of safety that can be created through the presence of policies, whilst Austin (2001) states that codes of practice are helpful but not sufficient for managing boundaries. The way in which the setting can influence the culture of working is also important for boundary maintenance and sets the context for practitioner behaviour ' … this is how we do things here … '. For example, requiring that all staff engage in some form of group-based reflective practice (Moore, 2012), helps foster the notion of an 'aware organisation'. However, forensic settings can also lead practitioners through a process of desensitisation, to reduce complexity to simple ideas (e.g. good and bad; right and wrong), to 'act without thought' and to accept situations that are problematic (Austin, 2001). Thus attending to the culture of the organisation is an important element of boundary maintenance.

Boundary maintenance in supervision – According to Moore (2012), supervision within specialist forensic personality disorder services has two core functions, boundary maintenance and attending to the supervisee's emotional and developmental needs. Therefore, it is critical that boundary maintenance forms part of the 'purpose of supervision' and is an explicit element of supervision.

Supervisors and supervisees are encouraged to use the supervision agreement to acknowledge the attention that will be given to boundaries. This parallels the suggestion by Evershed (2010) that therapy contracts can be used to enable boundaries to be discussed and reinforced with clients. It must also be remembered that some staff are 'supervision avoidant' (Evershed, 2010) and will fall outside arrangements for supervision unless there are mechanisms to support engagement. Therefore, supervisors may need to act on any emerging patterns of supervision avoidance in order to prevent this becoming ingrained. Supervisors also need to recognise that supervisees may feel ashamed when discussing boundaries, especially when problems arise (Schafer, 1997). These can be further exacerbated by a fear of blame and an anticipated negative organisational response (Evershed, 2010). Such factors can be significant barriers to addressing boundary problems (supervisee non-disclosure is discussed in more detail in Chapter 7). Supervisors therefore need to be attentive to any warning signs that may be present and create a supervision climate that is conducive to boundary maintenance discussions. As already discussed, supervisors are responsible for providing high quality supervision within which boundary management should take high priority (Evershed, 2010).

In order to help the supervisee maintain effective boundaries the supervisor should explore the complexity of situations, the cost and benefit of actions and pay attention to those situations, clients or aspects of work not being brought to supervision. This could be in the form of a regular full 'client' review where interactions are discussed and reviewed. 'Supervisors need also to focus on any slips and omissions in the supervisee's account of their work, including material that is raised in an unusual way or that has a degree of emotion attached to it' (Evershed, 2010, p. 142). Another approach to boundary maintenance is to introduce rules which are shared with, and 'taught to', clients (Love, 2001b). They present a framework of 'therapeutic rules' used within a hospital setting in which they describe a) boundaries; b) appropriate and inappropriate behaviour, and describe how c) 'staff-patient relationships are one-way helping relationships' (p. 7) that d) differ from friendships. Such an approach may have utility in other forensic settings.

A continuum of vulnerability – Through the discussion about staff, client and context above, it is possible to see that most boundary problems arise through a coming together of many factors. It may therefore be helpful for the supervisor to consider a 'vulnerability continuum' in relation to possible boundary problems. In this vulnerability continuum, supervisors should give weight to factors relating to the practitioner (e.g. a lack of or poor training, practitioner emotional distress, isolation and wishing to rescue), the client (e.g. past boundary problems, personality/style, motivations) and the context (e.g. policies and the physical environment). Thus, each of the arrows in Figure 8.1 could be seen to vary in 'vulnerability weighting' leading to different levels of boundary risk at different points in time. When considering vulnerability, supervisors should also help supervisees be attentive to possible bias and inattention within their decision making (e.g. Bazerman, 1990).

Boundary problem recognition – The supervisor needs to be attentive to possible boundary problems as there are many reasons why these might be missed. For example, staff may rationalise their behaviour and consequently miss warning signs, whilst team splits may develop which lead to unintentional collusion and a failure to recognise what is happening (Love, 2001b). To help identify problems, supervisors may wish to encourage the use of a boundary measure (e.g. Epstein and Simon, 1990; Love, 2001a; Schafer, 1997), however these need to be used in an 'atmosphere of support' (Schafer, 1997, p. 210). Supervisors and supervisees may wish to generate their own list of early indicators within their setting. The following markers may be a helpful start: 'strong feelings about a client'; 'extended sessions'; 'overdoing, overprotecting and over-identifying'; 'unplanned/out-of-hours telephone contact' (more likely in community contexts), 'gift giving/accepting', 'touching/comforting' and 'practitioner self-disclosures', (Love, 2001a; Walker and Clark, 1999) and departures from normal practice (Evershed, 2010). Moore (2012) describes 'toxic transference' as characterised by client behaviours such as vexatious complaints, raising questions about members of staff, giving different information to different staff members, flirting with or rejecting staff and comparing one staff member with another. Being 'tuned in' to such aspects of supervisee and client behaviour and emotions may allow indicators to be identified that reveal problems that need to be resolved. Sometimes it is also important to use supervision 'to aid in distinguishing the impact of a behaviour from its intent' (Gutheil and Gabbard, 1998), and to understand boundaries within the specific service and context. This can help to ensure that context appropriate boundaries are maintained.

Some client groups may prompt specific attention to be given to the potential for boundary difficulties. Moore (2012) notes that spending time in the company of people with personality disorders is emotionally demanding and that repeated exposure to disturbing material can impact on life outside work (e.g. choices made, response to situations). For example, practitioners working with borderline personality disorder need to be aware of their own feelings and responses and recognise issues such as splitting of staff into the 'good guys' and the 'bad guys' (Bland and Rossen, 2005).

Early intervention. In order to address problems it is essential to recognise signs early and take prompt action. Boundary violations may start very small, for example through prisoners or patients encroaching (perhaps through 'invitation') on staff duties and responsibilities. Across these warning signs of potential boundary violations, supervisors can aid the individual to understand and explore the relationship and the nature of what is taking place and consider ways of responding to protect the individual, the client and the service. This might include clarity in relation to policies, developing procedures and practices which reset the boundary, skills development for the supervisee and on-going monitoring and support.

Active boundary management. In their paper on professional boundaries and boundary problems, Walker and Clark (1999) suggest that without clear 'practice-specific' ethical guidelines and effective supervision, practitioners can easily lapse into boundary problems. They suggest that supervision offers a cost-effective method for managing risk through the early identification and response to potential boundary problems. As a foundation, they identify four major supervision principles for working within ethical boundaries, namely:

(1) Supervision should be proactive: supervision should be provided regularly, not just when problems arise.
(2) Supervision should be sensitive to individual circumstance: supervisors should know of personal factors/changes which may make the supervisee vulnerable.
(3) Supervision should consider specific information: details of the situation or 'case' should be explored.
(4) Supervision should be based on guided exploration: generally the use of Socratic and exploratory methods by the supervisor will be most useful.

They describe the importance of the early identification and response to possible boundary problems in order to avoid the 'slippery slope' from seemingly irrelevant to unethical behaviour occurring. A quick guide to boundary maintenance can be found in Box 8.2.

Managing boundary violations. Sometimes problems will only be noticed when a boundary violation has occurred. In such situations, a rapid, fair, supportive but clear response is needed. It is essential that local policy and professional guidelines give clear attention to this, as reactively developing solutions is unlikely to be helpful. Supervisors and supervisees need to be aware of the required responses and both should take assertive action. This may include reporting of the issue to managers as well as those outside the service. Avoiding or trying to fix the problem without due consideration of the appropriate policies is both problematic and ethically dubious. In cases of significant boundary violations, supervisors may be faced with many questions such as 'how was this missed?', 'what should I do now?' and 'how could I have prevented this?'. It is recommended that such issues be considered in their own supervision. They should also aid the supervisee to make provision for their own support.

BOX 8.2: A quick guide to boundary maintenance (based on Evershed, 2010; Faulkner and Regehr, 2011; Love, 2001a, 2001b; Love and Heber, 2001; Moore, 2012; Peternelj-Taylor and Yonge, 2003; Walker and Clark, 1999)

Boundary maintenance should form a core feature of supervision within forensic settings and requires input from the organisation, the supervisee and supervisor.

Organisational support for boundaries – the organisation needs to create a safe and responsive environment in which boundaries can be managed and difficulties addressed. The organisation needs to create policies, provide training and foster supervision that can help maintain boundaries in the difficult and sometimes hostile context of forensic settings.

Supervisee support for boundaries – when engaging with clients it is important to:

- carefully consider personal disclosure (how will this be helpful to the client)
- review own needs (why am I doing this now)
- challenge yourself (am I lying to myself)
- acknowledge the possibility of boundary problems
- discuss boundaries in supervision
- be proactive (awareness in order to avoid a slide into more problematic violations)
- consider using a measure of boundary problems
- remember why the individual is in the setting

Supervisor support for boundaries – when providing supervision it is important to:

- regularly explore boundaries through developing useful questions and prompts for this
- look for boundary adjustments, slips, inattention or crossing
- be aware of who is not talked about
- listen for over-protective or distancing language
- help the supervisee notice strong feelings about the client
- help the supervisee reinforce boundaries where necessary
- highlight, discuss and address small boundary violations
- be clear about own role and purpose
- attend to team splitting or inconsistencies
- focus on unrealistic expectations, demoralisation or personalisation
- promote comparing this client/situation with others the supervisee works with

It is important to think and reflect, and engage in the mindful application of policy and guidelines. Regularly discuss boundaries and workplace complexity.

Conclusion

The issues of risk and boundaries within forensic settings are highly complex and require procedural, physical and relational 'solutions'. Supervision should not be thought of as a mechanism to eradicate problems but rather as a tool to foster good risk management, the maintenance of safe boundaries and a mechanism through which boundary problems can be noticed, recognised and responded to when they arise. It is important that practitioners are supported to reflect on their actions, thoughts and feelings rather than being trained to follow simple rules without thought or consideration (Peternelj-Taylor and Yonge, 2003).

References

Allen, B. and Bosta, D. (1981) *Games Criminals Play: How You Can Profit By Knowing Them*, Roseville, CA: Rae John Publishers.

Austin, W. (2001) 'Relational ethics in forensic psychiatric settings', *Journal of Psychosocial Nursing and Mental Health Services* 39(9): 12–17.

Azar, S. T. (2000) 'Preventing burnout in professionals and paraprofessionals who work with child abuse and neglect cases: a cognitive behavioral approach to supervision', *Journal of Clinical Psychology* 56(5): 643–63.

Bazerman, M. H. (1990) *Judgment in Managerial Decision Making* (2nd edn), Oxford: John Wiley & Sons.

Beddoe, L. (2010) 'Surveillance or reflection: professional supervision in "the risk society"', *British Journal of Social Work* 40(4): 1279–96.

Bland, A. R. and Rossen, E. K. (2005) 'Clinical supervision of nurses working with patients with borderline personality disorder', *Issues in Mental Health Nursing* 26(5): 507–17.

Collins, M. and Davies, S. (2005) 'The security needs assessment profile: a multidimensional approach to measuring security needs', *International Journal of Forensic Mental Health* 4(1): 39–52.

Daffern, M., Jones, L. and Shine, J. (2010) *Offence Paralleling Behaviour: A Case Formulation Approach to Offender Assessment and Intervention*, Oxford: Wiley.

Elliott, W. N. (2006) 'Power and control tactics employed by prison inmates – a case study', *Federal Probation* 70: 45.

Epstein, R. S. and Simon, R. I. (1990) 'The exploitation index: an early warning indicator of boundary violations in psychotherapy', *Bulletin of the Menninger Clinic*.

Evershed, S. (2010) 'The grey areas of boundary issues when working with forensic patients who have a personality disorder', in P. Willmot and N. Gordon (eds), *Working Positively with Personality Disorder in Secure Settings*, Oxford: John Wiley & Sons, pp. 127–45.

Faulkner, C. and Regehr, C. (2011) 'Sexual boundary violations committed by female forensic workers', *Journal of the American Academy of Psychiatry and the Law Online* 39(2): 154–63.

Gutheil, T. G. and Gabbard, G. O. (1998) 'Misuses and misunderstandings of boundary theory in clinical and regulatory settings', *American Journal of Psychiatry* 155(3): 409–14.

Hamilton, L. (2010) 'The boundary seesaw model: good fences make for good neighbours', in A. Tennant and K. Howells (eds), *Using Time Not Doing Time*, Oxford: Wiley-Blackwell.

Kitchener, K. S. (1988) 'Dual role relationships: what makes them so problematic?', *Journal of Counseling & Development* 67(4): 217–21.

Love, C. C. (2001a) 'Staff-patient erotic boundary violations: Part 1 – Staff Factors', *On the Edge* 7(3): 4–7.

——(2001b) 'Staff-patient erotic boundary violations: Part 2 – Patient Factors', *On the Edge* 7(4): 4–8.

Love, C. C. and Heber, S. A. (2001) 'Staff–patient erotic boundary violations: Part 3 – Environmental Factors', *On the Edge* 8(1): 12–16.

Marquart, J. W., Barnhill, M. B. and Balshaw-Biddle, K. (2001) 'Fatal attraction: an analysis of employee boundary violations in a southern prison system, 1995–98', *Justice Quarterly* 18(4): 877–910.

Moore, E. (2012) 'Personality disorder: its impact on staff and the role of supervision', *Advances in Psychiatric Treatment* 18(1): 44–55.

Mothersole, G. (2000) 'Clinical supervision and forensic work', *Journal of Sexual Aggression* 5(1): 45–58.

Overholser, J. C. and Fine, M. A. (1990) 'Defining the boundaries of professional competence: managing subtle cases of clinical incompetence', *Professional Psychology: Research and Practice* 21(6), 462.

Peternelj-Taylor, C. A. and Yonge, O. (2003) 'Exploring boundaries in the nurse–client relationship: professional roles and responsibilities', *Perspectives in Psychiatric Care* 39(2): 55–66.

Power, S. (2007) 'Boundaries and responsibilities in clinical supervision', in J. Driscoll (ed.), *Practising Clinical Supervision*, Oxford: Elsevier Health Sciences, pp. 53–71.

Schafer, P. (1997) 'When a client develops an attraction: successful resolution versus boundary violation', *Journal of Psychiatric and Mental Health Nursing* 4(3): 203–11.

Strom-Gottfried, K. (1999) 'Professional boundaries: an analysis of violations by social workers', *Families in Society: The Journal of Contemporary Social Services* 80(5): 439–49.

Titterton, M. (2005) *Risk and Risk Taking in Health and Social Welfare*, London: Jessica Kingsley Publishers.

——(2010) *Positive risk taking*, HALE. Retrieved from www.haletrust.com/system/files/Positive+Risk+Taking.pdf.

Walker, R. and Clark, J. J. (1999) 'Heading off boundary problems: clinical supervision as risk management', *Psychiatric Services* 50(11): 1435–39.

Ward, T. and Maruna, S. (2007) *Rehabilitation*, Abingdon: Routledge.

White, E., Butterworth, T., Bishop, V., Carson, J., Jeacock, J. and Clements, A. (1998) 'Clinical supervision: insider reports of a private world', *Journal of Advanced Nursing* 28(1): 185–92.

Worley, R., Marquart, J. W. and Mullings, J. L. (2003) 'Prison guard predators: an analysis of inmates who established inappropriate relationships with prison staff, 1995–98', *Deviant Behavior* 24: 175–94.

9 Developing supervision in forensic practice
Structures, systems and audit

Much of content up to this point has focussed upon the delivery of supervision and the knowledge, skills and techniques associated with this. However, most employers want to be sure that their duties to their clients and their workers are met; this often includes ensuring adequate provision for training and supervision of staff. Although this chapter is relevant to those involved in the delivery of supervision, it is primarily aimed at those who are tasked with developing and implementing supervision policy and strategy within their organisations. This task is not an easy one as it requires careful analysis, planning and delivery if a robust and sustainable supervision approach is to be embedded within the system. Supporting this, authors such as Cheater and Hale (2001) and Coffey and Coleman (2001) have argued that effective structures for supervision are necessary for forensic community mental health nurses – this argument can easily be extended to other forensic practice settings. However, amongst the challenges in establishing a culture of supervision, is the all too familiar observation made by one of the participants in the study of supervision in prison health care by Freshwater, Walsh, and Storey (2002): 'it is the people that most need it that actually don't want to do it' (p. 18). On the other side of the equation are the findings that those who believe in self-care are more likely to engage in supervision and those who believe in supervision are much more likely to devote time to engaging in it (Bober and Regehr, 2006; Cheater and Hale, 2001; Coffey and Coleman, 2001; Freshwater *et al.*, 2002). Despite this, most of the staff who participate in supervision consider it to be valuable for all staff irrespective of grade or experience (Freshwater *et al.*, 2002; Mothersole, 2000).

Barriers and pitfalls in supervision implementation

In order to provide the best possible chance of successful implementation, learning lessons from the difficulties identified by others is a sensible first step. This should be supplemented by considering the local experience of introducing any new initiatives and change. Problems with implementation are very well documented and a number of themes have been found in several studies.

Staff engagement: Cottrell (2002) provides a very useful way of thinking about why and how attempts to establish supervision in an organisation might be thwarted and/or fail. He identifies the different 'vested interests' and relationships that may emerge between the supervisee, their manager, the supervisor and senior management, and presents four pairings that can negatively impact on supervision implementation. This is discussed in more detail in Box 9.1. Although used to discuss problems after they have occurred, this conceptualisation also serves to underline the importance of mutual engagement across all potential stakeholders at the earliest opportunity. Further, it emphasises the need for careful planning prior to implementation. Cottrell's observations provide some indication of the things to monitor as indications that supervision implementation is proving problematic. Pre-empting and responding to these might provide the best chance of success.

> ### BOX 9.1 Problem alliances (based on Cottrell, 2002)
>
> In this scheme there are four 'players' – the senior manager(s), the direct manager (e.g. ward manager, unit manager), the supervisees and the supervisor.
>
> *Tokenism* can occur when the manager and senior management implement supervision without adequately preparing staff who will be supervised and those who will supervise. As a result, the supervisee and supervisor may just go through the motions and supervisees may put up resistance by being ill-prepared or only presenting 'safe work'. Supervision gradually fizzles out as all parties grow weary of it.
>
> *Resistance* may be seen when supervisees and their manager group together to stave off the imposition of supervision. These situations are enacted through staff being unavailable for supervision, work schedules being changed and urgent matters and crises occurring that result in supervision being cancelled. Dispirited supervisors formally suspend attempts at supervision.
>
> *Mutiny* can occur when supervisor and supervisee are seen to form a special group or 'clique', or when managers feel excluded. Such alliances may be formed between recently qualified (and enthusiastic) staff wanting to 'get going', or where there is an absence of direction from managers or the organisation. Managers or those not accessing supervision bring supervision to a stop.
>
> *Suspicion* can be fostered when the supervisor and the senior manager are 'in the know', but others are not. This can result when, for example, the desire to get supervision established (often borne from good intentions) has resulted in supervisor training taking place but others not being adequately informed and involved. In this scenario supervision can feel unsafe as supervisees are unsure how confidentiality will be managed. Supervision fails to thrive, time is spent organising it, however negative propaganda builds against it. As Cottrell warns, 'another short-lived fad bites the dust'.

The observations in Box 9.1 are important for anyone developing supervision systems or attempting to embed supervision in an organisation. His suggestions for avoiding these are based on focusing on building the factors at the opposite 'pole' to the problem. Therefore, establishing *commitment* from all those involved directly and indirectly will help to combat tokenism; sharing information and embedding a rationale for supervision helps foster *acceptance* – an important factor in mitigating resistance; ensuring widespread inclusion and a sense of ownership and *loyalty* will help pre-empt possible mutiny; creating a sense of control and *trust* can address suspicion. These positive conditions can be fostered by doing 'the groundwork', i.e. ensuring that sufficient time is taken to share information; clarify and agree responsibilities; discuss each 'player's' motivations and expectations. Thus, all of those with an interest – supervisees, supervisors, managers and senior managers, need to be involved throughout the process to minimise the likelihood of supervision being seen as 'something else that is thrust upon us' (Cheater and Hale, 2001, p. 127), and to provide a means to identify and resolve issues and concerns early.

Practical and system factors: There are many practical and systemic barriers which need to be considered and addressed before supervision is rolled out across the workforce. In a study of supervision provision within a forensic mental health service, Long *et al.* (2013) identified barriers to supervision at the individual level (such as a lack of confidence, a lack of understanding of supervision), and at the organisational level (e.g. lack of resources – such as suitably trained supervisors, poor management support). In this study, and in a study of staff working in prison healthcare, work pressures and safeguarding time for supervision proved to be difficult which hampered supervision provision (Freshwater *et al.*, 2002). Careful planning is also essential. For example, in a study by Cheater and Hale (2001), they concluded that the deployment of the supervision resource may have taken place before sufficient ground work had been completed to promote the benefits of supervision, establish commitment, overcome misconceptions and to ensure there was the facility for protected time. After 12 months of the programme, they found a reasonable level of understanding of the scheme, however a much lower than expected level of uptake. It is important to note that when there are time pressures, supervision may cease even though this period may be when it is most useful (Jenkins, 2000).

Maximising successful implementation: developing a service strategy

As shown above, and in other chapters of this text, there are many factors that need to be considered in order to maximise the chances of implementing supervision successfully. These are discussed in this section, however readers should also consult Box 9.2 which provides an eight-step plan for implementing supervision. This approach has a number of similarities to the Lynch Model of Implementation (Lynch and Happell, 2008) which was developed from experiences gathered during the introduction of supervision into a rural mental health service in Australia. The Lynch model describes six steps:

(1) *Clinical supervision or [an alternative?]* (why is supervision being considered).
(2) *Initial assessment of the culture* (identifying 'pushing and resisting' forces and placing these in order of priority).
(3) *Obtaining organisational support* (identifying and gaining the support needed).
(4) *Developing the strategic plan* (involving stakeholders and producing a document).
(5) *Operationalising the strategic plan* (education and training; communication and 'marketing').
(6) *Reflection and evaluation* (sustainability, outcomes, next steps).

> **BOX 9.2 Steps in developing and implementing supervision (based on Hawkins and Shohet, 2006)**
>
> In most services a system of, and structures for supervision will be 'retro-fitted' i.e. being introduced into an organisation that is already 'up and running'. These steps address such a situation. In a new service, it is possible to introduce supervision as a requirement across all roles, as a component of the service specification. In such a case, the latter stages of this list (steps 5-8) are most relevant, as is the need to support 'supervision leaders' across the organisation.
>
> **1. Understand and harness what is already in place**
>
> It is likely that some form of supervision is already taking place in some parts of the service/organisation and that elsewhere many have found ways to meet some of the same needs (e.g. personal learning and skills development). Start by discovering what is already happening – this might help identify how to best garner interest and where to carry out a pilot of supervision. Identifying workers who are mandated to have supervision as part of their registration or licence to practice can equally be helpful.
>
> **2. Engage with all stakeholders and develop interest**
>
> Managers and workers need to be involved from an early stage. Knowledge of the organisation is necessary to locate which structures or governance groups will need to provide 'permission' for the development of supervision. Discussions will also need to be fostered to help staff pinpoint what benefit it might have to them. Addressing myths such as 'experienced people don't need it' and 'it's only for those with problem practice' will need to be undertaken from the start.

3. Provide initial training and information

Provide training to 'would-be' supervisors and supervisees, but also to managers – this should cover the 'why', 'how' and 'who' and the ways in which supervision links with the organisation (e.g. client outcomes, safe services) and personal (e.g. skills development and wellbeing) goals. Information can be shared through attending service area meetings, existing in-service staff training sessions, via the service intranet and by providing access to leaflets or books on supervision (such as this one!) within the practice area.

4. Start small in a well-supported pilot area

Capitalise on those who are already interested and engaged. Make sure there is adequate practical and managerial support for all those in the pilot area at all levels. Ensure that the pilot is evaluated (see later in this chapter) and supervisors, supervisees, clients, other staff and local managers are asked for information on what works and what needs to be overcome. Pre-empt challenges from other areas of the service, e.g. 'why are they getting this'. Such difficulties (see also step 5) could be converted into enthusiasm to extend the pilot to that service area.

5. Anticipate, identify and address barriers

A number of potential barriers to supervision have already been identified through this chapter including resistance, tokenism, scepticism and potential mutiny. Before delivering supervision it is important to 'do the groundwork' in order to pre-emptively deal with possible barriers. Planning and preparation are essential, however it is important to remain focused on the goal of action. Issues such as lack of supervisor availability and lack of time (especially within a small pilot area) suggest a serious failing at the planning stage.

6. Develop a detailed strategy and associated policies

Supervision will need to be supported through appropriate policies – this provides one mechanism for the organisation to 'sign up' to the investment in supervision. More practically, a strategy for how supervision will be delivered and the associated resources required (e.g. staff time, training) should be detailed. Methods of recording and reporting need to be covered (see point 8).

7. Support on-going supervision training and development across the service

Establishing supervision is an important first step. Once a pilot area has been developed, consideration should be given to how this practice (or a differently tailored approach) could be spread across other areas. Consider how new staff will receive training and have access to supervision. Through practice, supervisees and supervisors may have identified training needs, so it is important to consider on-going training and skills building/update workshops. Consider supporting some staff to undertake advanced training or study in supervision to help build local expertise from both practice and academia. Chapter 10 focuses on training supervisors and supervisees.

8. Audit and evaluation, commission and support research

Having a system to audit supervision is important to monitor what is taking place, identify what works and record where difficulties may lie (e.g. through noting reasons for cancellations). In addition, practice evaluation could be established to gather information from supervisees and supervisors about such things as changes that have followed from the introduction of supervision to the service. Other elements such as training should be evaluated, and can be informed and shaped by the audits, research and evaluation taking place. Finally, as outlined in Chapter 2, there is a great deal of scope for undertaking research in this area and this could/should be fostered as part of developing and delivering supervision.

To complement the information contained in Box 9.2, the section below will explore what might need to be done by considering how a supervision strategy could be approached and some of what it may contain. This will need to be both sensitive and relevant to the local context.

Features of successful supervision: Authors and researchers have identified several features associated with successful supervision. Observations made include:

(1) Higher scores on the Manchester Clinical Supervision Scale (MCSS) (see Special Topic 8) have been associated with sessions that last at least *60 minutes, occur monthly*, where the *supervisee chose their supervisor* and where sessions were held *away from the workplace* (Winstanley and White, 2003). Some of these elements were also investigated (and supported) in a high secure hospital setting (Carthy, Noak and Wadey, 2012).
(2) Supervision should be provided to all grades and levels of staff. For experienced staff, supervision can help guard against over confidence and omissions (Mothersole, 2000).
(3) Supervision needs organisational and managerial support and should include training for staff and an audit of activity (Long *et al.*, 2013).
(4) 'Good supervisors were as unlikely to achieve a desired clinical supervision effect in unhealthy cultures, as were poor supervisors in healthy cultures' (White and Winstanley, 2012).
(5) Supervisors who are trained have been evaluated more highly than those who were not (Hyrkäs, Appelqvist-Schmidlechner and Haataja, 2006).

(6) Higher scores on the MCSS were found in those who selected their supervisor and where the supervisor and supervisee were from the same organisation (Hyrkäs et al., 2006).
(7) It is essential that the purpose and goal(s) of supervision are spelt out (Day, 2012).
(8) The use of a supervision contract, a session record (for audit) and staff training is important (Davies, Maggs and Lewis, 2010).
(9) Through a carefully planned and implemented improvement programme (including the introduction of a policy and training workshops) Carthy et al. (2012) were able to ensure that the vast majority of staff (89 per cent) received clinical supervision on a monthly basis.
(10) Supervision provides a mechanism for 'on the job' learning and staff development (Davies and Tennant, 2003).

Core features: From the list above, a number of basic features are highlighted which should form part of the strategy. These elements could be seen as the 'must-haves'; they are not discussed in detail here as they are described more fully elsewhere in this text:

(1) Time – at least an hour on a monthly basis (see above).
(2) Purpose – that the goals and approach to supervision be agreed (see Chapter 3).
(3) Agreement – a written agreement be in place (e.g. see Chapter 3).
(4) Audit – a mechanism for basic audit be supported (e.g. see later in this chapter).

Getting 'buy in' across the system: To stand any chance of supervision being successfully implemented, it is important to involve and engage others – supervision must be owned by the staff (Freshwater et al., 2002). This is likely to require formal meetings, but it is important not to underestimate the importance of informal discussions and contact at this early stage. Part of this process includes identifying allies who can help determine, develop and implement the strategy (see next section). The importance of engaging with staff and managers cannot be overstated. As found by Cheater and Hale (2001), key management staff need to be 'targeted' and some form of marketing may be necessary to engage workers and managers across the system.

Strategic and managerial support: In most organisations, there are individuals who have the authority and leadership skills to promote change or to stifle it. Although, as argued by Cottrell (2002), a range of groups need to 'sign up' in order for supervision to be successfully implemented; someone with sufficient authority and seniority is certainly needed (Freshwater et al., 2002). Underscoring the importance of strategic support is an observation by White and Winstanley (2012) who stated that 'Control and management of the roster was found to be the bellwether mechanism by which [clinical supervision] was both facilitated and stymied' (p. 87). To add further weight to the importance of managerial and organisational support, Butterworth et al. (2008) notes that supervision is not always given the organisational support it needs. This has been reported in a number of studies including Paget (2001) and earlier Scanlon and Weir (1997), who noted that supervision was not given sufficient priority by managers who did not seem to view supervision as 'proper work', possibly because of a lack of understanding. However, it is important to stress that this support needs to be based on commitment; unless support is translated into action, staff may find that it is difficult to fit supervision into work time for example (Kenny and Allenby, 2013). However, care must be taken to ensure that supervision is not (or is not seen to be) used as a punitive management tool (White et al., 1998). As well as initial support, the participants in the study by Kenny and Allenby (2013) highlighted the need for support from management to be on-going. Therefore, part of the strategy needs to be engaging those in strategic positions both 'on the ground and on the board'.

Supervision leadership: A number of key individuals need to be identified to lead a supervision development. Ideally what is needed is a supervision advocate or champion who has leadership skills and is therefore able to support implementation (Freshwater et al., 2002). Such leadership may well be self-selecting based on individual interest and drive to embed supervision. In addition to an individual providing overall leadership, it might be necessary to appoint someone to lead on components of the strategy, such as training and audit/evaluation.

Growing the idea ... from little acorns: Developing supervision in one area of a service may be the best way to galvanise support and begin to develop local evidence. It may be that, initially, staff are self-selected or that an area volunteers to act as a pilot. It can also be helpful to draft a basic proposal to communicate the plan and gauge the reception of others. This might give an early indication of the interest and barriers from managers and senior staff. It can also help establish the level of 'readiness for supervision' within the system. On a related note, establishing supervision is likely to take time as it may involve both the introduction of a system and a change in culture. This is supported by the findings of Carthy et al. (2012), who evaluated the implementation of a supervision approach within a high secure hospital setting. They found that the area where the roll-out of supervision began had the highest scores on the Manchester Clinical Supervision Scale (e.g. Winstanley and White, 2011). From this they concluded that the process of socialisation into supervision and the subsequent effects of supervision on staff outcomes and the system take time.

Models of supervision: The supervision strategy and the associated training for staff should include information about models and approaches to supervision. This might also be supplemented by providing this information in the form of 'supervision packs' for staff or by placing posters in areas used for supervision. Chapters 3 and 4 provide information relevant to this.

Arguments concerning impact: There are many general arguments that can be made in support of supervision, including the research evidence contained in

Chapter 2. However, as also outlined in that chapter, the case for the benefits can be complex. Despite this, it can be helpful, and important, to provide information on the findings relating to the potential impact on client outcomes and the effects on staff as found in other settings. These may need to be accompanied by appropriate caveats because of the differences in the work being supervised or the difference in the setting in which the study took place. Arguments concerning the benefits of providing supervision include:

(1) Supervision can improve care and can reduce the number of complaints, as well as developing staff confidence, competence and knowledge.
(2) Supervision can reduce worker stress and increase the perception of support, and staff retention (Sloan, 1999).
(3) 'Employees who are supported and are allowed time to reflect and develop will make a significant contribution to patient well being and safety and employers bear a considerable responsibility in sustaining and developing this activity in their organisations' (Butterworth et al., 2008, p.270).
(4) Where supervision had taken place, a reasonable proportion were able to give concrete examples of how supervision had impacted on their practice, for example in relation to improvements in patient care and confidence to make changes to systems (Cheater and Hale, 2001).
(5) Those who engage in supervision generally report that they find it valuable (e.g. Cheater and Hale, 2001; Freshwater et al., 2002).
(6) Supervision can help practitioners to identify and address bias and thus maintain necessary independence/impartiality. Further, supervision can help workers recognise and manage emotional reactions, maintain up-to-date knowledge, and foster and enhance ethical practice (Day, 2012).
(7) Training supervision is important as it is often one of the mechanisms by which individuals enter a profession, thus it can fulfil a gate-keeping role. In addition, the role of the supervisor in such circumstances is also to safeguard the client and society (Falender, 2014).

Detail the costs: One aspect of building a case for supervision is through careful consideration of the likely costs (e.g. financial, human resources) and the possible gains (e.g. client outcomes, staff development). Some of these are easy to articulate, for example the cost of releasing staff to undertake supervision based on salary costs, costs associated with training and 'back-fill'. Therefore, time should be taken to identify these if such factors are important to getting approval. A detailed framework provided by Hyrkäs, Lehti and Paunonen Ilmonen (2001) might be useful for establishing a methodology to evaluate the costs and gains associated with supervision within the service.

Supervision alongside existing strategies: it is important to recognise that other mechanisms may already exist which have been created to meet some of the needs of the workforce. This might include staff support sessions and information support, both of which might be referred to as 'supervision'. Delineating these activities, for example by identifying their different functions, whilst acknowledging and accepting their value is important. Stating how supervision might sit alongside, complement and/or enhance these arrangements is also vital. For example, a study by White et al. (1998) found that nurses who had not previously received supervision reported that some of the functions of supervision had been previously met by other means. Additionally, in a study of supervision for nurses, Teasdale, Brocklehurst and Thom (2001) found that supervision was used for reflecting on their work, whilst other more informal mechanisms were used for immediate advice and support. They suggested that both these approaches may be needed, however they recognised that in some circumstances it may be necessary to target supervision. Where resources are limited they suggest targeting supervision to more junior staff. Gathering information about existing practice and what already works can form part of the task of canvassing interest and engaging staff.

Supervision for all staff: Mothersole (2000) cautions against seeing supervision as the domain of junior staff only, and comments that good supervision is challenging of both attitudes and actions. The importance of post-qualification supervision has been echoed by Day (2012) in a paper focused on qualified forensic psychologists. Of equal importance is ensuring that those staff who are not 'qualified' (e.g. unregistered/unlicensed practitioners) also access supervision. In an inpatient setting, Long et al. (2013) found the unqualified staff were much less likely to engage in supervision than their qualified contemporaries. It is important to recognise that in many service areas and settings those workers who are unqualified or only hold basic training often have a great deal of unsupported and/or unstructured contact with clients. Supervision provides a method to provide support and training 'on the job' at the same time as ensuring possible risks are appropriately managed and safeguards are in place for the worker.

Supervisor choice (and within and cross-discipline supervision): The evidence points towards advantages associated with supervisor choice, however this may not be feasible (e.g. due to the configuration of the workforce) or desirable (e.g. for a new member of staff such a choice is likely to be daunting and meaningless). However, part of the consideration in relation to choice needs to be whether or not the supervisor should come from the same discipline or profession (e.g. Cutcliffe and Lowe, 2005; Scanlon and Weir, 1997). This 'dilemma' has its roots in the therapy, social care and mental health field. There appears to be no solid evidence for or against 'within profession' supervision, although there appear to be strong advocates on either side with possible practice differences in different areas of the world (see Cutcliffe and Lowe, 2005). Hair (2013) suggests that cross-discipline supervision provided to newly qualified social workers might result in social work specific skills being devalued and ethical issues associated with social work practice being inadequately addressed. In her research she found that most of her respondents agreed that social workers 'need', 'should' or 'must' be supervised by other social workers. However, Cutcliffe and Lowe (2005) note that cross-discipline supervision may (a) foster the supervisee having greater power within the relationship, and (b) result in the supervisor moving away from a profession expert position where the supervisee is schooled and developed to be like the supervisor and to fit within their profession as it currently exists. This position might be further complicated by how differences are rated by supervisees. For example, in one study, OT supervisors were rated most highly and psychologist supervisors the lowest! (Hyrkäs, Appelqvist-Schmidlechner and Haataja, 2006). Davies et al. (2004) argue that supervision should be provided by the most suitable person, regardless of their profession, but attention should be paid to ensuring that professional requirements and profession specific difficulties can be met/addressed. This could be through, for example, 'specific supervision' (see Chapter 3) or through line management supervision.

Whether supervisors should come from within the service or externally is another important choice. External supervision arrangements can enable an 'outside perspective' to be brought to both work with clients and considerations of team difficulties. As reported by Mothersole (2000), supervision with someone outside the organisation will reduce the likelihood of 'slipping into organisational blind spots'. However, where this line is taken, a clear contract of roles and responsibilities is needed and careful attention must be given to the boundaries and the relationship between the supervisor and the organisation in relation to such factors as accountability, confidentiality and cost (Scanlon and Weir, 1997 and see Beddoe and Davys, 2010). A half-way position is that of Davies et al. (2004) who suggest that supervisors are drawn from within the service, but from outside the immediate environment. This might help to overcome some of the contracting issues noted by Beddoe and Davys (2010), but is unlikely to be feasible in small services.

As noted by Jones (2006), there are a number of points, framed here as questions, which might be worth detailing, such as, 'How will staff be prepared for supervision?'; 'How should supervisee and supervisor be matched?'; 'Are protocols needed for who should and shouldn't work together?'; 'How long should supervisee and supervisor work together?'. The service strategy should consider these.

Staff preparation and training: Preparing and training staff is critical and is discussed in detail in Chapter 10. Identifying who will be responsible for preparing staff should take place early in order for the necessary arrangements to be ready to be delivered once implementation of the strategy begins. As a minimum, it is suggested that at least one day of training for supervisors and half to one day of training for supervisees. However, this should be a starting point with attention given to on-going training. It is also important to provide training and information to managers to help their understanding of supervision. The availability of 'supervision of supervision' also needs to be considered (Davies et al., 2010).

Method of delivery – group or individual: As discussed in Chapter 3, there are benefits and drawbacks to both individual and group supervision which will need to be considered in order to inform the strategy for delivering supervision. Where group supervision is to be provided, Kenny and Allenby (2013) suggest that it may be beneficial to prepare and induct supervisees through individual supervision and to ensure that there is a clearly agreed purpose, focus and process for group supervision. Further, White and Winstanley (2012) suggest that where groups are used, a ratio of fewer than 9:1 supervisees:supervisor be adopted.

Supervisor 'accreditation': Thought should be given to whether or not the service will develop any form of 'in-house' register or accreditation system for supervisors. At one end of the scale this might simply be a list of people who have completed some form of training and who are willing to supervise others. At the other end of the scale this might be based on assessing competence and registering supervisors at different levels or to work in with different groups (e.g. individual but not group supervision; newly qualified but not experienced staff). Accreditation should also be thought of in relation to professional requirements (below).

Line management and supervision: Sometimes it is necessary and desirable for the line manager to take on the role of practice supervisor (dual role supervision), as might be the case in a small service area, however this is not without its difficulties. For example, Hair (2013) cautions that when a single person is providing line management and supervision, those in the supervisor role need to resist possible pressures to narrow the focus of supervision to the management functions (such as case numbers and operational issues). This can be particularly difficult (especially in times of austerity!) when there are organisational pressures to change working practice or take on more work. However, this pressure might also come from the manager themselves as found in the study by Manthorpe *et al.* (2013) where managers considered case management to be the main purpose of supervision. The skill of the dual role supervisor to remain focused on providing collaborative, critically reflective and supportive supervision is therefore important. There can also be other compromises in this arrangement. For example, the supervisee has a single point of contact for both management and supervision, which means that this relationship must be effective. It takes away the possibility of the supervisee being able to consult with someone 'more independent' if there are things they need to raise with their supervisor or line manager. Supervisees might also be less inclined to expose their weaknesses or discuss difficulties they are facing in a frank and open manner where the supervisor is also their line manager, if they are concerned this will be evaluated in some way or may impact on their prospects of promotion, for example. In a multiprofessional study of staff who had participated in a training course, Cutcliffe and Hyrkäs (2006) found that most respondents thought their supervisor should not also be their manager. This led the authors to argue that these functions (management and supervision) should be kept separate, with managers taking on the roles of supporting, evaluating and facilitating supervision. Based on the issues and complexities such as those listed here, this suggestion for separate roles has also been made in a forensic context (Davies *et al.*, 2004).

Professional requirements: Many professional bodies require their members to demonstrate on-going professional development. In addition to supervision being one mechanism to achieving this, some organisations stipulate requirements in relation to supervision. The service strategy should include these relevant requirements and this can form part of the basis for developing an implementation strategy. In addition, some professional organisations have a voluntary register of supervisors (e.g. within the UK the British Psychological Society has a Register of Applied Psychology Practice Supervisors) whilst other bodies require that staff be supervised by an accredited supervisor. This is very common where an individual is learning or practicing a specific psychological therapy (e.g. those training in Cognitive Analytic Therapy, Schema Therapy or Cognitive Behaviour Therapy).

Political and contextual differences: The ways in which supervision is viewed and the relative importance attached to the different functions supervision might provide, may be influenced by wider societal and governmental factors, as well as differences in the ways in which different professionals practice in different areas of the world. For example, through their descriptions of supervision within social work in England and Sweden, Bradley and Höjer (2009) provide examples of this. Within England, the focus in social work supervision takes more of an administrative approach with performance, targets and standards viewed as important, and often a view that reflection is neglected. In England, line managers often fulfil this role. In contrast, the approach in Sweden largely separates the administrative function (which remains with the manager) from work and emotional support and a client focus which is typically provided by an external supervisor. They conclude that the English approach may be well suited to newly qualified practitioners, whilst the reflective approach (more evident in the Swedish model) may be important in fostering a learning organisation.

Using technology: In some cases it may be necessary to provide supervision remotely via phone or video link (Day, 2012). This may be the case where individuals or services are isolated or where particular expertise is wanted. Where this is used, issues such as contracting, boundaries and confidentiality (e.g. use of secure communication link) need careful thought. Engaging in supervision in this format is also very different to the more typical face-to-face method and therefore procedures and training may be needed to manage this.

Maximising success: thoughtful implementation

As already emphasised, careful thought needs to be given to how supervision will be introduced within the service. As White and Winstanley (2012) suggests, supervision should be introduced in a planned manner in a specific location where it is 'owned' by all, supervisors are prepared, systems are in place to support all staff in receiving it and common standards are agreed (e.g. in relation to session length and frequency). This will need to be informed by local conditions, such as the capacity and availability of would-be supervisors, and the decisions made when the strategy was being developed (e.g. will there be a pilot and if so where).

As noted by Fowler (1996), 'Where the demand is small, the criteria can be precise. Where the demand is high or the ideal qualities scarce, the criteria become more general' (p. 476). This should be borne in mind when developing a strategy for supervision, as the more precise the criteria, training and audit processes, the more robust the supervision framework and provision is likely to be. Therefore, compromises to this should be explicit.

Audit, evaluation and research

Part of the strategy needs to address how audit, evaluation and research will feature in the development of supervision to provide information about supervision in *this* service. Although audit, evaluation and research activities are related, they are distinct and usually require different considerations in relation to ethical approvals, governance and resourcing. Detailed consideration of the differences between these is beyond the scope of this chapter, however, for the interested reader there are many online sources of information (e.g. www.nres.nhs.uk/EasySiteWeb/GatewayLink.aspx?alId=355 [accessed 26 April 2014]). In this section we will briefly consider the importance of these activities and how they can be integrated into the development and delivery of supervision.

Audit

Audit is concerned with assessing service delivery against pre-determined standards such as those contained within a service strategy document as discussed above. It is important to establish an audit system from the start (Davies *et al.*, 2004), and to ensure audit is included within any pilot. Supervision audit data might include whether or not supervision took place, how long it lasted and how often it has occurred. Developing an audit strategy can be relatively simple and can be introduced in such a way that information is collected routinely. This requires a data collection form (see example in Box 9.3) and agreement about who should complete them, where they will be stored, when the data will be analysed and who will be responsible for this. In addition, storing copies of supervision contracts in a central location can help monitor that these are in place. Such audit information can help identify if standards are being met and enable areas of difficulty or good practice to be easily identified.

BOX 9.3 Example audit form (Davies and Williams, unpublished)

Audit forms can be developed and used to collect data to assist with routine audit and evaluation of supervision. The functions of the tool presented below are threefold:

- A record for the supervisor/supervisee to monitor against their agreement.
- A method for managers to monitor supervision taking place and levels of cancellation/rescheduling.

- A method to identify common supervision themes in order to inform wider staff training and reflection through group staff support structures.

**Clinical Supervision Routine Audit
Event Record – Example**

Please complete this form at the end of each scheduled clinical supervision session or when a session has been cancelled. Completed forms should be given to the administrator. It is the supervisee's responsibility to complete this event record. THANK YOU.

1. Supervisee name _____
2. Supervisor name _____
3. Regular supervisor (please circle)   Yes   No
4. Format of supervision (please circle)

   Individual   Group   Other (specify) _____

5. Date _____/_____/_____

6. Length of session _____

   (place X if cancelled)

7. Type of supervision (please circle)

   Scheduled   Ad hoc   Handover   Emergency/crisis
   Other (e.g. reflective practice group) _____

8. Core topics (circle all that apply)

   Patient issues   Groupwork   Care plans   Supervision of others
   Interpersonal   Ward issues   Staff issues   Other _____

9. If cancelled, please state reason _____
10. Date of next supervision _____/_____/_____

Evaluation

The importance of establishing ways to evaluate and monitor supervision has been highlighted by many authors (e.g. Cheater and Hale, 2001; Jones, 2006; Long *et al.*, 2013; White and Winstanley, 2012). Local evaluation is necessary in order to help determine whether supervision as it is currently offered in the setting is useful and/or effective. This will help support and inform future decision making about the delivery of supervision along with the content of training. In addition to regular feedback and the evaluation of training offered to staff, some elements of evaluation can be readily incorporated alongside the delivery of supervision. For example, by including some multiple choice or open-ended questions within the approach used for routine audit data collection, information can be gathered which can be later analysed to reveal themes – such as the types of work brought to supervision. In addition, routine data collected for other purposes (e.g. staff sickness rates or client outcomes) might also be relevant information as part of a carefully designed evaluation. More explicit evaluation methods (e.g. surveys or focus groups) might also enable information such as 'what is useful' and 'how supervision impacts on practice' to be gathered.

Research

As outlined in Chapter 2, there are numerous opportunities for engaging in evaluation or research. Such work could be based on local replication of findings from elsewhere, but might also focus on questions that are important to the stakeholders involved in the service. High quality supervision research is badly needed especially within the context of forensic practice. In addition to the many questions that have been identified in relation to supervision generally, e.g. what impact does it have on client/task outcomes; what models are used and in what ways, there are important questions that are especially pertinent to the forensic context. Three obvious areas for forensic supervision research are 'how risk is monitored and addressed in supervision'; 'how boundary issues are noticed and managed'; and 'the nature and resolution of ethical issues brought to supervision'.

Conclusion

Introducing supervision and embedding it within the custom and practice of a work area is a challenging task which requires support and commitment from those in positions of authority. Winstanley and White (2003) note that implementation often starts in specific areas before being generalised and that embedding supervision within an organisational context is often a lengthy process. Further, it should also be borne in mind that those who might be in most need of supervision may be the least likely to engage with it (Winstanley and White, 2003). As described in this chapter, creating an infrastructure will be necessary if supervision is to succeed.

References

Beddoe, L. and Davys, A. (2010) *Best Practice in Professional Supervision*, London: Jessica Kingsley Publishers.
Bober, T. and Regehr, C. (2006) 'Strategies for reducing secondary or vicarious trauma: do they work?', *Brief Treatment and Crisis Intervention* 6(1): 1–9.
Bradley, G. and Höjer, S. (2009) 'Supervision reviewed: reflections on two different social work models in England and Sweden', *European Journal of Social Work* 12(1): 71–85.

Butterworth, T., Bell, L., Jackson, C. and Pajnkihar, M. (2008) 'Wicked spell or magic bullet? A review of the clinical supervision literature 2001–7', *Nurse Education Today* 28(3): 264–72.

Carthy, J. Noak, J. and Wadey, E. (2012) 'Clinical supervision in a high secure hospital', *British Journal of Mental Health* 1(1): 24–32.

Cheater, F. M. and Hale, C. (2001) 'An evaluation of a local clinical supervision scheme for practice nurses', *Journal of Clinical Nursing* 10(1): 119–31.

Coffey, M. and Coleman, M. (2001) 'The relationship between support and stress in forensic community mental health nursing', *Journal of Advanced Nursing* 34(3): 397–407.

Cottrell, S. (2002) 'Suspicion, resistance, tokenism and mutiny: problematic dynamics relevant to the implementation of clinical supervision in nursing', *Journal of Psychiatric and Mental Health Nursing* 9(6): 667–71.

Cutcliffe, J. R. and Hyrkäs, K. (2006) 'Multidisciplinary attitudinal positions regarding clinical supervision: a cross–sectional study', *Journal of Nursing Management* 14(8): 617–27.

Cutcliffe, J. R. and Lowe, L. (2005) 'A comparison of North American and European conceptualizations of clinical supervision', *Issues in Mental Health Nursing* 26(5): 475–88.

Davies, E. J., Tennant, A., Ferguson, E. and Jones, L. (2004) 'Developing models and a framework for multi-professional clinical supervision', *The British Journal of Forensic Practice* 6(3): 36–42.

Davies, J. and Tennant, A. (2003) 'Dangerous and Severe Personality Disorder (DSPD). Integrating education, training, teamwork and supervision', *Issues in Forensic Psychology* 86–96.

Davies, J., Maggs, R. G. and Lewis, R. (2010) 'The development of a UK low secure service: philosophy, training, supervision and evaluation', *International Journal of Forensic Mental Health* 9(4): 334–42.

Day, A. (2012) 'The nature of supervision in forensic psychology: some observations and recommendations', *The British Journal of Forensic Practice* 14(2): 116–23.

Falender, C. A. (2014) 'Clinical supervision in a competency-based era', *South African Journal of Psychology* 44(1): 6–17.

Fowler, J. (1996) 'The organization of clinical supervision within the nursing profession: a review of the literature', *Journal of Advanced Nursing* 23(3): 471–78.

Freshwater, D., Walsh, L. and Storey, L. (2002) 'Prison health care: developing leadership through clinical supervision', *Nursing Management – Harrow* 8(9): 16–20.

Hair, H. J. (2013) 'The purpose and duration of supervision, and the training and discipline of supervisors: what social workers say they need to provide effective services', *British Journal of Social Work* 43(8): 1562–88.

Hawkins, P. and Shohet, R. (2006) *Supervision in the Helping Professions* (3rd edn), Buckingham: Open University Press.

Hyrkäs, K., Appelqvist-Schmidlechner, K. and Haataja, R. (2006) 'Efficacy of clinical supervision: influence on job satisfaction, burnout and quality of care', *Journal of Advanced Nursing* 55(4): 521–35.

Hyrkäs, K., Lehti, K. and Paunonen Ilmonen, M. (2001) 'Cost–benefit analysis of team supervision: the development of an innovative model and its application as a case study in one Finnish University Hospital', *Journal of Nursing Management* 9(5): 259–68.

Jenkins, E. (2000) 'Clinical supervision: what is going on in West Wales? Results of a telephone survey', *Journal of Research in Nursing* 5(1): 21–36.

Jones, A. (2006) 'Clinical supervision: what do we know and what do we need to know? A review and commentary', *Journal of Nursing Management* 14(8): 577–85.

Kenny, A. and Allenby, A. (2013) 'Implementing clinical supervision for Australian rural nurses', *Nurse Education in Practice* 13(3): 165–9.

Long, C. G., Harding, S., Payne, K. and Collins, L. (2013) 'Nursing and health-care assistant experience of supervision in a medium secure psychiatric service for women: implications for service development', *Journal of Psychiatric and Mental Health Nursing* 21(2): 154–62.

Lynch, L. and Happell, B. (2008) 'Implementation of clinical supervision in action: Part 3: The development of a model', *International Journal of Mental Health Nursing* 17(1): 73–82.

Manthorpe, J., Moriarty, J., Hussein, S., Stevens, M. and Sharpe, E. (2013) 'Content and purpose of supervision in social work practice in England: views of newly qualified social workers, managers and directors', *British Journal of Social Work*, available at http://bjsw.oxfordjournals.org/content/early/2013/06/03/bjsw.bct102.abstract.

Mothersole, G. (2000) 'Clinical supervision and forensic work', *Journal of Sexual Aggression* 5(1): 45–58.

Paget, T. (2001) 'Reflective practice and clinical outcomes: practitioners' views on how reflective practice has influenced their clinical practice', *Journal of Clinical Nursing* 10(2): 204–14.

Scanlon, C. and Weir, W. S. (1997) 'Learning from practice? Mental health nurses' perceptions and experiences of clinical supervision', *Journal of Advanced Nursing* 26(2): 295–303.

Sloan, G. (1999) 'Understanding clinical supervision from a nursing perspective', *British Journal of Nursing* 8: 524–9.

Teasdale, K., Brocklehurst, N. and Thom, N. (2001) 'Clinical supervision and support for nurses: an evaluation study', *Journal of Advanced Nursing* 33(2): 216–24.

White, E. and Winstanley, J. (2012) 'Clinical supervision for mental health professionals', *Social Work and Social Sciences Review* 14(3): 77–94.

White, E., Butterworth, T., Bishop, V., Carson, J., Jeacock, J. and Clements, A. (1998) 'Clinical supervision: insider reports of a private world', *Journal of Advanced Nursing* 28(1): 185–92.

Winstanley, J. and White, E. (2003) 'Clinical supervision: models, measures and best practice', *Nurse Researcher* 10(4): 7–38.

——(2011) 'The MCSS-26©: Revision of the Manchester Clinical Supervision Scale© using the Rasch Measurement Model', *Journal of Nursing Measurement* 19(3): 160–78.

10 Supervisor and supervisee training and development

Many of the qualities and tasks demonstrated in effective supervision overlap with those of an effective forensic practitioner, therapist, educator, leader or manager. However, these roles are discrete which leads to the question of how best to support and develop people to undertake the supervisor role. In common with many leadership and management roles, individuals often take on supervising others because of their position within an organisation rather than through specific training or expertise. Thus, it is relatively common in practice settings for supervisors to be experienced practitioners but not necessarily to possess specific training, skills or knowledge in supervision. In spite of this common approach, many authors and researchers have advocated training for both the supervisor (e.g. Davies, 2008; Hair, 2013; Hyrkäs, Koivula and Paunonen, 1999; Landmark *et al.*, 2003) and the supervisee (e.g. Cutcliffe and Proctor, 1998a, 1998b). As with supervision practice within forensic settings, to date supervisor training has been a significant area of neglect. This chapter will focus on the reasons for investing in supervisee and supervisor training and development and provides an example outline of a training programme for forensic practitioners. First, however, it is important to consider the routes to becoming a supervisor which are commonly found in practice settings.

Supervisor development paradigms

There are four broad approaches to supervisor development, namely natural progression, self-directed learning, taught programmes and a hybrid approach.

The natural progression

In many organisations, people become supervisors because of their experience of 'doing the job they are supervising' or because of their place in the organisational hierarchy. This could be thought of as a 'master craftsman' or 'shop-floor supervisor' approach to the role. In the natural progression approach, the supervision of staff is viewed just as any other task the supervisor undertakes. The advantages of this approach are that the supervisor has 'time served' in the role being supervised and therefore usually possesses relevant knowledge and skill about the supervisee's job role. This approach can also be cost-efficient, as it doesn't require any 'time out' for specific supervision training or development. It also has an aspect of equity in that all staff of a particular level or grade can adopt the supervision role. However, there are a number of possible limitations and disadvantages of this approach. These include the assumption that doing the job is the same as supervising others who are doing the job and that those who are 'good' at doing the job will be 'good' at supervising others. Falender (2014) states that supervision training is essential as it cannot be assumed that because someone is competent and knowledgeable in their area of practice they will be competent in supervising others. In a similar vein, Hair (2013) states that training is necessary to be effective as a supervisor, as experience 'on the job' is not sufficient. This approach also neglects the fact that supervision is generally broader than 'task completion' and therefore doesn't support the supervisor in addressing the range of functions within supervision. Finally, it assumes that there is no requirement for the range of supervision specific skills or knowledge as outlined in this book.

Self-directed learning

Although self-directed learning is likely to be a feature of both the taught programme and hybrid options below, it is also a discrete approach to development in itself. This approach is led by the interest and motivation of the individual and is likely to include reading (e.g. texts such as this) and possibly developing skills and knowledge through receiving supervision. This approach often follows from the natural progression approach above – someone takes on the role of supervisor and decides that they would benefit from additional knowledge and skill. There are several advantages to this approach including its cost-efficiency and that it leads to a very bespoke and individualised training for the supervisor. However, the downsides include the potential to become swamped with information or to be isolated in developing supervision skill and knowledge.

The taught course model

Some authors argue for the need for postgraduate education programmes for supervisors (e.g. Landmark et al., 2003) and many professional bodies and employing organisations provide some form of training course for those undertaking the supervisor role. These range from one day 'in-house' 'educational' events; through short courses (e.g. 2–5 days of training) run either 'in-house' or by professional bodies or universities, through to university based modules and postgraduate courses. Some of these will qualify the individual to membership of a professional register (e.g. the Register of Applied Psychology Practice Supervisors run by the British Psychological Society). The underpinning assumption is that developing supervision knowledge and skill will positively impact on supervisor performance and thus the supervisee experience of supervision and ultimately their outcomes. The advantages of taught programmes include that they focus attention onto the specific features of supervision and specifically the skills and knowledge associated with these, and that they can be relatively cheap (especially one day 'in-house' courses). However, their disadvantages include potentially limiting the availability of supervisors (e.g. if training isn't available or can't be easily accessed by would-be supervisors) and the assumption (especially on the shorter courses) that 'teaching' knowledge will translate into skill.

The hybrid model

The hybrid model is commonly found in the longer courses in supervision (e.g. a 15-week university module as described by Rafferty and Coleman, 1996, and a postgraduate diploma provided by Sheffield University, n.d.) and combines a variety of learning and development methods such as formal teaching, self-directed learning and skills practice under supervision. This enables the developing supervisor to obtain feedback in a number of ways in order to build competence. Such approaches may lead to formal accreditation with a body (e.g. accredited supervisor with the British Association for Behavioural and Cognitive Psychotherapies). The advantages of this model are that it is comprehensive and enables supervisors to develop and demonstrate competence, however this approach tends to be more expensive both in course fees and staff time.

Why bother with training and development?

Having outlined the options for supervision training and development, it is necessary to consider why any formal process may be worth investing in. It is widely acknowledged that 'supervision is a complex undertaking ... requiring the acquisition of skills and competencies to make it work effectively' (Jones, 2006, p. 579) and can be considered to be 'a task which requires training, accrediting, on-going support and continual development' (Davies, Salmon and MacDonald, 2000, p. 19). Kilminster and Jolly (2000), report that the need for training in relation to supervision is well supported. In addition to these general arguments, supervisees want to be supervised by someone who is skilled in this task, and training may assist with this. For example, studies have found that supervisors who were trained were evaluated more highly than their non-trained counterparts (Hyrkäs, Appelqvist-Schmidlechner and Haataja, 2006). Arguments are also made from the supervisor perspective; Landmark et al. (2003) found that supervisors reported needing education and development for their role facilitating reflective practice. It is also important to consider that some individuals providing supervision to others are not very effective or responsive or are less effective than they could be. This observation, however, has individual implications (i.e. someone not being deployed as a supervisor) and organisational implications (e.g. not sufficient supervisors for the staff group). Taylor et al. (2012) showed that supervisor self-assessment of supervisory competence increased over time which they suggest could have stemmed from the five-day supervisor training they introduced.

Training might also be important where research or evaluation is to be undertaken into supervision. For example, in a number of published studies there is no mention of the training received by supervisors, their approach to supervision or the quality of the supervisor. Training may provide a way of ensuring a minimum level of competence amongst the supervisors in any study.

What do we know about providing supervision training?

It is 20 years since Russell and Petrie (1995) reported that little attention had been given to supervisor training, however this remains the case especially in the field of forensic practice. The role of the supervisor largely continues to be one that is acquired by default with skills being acquired through the supervisor's own experiences of supervision or just through being 'thrown in at the deep end' (the natural progression and self-directed learning approaches above). This inevitably results in a hit-and-miss approach to supervision provision which is likely to do a disservice to those being supervised and fails to recognise the role of supervision as a learning, reflection and development tool. Even in professional training courses, supervision skills may not be included. For example, a survey of supervision training within clinical and counselling psychology programs in the US found that there was a paucity of information about the nature and impact of training in supervision and different views on how best to deliver training even though there was general support that training was needed (Scott et al., 2000). In their study, less than a third of the programmes mandated training usually because there was no space in the curriculum. This observation has also been made in relation to nurse training where training for supervisees was advocated as an alternative (see Cutcliffe and Proctor, 1998a, 1998b). Scott et al. (2000) also found that where supervision was taught, at least one-fifth of the programmes didn't undertake any form of assessment of supervision knowledge, skills or competence.

There is little guidance as to how best to approach training. From a pragmatic standpoint it is likely that extended training (possibly at postgraduate level) is necessary for those who will be developing and delivering a supervision strategy within an organisation, with shorter training provided to others as appropriate. However, it is worth noting that in the supervision studies reported by Hyrkäs et al. (1999) supervisors appeared to have received post-registration training in supervision ranging from 2–4 years, whilst participants in Hair's (2013) study suggested that a one year training was necessary. Cutcliffe and Proctor (1998a) observed that focusing training on supervisors requires that there is a culture of wanting to engage in supervision and thus training students to be supervisees may be more productive and provides a foundation for future supervisor training. They also note the cost to the organisation of releasing staff and questions whether brief training (e.g. 1–3 days) is enough.

Providing training and development

Training supervisees

Training supervisees may seem an unusual concept, however Cutcliffe and Proctor (1998b) make a strong case for the training of supervisees as part of core professional training (in their paper they focus on nursing specifically). They suggest that training supervisees brings with it numerous potential benefits including:

(a) empowering supervisees, which can result in a shift from passive recipient to adult learner with a say over their development and supervision;
(b) enabling some sharing of responsibility;
(c) underscoring that supervision is for the supervisee and their work;
(d) greater equality in the supervisory relationship and therefore more ownership of their supervision;
(e) building a foundation for openness and honesty (and later supervisor training);
(f) giving explicit recognition to the 'impact of emotionally charged experiences'; and
(g) increasing awareness of benefits and shared values, ground rules, goals etc.

It would appear that these benefits could be easily applied to all supervisees. Thus providing training in some of the key aspects of supervision may help to ensure that supervisees are aware and skilled participants in supervision, empowered to ensure that supervision meets their needs and develops practice. Chapters 3, 4 and 6 are useful starting points for this. Cutcliffe and Proctor (1998b) suggest that for students or trainees, supervisee training should be in the form of education followed by experience which is then consolidated through course work. This 'knowledge then experience' approach could be easily adopted for 'in-house' training.

Training supervisors

As shown throughout this book, there are a broad range of knowledge, skills and competencies associated with supervision. However, when considering supervisor development it is important to consider what is being aimed for. Whilst everyone might have a notion of a 'perfect supervisor', what is most likely to be needed is a 'good enough' supervision experience within which an individual can develop, benchmark their practice, recharge their batteries and deliver effective and efficient services.

Supervisors are likely to go through a process of development over time. For example, Russell and Petrie (1995) suggest that supervisors move from self-conscious and anxious to integrated and secure. Others have also argued that there is a need to attend to the level of development of both supervisor and supervisee in order to ensure appropriate 'matching' (e.g. Davies et al., 2004). However, it may also be that training needs are also influenced by developmental level – it may be that foundation and more advanced training are appropriate for supervisors with different levels of experience.

Mor Barak and colleagues (Mor Barak et al., 2009) argue for supervisors to be trained in three supervisory dimensions, namely: task assistance; social and emotional support; and supervisory interpersonal interaction. As shown in Figure 4.1 (Chapter 4), these, and the additional function of the administrative (normative) aspects of supervision, form a solid foundation for what supervision needs to provide. Others have also argued for supervisors to be trained in alliance management principles (Bambling et al., 2006), as supervision requires the establishment of a good relationship between supervisee and supervisor (Falender, 2014). Furthermore, supervision training is necessary to ensure that 'supervisors have a knowledge of and sensitivity to the interpersonal processes that can occur between individuals and groups and may impede the therapeutic nature of patient-nurse, supervisor-supervisee and collegial relationships' (Ayer et al., 1997). Where supervision is to be facilitated in a group format, supervisors will also need to have knowledge and skills in group dynamics (Cleary and Freeman, 2005). As noted by Fowler (1996), supervisor training may also need to explicitly facilitate the transfer of skills from other settings and areas of practice to supervision. However, this skills transfer should be careful not to unintentionally promote the idea of supervision as just like another process, e.g. patient care or therapy (see natural progression above). Falender et al. (2004) identify four areas of supervision competence, namely:

(1) knowledge – this concerns what needs to be known and understood and might include supervision specific knowledge (e.g. supervision models), or profession, role and organisation knowledge (e.g. how to perform a specific task that the supervisee needs to undertake);
(2) skills – this covers a range of abilities that the supervisor needs in order to provide effective supervision (e.g. the ability to form a supervisory relationship; the ability to provide constructive feedback);
(3) values – this relates to the approach of the supervisor towards the supervisee, the task of supervision and the work being undertaken by the supervisee (e.g. being respectful and empowering; being sensitive to diversity; recognising one's own limits); and
(4) social context – this addresses a broad range of elements such as ethical and legal issues; understanding and using developmental processes.

Carefully designed training programmes would be expected to lead to enhanced supervisory skills, knowledge and competence.

What to include in training – building on the broad ideas above, it is possible to provide a more detailed description of supervision training. Ideally, supervision training should include training in supervision models, an understanding of the research and the evidence base and ethics (Russell and Petrie, 1995). Falender (2014) describes a number of competencies that are required in supervision, these include the ability to establish a supervisory relationship, competence in technology in supervision, competence in managing roles and responsibilities and competence in relation to diversity. Within forensic settings, Davies (2008) has provided a possible training outline that could be delivered in a range of formats from a one-day introduction through to a postgraduate university course, depending on the depth and breadth of coverage. In addition, Roth and Pilling (n.d.) present a framework of supervision competencies developed as part of the Improving Access to Psychological Therapies initiative in England (UK). In the framework, the authors identify four sets of competency: (1) 'generic supervision competencies' (e.g. forming a good supervisory alliance); (2) 'specific supervision competencies' (e.g. conducting supervision in group formats); (3) 'application of supervision to specific models or contexts' (e.g. supervision of Cognitive Behavioural Therapy); and (4) 'meta-competencies' (e.g. applying professional judgement). A possible outline for supervision training in forensic settings is provided in Box 10.1.

> **BOX 10.1 Supervision training programme outline (based on Davies, 2008; Falender, 2014; Falender *et al.*, 2004; Roth and Pilling, n.d.; Scaife, 2013)**
>
> Despite the absence of published competencies for providing supervision in forensic settings, it is possible to distil from the literature a number of elements that are likely to prove useful for equipping would-be supervisors. In many ways the chapters and special topics of this book provide the basis for a training programme.
>
> Many of these areas of knowledge, skill and competence could be delivered to both supervisee and supervisor, however the level of detail and precise content may well differ. A training programme for forensic practice supervision should include (in no particular order):
>
> *An overview of supervision* – this needs to include a definition of supervision, and outline of the rationale for practice supervision in a forensic context, and the relevant research evidence.
> *The supervision relationship* – this should explore the central importance of the relationship as the foundation for the task of supervision and outline the supervisor and supervisee factors which can help build and maintain an effective supervision relationship.
> *Types of supervision* – this should provide an outline of the ways in which supervision can be delivered (e.g. expert, group, individual) along with their strengths and limitations.
> *Core supervision skills* – this needs to cover elements such as the supervision agreement, using agendas and record keeping.

> *Supervisee skills* – this should provide guidance on supervisee induction, preparing for supervision and presenting work in supervision.
> *Learning, reflection and creativity* – this should explore different learning styles and how these can be harnessed in supervision; approaches to reflection and how this links to learning and development, and the use of creative approaches in supervision (e.g. Lahad, 2000). This might also include a focus on using your own supervision/supervision of supervision.
> *Successes and good practice* – this deserves specific attention as without it supervision can easily be drawn into a troubleshooting arena and a forum for focusing solely on difficulties.
> *Safe practice* – this should include a focus on risk issues and boundary maintenance/violations.
> *Ethical issues in supervision* – this should include identifying ethical issues and ways to approach/address them.
> *Difficulties, (constructive) challenge and feedback* – this should include approaches to providing and receiving regular feedback. It should also explore common difficulties and how these might be resolved.
> *Audit and evaluation in supervision* – this should outline any local approaches to supervision as well as provide guidance on evaluating supervision practice.
>
> Roles and responsibilities in relation to students and trainees (e.g. student assessment) should be the responsibility of training organisations, and would need to suppliment the above.
>
> Source: some small parts of the above text originally appeared in J. Davies (2008), 'Supervision in forensic psychology practice: Issues for supervisor development'.
> *Forensic Update* 95: 42–5.

How to deliver training – formal courses in supervision should comprise didactic, experiential and coursework elements (Russell and Petrie, 1995), whilst in-house training should, where possible, combine teaching with practice elements. With in-house training, careful consideration should be given to the overall training process, policies, core texts or a handbook and supervisor recognition or 'accreditation' (Davies et al., 2004). Falender (2014) proposes a sequence for supervisor training comprising of (a) developing competence as a supervisee; (b) formalised training in supervision; (c) providing supervision to a peer or a less experienced colleague (with supervision for this to support skills development); leading to (d) formal assessment of supervision competence. In addition, 'meta-competence' (i.e. identifying what you don't know; i.e. your deaf, dumb, blind and numb spots) needs to be developed. This may require the use of audio or video recording of sessions in order to review what actually took place rather than relying on what can be recalled. Falender et al. (2004)

provide guidance on how supervision competence might be trained (e.g. coursework; supervision of supervision) and how competencies might be assessed (e.g. completion of a course; documented supervisee feedback; assessment of outcomes). As reported by many authors (e.g. Davies, 2008), supervisor training should be delivered in the context of supervision and on-going development for the supervisors and a local policy.

In most settings it will be necessary to develop a range of supervision training options ranging from introductory training for supervisors and supervisees through to access to advanced training such as a postgraduate university programme. It may be that a small number of individuals (perhaps those who will be responsible for developing, implementing or maintaining supervision across a workforce) are trained to an advanced level and it is these individuals who then provide 'in-house' training that is shorter in duration. Consideration needs to be given to how competence etc. will be assessed.

Supervising the supervisors

Whilst training may be necessary in order to equip supervisors, skilled practice is likely to only be achieved and maintained if the supervisors themselves receive supervision for this area of practice. Azar (2000) argues that supervision of supervision should be sought, and in a survey of accredited counsellors and accredited counsellor supervisors, Wheeler and King (2000) found that most individuals found supervision of supervision 'helpful, important and necessary'. Only 15 per cent of the respondents said they would not engage in this activity if they didn't have to. Half of the sample had the same supervisor for all of their work (including their supervision practice) and in such situations they reported that around a third of the time was focused on supervision of supervision. When examining what was taken to be supervision Wheeler and King (2000) found that ethical issues, boundaries, competence of their supervisees, training, agreements and the supervisee/client relationship (i.e. an aspect of the work of the supervisee) were common features. However, they also noted that it was possible that individuals brought their own dilemmas to their supervision of supervision disguised as those of a supervisee. As with all other forms of supervision, an agreement is important; as Wheeler and King (2000) note, there needs to be clarity about the accountability of the supervisor of the supervisor.

In her exploration of 'supervision of supervision', Power (2013) notes that (as with other supervisory relationships) the 'value of supervision is only as great as the two participants' ability to use it; key ingredients will be the supervisee's capacity to learn and the ability of the supervisor to support this'. Further, as with supervision more generally, it would appear that supervision of supervision needs an effective alliance upon which reflection and learning can take place. She spotlights the need for the 'consultant supervisor' to be aware of what is and isn't being presented for consideration. Thus in common with the work being supervised, 'blind, deaf, dumb and numb' spots may also be present in supervision of supervision (c.f. Gordon, Beckley and Lowings, 2010).

The developmental model by Stoltenberg and McNeill (2010) includes within it supervisor competence and development. This has implications for who might supervise who, and how the needs of a supervisor may be met through the supervision they receive. Their model also suggests that the supervisor pool at the highest level of skill and experience will be limited which may be very evident in a relatively new profession such as forensic psychology where the number of trainees is large relative to the number of practising members. Clearly, regular supervision of supervisory practice can serve a number of functions including supporting CPD, considering legal and ethical issues/dilemmas, building competence and overcoming barriers to and constraints on supervision. This can be facilitated by individuals providing self-report and bringing audio tapes of their supervisory practice for review and discussion, as well as through live review whereby a supervision session is observed by a more experienced supervisor in order to help shape practice and enhance learning. If we are to take a developmental stance in relation to supervision it may be that supervisors could (and maybe should) be accredited at different levels (Davies et al., 2000).

Conclusion

The need for training is likely to be high, whilst the availability of specialist training at basic and advanced levels is currently limited. However, there is growing consensus about the areas of competence relevant to supervision and the ways in which these might be developed. In order to develop high quality supervision, services will need to invest in training and development in this area. However, several professional organisations have already taken that step, so that over time, forensic services will have high quality supervision as part of their portfolio of staff support, training and development. Given the paucity of evidence relating to supervision in forensic settings, it is important that investment in training and the development of supervision practice is coupled with research to assess the impact of supervision training in forensic settings.

References

Ayer, S., Knight, S., Joyce, L. and Nightingale, V. (1997) 'Practice-led education and development project: developing styles in clinical supervision', *Nurse Education Today* 17 (5): 347–58.

Azar, S. T. (2000) 'Preventing burnout in professionals and paraprofessionals who work with child abuse and neglect cases: a cognitive behavioral approach to supervision', *Journal of Clinical Psychology* 56(5): 643–63.

Bambling, M., King, R., Raue, P., Schweitzer, R. and Lambert, W. (2006) 'Clinical supervision: its influence on client-rated working alliance and client symptom reduction in the brief treatment of major depression', *Psychotherapy Research* 16(3): 317–31.

Cleary, M. and Freeman, A. (2005) 'The cultural realities of clinical supervision in an acute inpatient mental health setting', *Issues in Mental Health Nursing* 26(5): 489–505.

Cutcliffe, J. R. and Proctor, B. (1998a) 'An alternative training approach to clinical supervision: 1', *British Journal of Nursing* 7(5): 280–5.

——(1998b) 'An alternative training approach to clinical supervision: 2', *British Journal of Nursing* 7(6): 346–50.

Davies, J. (2008) 'Supervision in forensic psychology practice: issues for supervisor development', *Forensic Update* 95: 42–5.

Davies, J., Salmon, A. and MacDonald, F. (2000) 'Supervision: what works for whom?', *Clinical Psychology Forum* 146: 17–20.

Davies, J., Tennant, A., Ferguson, E. and Jones, L. (2004) 'Developing models and a framework for multi-professional clinical supervision', *The British Journal of Forensic Practice* 6(3): 36–42.

Falender, C. A. (2014) 'Clinical supervision in a competency-based era', *South African Journal of Psychology* 44(1): 6–17.

Falender, C. A., Cornish, J. A. E., Goodyear, R., Hatcher, R., Kaslow, N. J., Leventhal, G., et al. (2004) 'Defining competencies in psychology supervision: a consensus statement', *Journal of Clinical Psychology* 60(7): 771–85.

Fowler, J. (1996) 'The organization of clinical supervision within the nursing profession: a review of the literature', *Journal of Advanced Nursing* 23(3): 471–8.

Gordon, N., Beckley, K. and Lowings, G. (2010) 'Therapists' Experiences of Therapy', in N. Gordon and P. Willmot (eds), *Working Positively with Personality Disorder in Secure Settings: A practitioner's perspecitve*, Oxford: Wiley & Sons.

Hair, H. J. (2013) 'The purpose and duration of supervision, and the training and discipline of supervisors: what social workers say they need to provide effective services', *British Journal of Social Work* 43(8): 1562–88.

Hyrkäs, K., Appelqvist-Schmidlechner, K. and Haataja, R. (2006) 'Efficacy of clinical supervision: influence on job satisfaction, burnout and quality of care', *Journal of Advanced Nursing* 55(4): 521–35.

Hyrkäs, K., Koivula, M. and Paunonen, M. (1999) 'Clinical supervision in nursing in the 1990s – current state of concepts, theory and research', *Journal of Nursing Management* 7(3): 177.

Jones, A. (2006) 'Clinical supervision: what do we know and what do we need to know? A review and commentary', *Journal of Nursing Management* 14(8): 577–85.

Kilminster, S. M. and Jolly, B. C. (2000) 'Effective supervision in clinical practice settings: a literature review', *Medical Education* 34(10): 827–40.

Landmark, B. T., Hansen, G. S., Bjones, I. and Bøhler, A. (2003) 'Clinical supervision – factors defined by nurses as influential upon the development of competence and skills in supervision', *Journal of Clinical Nursing* 12(6): 834–41.

Mor Barak, M. E., Travis, D. J., Pyun, H. and Xie, B. (2009) 'The impact of supervision on worker outcomes: a meta-analysis', *Social Service Review* 83(1): 3–32.

Power, A. (2013) 'Supervision of supervision: how many mirrors do we need?', *British Journal of Psychotherapy* 29(3): 389–404.

Rafferty, M. and Coleman, M. (1996) 'Educating nurses to undertake clinical supervision in practice', *Nursing Standard (Royal College of Nursing (Great Britain): 1987)* 10(45): 38–41.

Roth, A. and Pilling, S. (n.d.) 'A competence framework for the supervision of psychological therapies', retrieved 13 May 2014, from www.ucl.ac.uk/clinical-psychology/CORE/supervision_framework.htm#Description.

Russell, R. K. and Petrie, T. (1995) 'Issues in training effective supervisors', *Applied and Preventive Psychology* 3(1): 27–42.

Scaife, J. (2013) *Supervision in Clinical Practice*, Abingdon: Routledge.

Scott, K. J., Ingram, K. M., Vitanza, S. A. and Smith, N. G. (2000) 'Training in supervision: a survey of current practices', *The Counseling Psychologist* 28(3): 403–22.

Stoltenberg, C. D. and McNeill, B. W. (2010) *IDM Supervision* (3rd edn), Abingdon: Routledge.

Taylor, K. N., Gordon, K., Grist, S. and Olding, C. (2012) 'Developing supervisory competence: preliminary data on the impact of CBT supervision training', *The Cognitive Behaviour Therapist* 5(04): 83–92.

University of Sheffield (n.d.) 'PG Cert – Postgraduate Diploma Clinical Supervision – Courses – Clinical Psychology Unit – The University of Sheffield', retrieved 14 May 2014, from www.shef.ac.uk/clinicalpsychology/programmes/clinicalsup/intro.

Wheeler, S. and King, D. (2000) 'Do counselling supervisors want or need to have their supervision supervised? An exploratory study', *British Journal of Guidance and Counselling* 28(2): 279–90.

Special topics

This section addresses 10 topics in a series of short self-contained chapters. In this way, the contents of this section could be likened to a quick reference guide. The special topics covered are:

1. The impact of the setting on supervision
2. Ethical issues
3. Supervising group work
4. Supervising non-client work
5. Critiques of supervision and reflective practice
6. Overcoming problems in supervision
7. Creative approaches to supervision
8. Assessments and measures for use in supervision and research
9. Team supervision
10. Reflective practice

Special Topic 1
The impact of the setting on supervision

The setting within which forensic practice and thus forensic supervision takes place can impact on the work being done and have numerous implications for supervision. The purpose of this special topic is to highlight the importance of the setting and to alert the reader to the need to consider the context routinely within supervision. It is beyond the scope of this discussion to identify each setting and the likely impact on supervision, rather it is hoped that the brief discussion here will enable the supervisor and supervisee to view their setting afresh with attention to the ways in which it both frames and influences practitioners and supervision.

The setting provides the context within which the practitioner practices and, as we have seen in The Process Model of Supervision (Hawkins and Shohet, 2006), the context is worthy of attention in its own right. The setting might well influence directly and indirectly such factors as the attitudes, actions and interactions of those within it. This may include setting limits on practice or giving rise to specific issues. The setting also defines the parameters of the clients who are placed within it. This might include the gender, age and common needs of the clients. For example, adult offenders may be in a prison, community or hospital setting and each of these will exert specific influences on expectations and daily life. Further, the setting is likely to give rise to specific clusters of clients (e.g. by offence type, level of risk, presenting mental health problem) which may result in practitioners becoming specialist in some areas of practice. However, this strength may also be accompanied by limitations on the practitioner and, more importantly, within the workforce. This can include being blind to certain events or having limited responses or options when things outside the norm take place. The context also influences the policies and procedures of the setting. For example, the balance between physical security, procedural security and relational security will be setting dependent. Ethical issues are also likely to be impacted upon by the setting.

The setting might also have a direct impact on the practitioner; for example, some settings may be more inherently stressful than others or may have differing effects on the worker. By way of example, Butterworth *et al.*, (1999) found that staff working in community settings found their work more emotionally draining than their hospital colleagues although they reported less depersonalisation (a cynical and detached response). Therefore, it is worth considering the possibility of 'setting effects' when supervising staff or when transferring research findings from one setting to another.

The following three setting examples provide observations about some of the specific influences that may be associated with each. It is not intended to be exhaustive but to provide some illustrative accounts which might become the basis for discussions between supervisor and supervisee in relation to the setting and context in which the supervisee works.

Example setting 1 – a forensic mental health inpatient service

The supervisor needs to be attentive to such issues as:

- practitioners within such services becoming highly experienced at working with specific types of need and therefore pushing the client to fit with expectations or becoming less familiar or skilful at working with other presenting difficulties;
- practitioners may focus on health issues and lose sight of key risk factors associated with the client;
- practitioners may take on multiple roles with clients increasing the likelihood for problematic dual roles and boundary crossings to take place; and
- many practitioners (often those with a great deal of direct client contact) have no professional body or formal training and are often not prioritised to engage in supervision.

Example setting 2 – a probation service

The supervisor needs to be attentive to such issues as:

- the challenge of balancing the functions of monitoring the individual with providing support and sometimes treatment and the conflicting messages this can send to the client;
- the risk associated with 'lone working' sometimes undertaken and the possibility of 'numbing' or 'complacency' to personal risk over time;
- the discretion given to the practitioner and how this is used by them in a fair and appropriate way; and
- the practitioner being aware of the multiple issues outside the focus of probation (e.g. inadequate housing, poor job prospects) leading the practitioner to feel disempowered or despondent.

Example setting 3 – a child secure care unit

The supervisor needs to be attentive to such issues as:

- the short duration of stay for many of those placed within such units limiting the work that can be engaged in;

- the multiple interpersonal challenges (and attachment issues) such as peer influence, the possible dislocation from family and friends and a possible history of time in care frequently faced by the young people within the service. There is also the possibility of the practitioner experiencing transference (i.e. the young person engaging with them as they would have engaged with their mother for example) – the practitioner's ability to manage this is critical;
- the emotional distress of many clients and the impact of this on the practitioner including the potential for the practitioner to be drawn into 'trying to rescue' some individuals; and
- the developmental and educational needs of the individuals and how the practitioner ensures that they engage with the individual in ways that are consistent with their cognitive and emotional development.

Conclusion

This special topic has tried to cue the reader into the complex nature of the setting and the need for it to be given attention within the supervision context. It is essential that the supervisor and supervisee remain aware of the influence of the setting and regularly consider the impact it has on supervision and the practitioners' role. A useful question to ask is: 'if this was taking place in [a different setting] what would be different?'

References

Butterworth, T., Carson, J., Jeacock, J., White, E. and Clements, A. (1999) 'Stress, coping, burnout and job satisfaction in British nurses: findings from the clinical supervision evaluation project', *Stress medicine* 15(1): 27–33.

Hawkins, P. and Shohet, R. (2006) *Supervision in the Helping Professions* (3rd edn), Buckingham: Open University Press.

Special Topic 2
Ethical issues

Supervision within forensic practice will often need to consider and address complex ethical and legal issues. In non-forensic settings, Johns (1993) noted that many experiences brought to supervision have ethical and decision-making components and this is certainly true for forensic practice. However, as with many other areas of forensic practice, there are very few issues for which there are clear and scripted solutions. Rather, the approach to addressing difficulties and concerns within supervision will generally rely on adopting a framework within which such questions and dilemmas can be considered. Many of the ethical issues presented in forensic settings arise because of the tensions created through competing and sometimes conflicting expectations. These might relate to tensions between the responsibility to the client, the profession, the setting and society and associated conflicts in roles and duties (e.g. Bonner, 2006). It is also important to recognise that some tensions and difficulties might arise because 'services provided in one value system could potentially be interpreted differently by another' (Haag, 2006, p. 95) even though a common set of ethical principles should close this gap (Ward and Syversen, 2009). It must be acknowledged that in forensic settings, there are numerous power differentials and clients who are vulnerable in multiple ways. There may also be multiple issues of difference (including cultural and racial factors) which may further add to the possible complexity of everyday situations.

Ethical supervision

The notion of ethical supervision is used to capture the need for the supervisor to consider the ethical dimension of the work that takes place within supervision and the work conducted by the supervisee. In this regard, the ethical framework outlined here should apply as equally to the supervisee's experience of supervision as it does to the work of the supervisee in their job role. Within supervision this should include understanding relevant ethical codes, applying this knowledge and appropriate skills and modelling by the supervisor (Bernard and Goodyear, 2014). Newman (1981), writing about the supervision of psychotherapists, identified ten ethical questions concerning the supervisory relationship and process. These provide a starting point for considering ethical issues and to give ethics a substantive place within the supervision experience as suggested by the 'normative' function within the Proctor (1986) model (see Chapter 4):

(a) Is the supervisor qualified to supervise?
(b) Does the supervisor accept the responsibilities associated with the functions and roles?
(c) Have the supervisee's interests been considered?
(d) Has the particular pairing of supervisor and supervisee been considered?
(e) Have the goals of supervision been adequately considered?
(f) Has the choice of supervisory methods been considered?
(g) Have the limits of confidentiality been specified?
(h) Have the supervisor's expectations been considered?
(i) Has student/trainee progress been evaluated?
(j) Has the adequacy of supervision been evaluated?

Considering ethical issues more broadly, there are multiple ways in which this can be approached. In this special topic two steps will be taken – the first is to identify 'ethical expectations', i.e. common behaviours and expectations in forensic settings, the second is to outline a framework for considering ethical issues.

Ethical expectations

Ethical practice is a requirement of professionals and is typically described within professional codes and regulations. However, these tend to be profession specific and do not cover the many practitioners in forensic settings who do not have an identified profession to which they belong (e.g. health care support practitioners).

From the commonalities within professional ethical codes, and from features of professional competence (e.g. Bernard and Goodyear, 2014; Bonner, 2006; Haag, 2006; Overholser and Fine, 1990; Ward and Syversen, 2009; Wosket and Page, 1994), it is possible to identify a number of qualities, competencies and approaches to work that form a core of ethical expectations. Typically these are described in relation to work with clients, however they are equally relevant to supervision:

(a) *Beneficence* – striving to benefit clients and the associated idea of *non-maleficence*, i.e. not causing harm; within supervision these relate also to the supervisor's treatment of the supervisee.
(b) *Dignity and respect* – showing respect for the worth of all people and their right to *privacy* and *confidentiality*. Within supervision these would also include confidentiality regarding supervisee information and what they share/disclose and the management of client information. It also requires that the client understands that their contact with the practitioner will be subject to supervision.

(c) *Autonomy and self-determination (choice)* – this includes the notion of *informed consent* (making a free choice based on adequate information), and in the context of supervision this relates to the supervisee's choice to make decisions (e.g. to participate in a role play or reflection).
(d) *Maintaining competence* – including competence in relation to ethical practice and for supervisors in relation to supervision practice. This will include *'fitness' to practice*, i.e. being aware of any factors which may (temporarily) impair one's ability to engage in (ethical) practice.
(e) *Practice within the scope of their training and expertise* – although self-explanatory, within supervision this applies to both supervisor and supervisee actions and behaviours.
(f) *Maintaining appropriate boundaries (avoiding boundary violations) and managing dual relationships* – this is discussed in more detail in Chapter 8.
(g) *Fidelity and responsibility* – which would include honouring agreements (e.g. need for confidentiality, ground rules and boundaries), the ability to establish trusting relationships and manage conflicts of interest. It might also include dual roles and business relationships especially where the supervision arrangements involve a private contract.
(h) *Due process* – having procedures that use fair criteria and warn of situations which might give rise to a right being removed; within supervision this might concern placement failure – due process would require that the supervisee was aware of the expectations and had been given warning and opportunity to address failings (a supervision agreement should contain role information, expectations, goals and consent information relevant to this).
(i) *Integrity* – this concerns accuracy, honesty and truthfulness; in supervision this requires that the supervisee present both positive and problematic aspects of their practice (including ethical and boundary issues) and the supervisor to provide honest and accurate feedback and information.
(j) *Justice* – respect for fairness and justice; in supervision attention to social responsibilities such as ensuring that ethical issues are attended to, prejudice is avoided and that there is a 'fair allocation of resources' to the supervisee.

However, it is important to be aware that each of these is itself complex – what are the bounds of confidentiality? who is the client? how voluntary is informed consent? (see Bernard and Goodyear, 2014; Haag, 2006, for thought-provoking descriptions of a number of such ethical dilemmas). Further, a stance which involves caution, scepticism and a general questioning of client motives (perhaps understandably common in forensic settings) can in themselves pose ethical challenges (Austin, 2001; Newman, 1981).

The term 'ethical blindness' has been used to describe the situation in which ethical issues are overlooked (Barnao, Robertson and Ward, 2012). These authors argue that this might occur because a code of practice doesn't cue the individual to see an ethical issue or when an individual becomes acculturated into a system that doesn't facilitate ethical awareness or discussion. Such blindness can lead to inappropriate action or inaction on the part of the practitioner. However, this blindness may also result from a process of desensitisation to the setting, the clients and the work being undertaken. As noted by Austin (2001), over time, situations, responses and practices can be accepted as normal and sight lost of the ethical and personal dimensions of each of these. Supervision therefore can be an important feature in the management of such processes.

Ethical dilemma frameworks: being ethical

Within supervision, a foundation for being ethical is being competent. In their paper concerning 'subtle cases of clinical incompetence', Overholser and Fine (1990) argue that professional competence is comprised of ability (knowing/having skill) and performance (deploying that ability) the latter of which they place on a continuum. Based on this they argue there are four possible 'sources' of incompetence each of which may be identified and sometimes remain (solely) within supervision:

(1) Incompetence due to lack of knowledge – can be readily evaluated and is likely to be defined by each profession. However, they note that knowledge can be obsolete within a decade and therefore professional training needs to instil lifelong learning and the ability to assess one's own competence regularly.
(2) Incompetence due to inadequate skill – this comprises a range of skills which may be generic (e.g. obtaining consent, responding to personal questions) or may be specific (e.g. not setting homework, failing to assess links between offences).
(3) Incompetence due to poor judgement – these are more sophisticated skills as they concern the appropriate selection and use of skills for a specific case or problem whilst taking account of contextual and other relevant factors (e.g. failure to apply a skilful response in a given situation).
(4) Incompetence due to disturbing interpersonal attributes – this focuses on the professionalism of the practitioner and may show itself in various ways (e.g. avoiding challenging a threatening client or establishing inappropriate boundaries with a client). In some respects this is the most challenging to address through supervision.

Overholser and Fine (1990) suggest that managing such problems should initially be through informal means where possible (in the case of supervision, this would be between the supervisor and the practitioner via such strategies as supportive confrontation); ongoing training and knowledge re ethical codes. However, their approach to managing incompetence assumes an openness to learning and reflection on the part of the supervisee and a timely and skilful response on the part of the supervisor to avoid collusion or omission.

Being ethical is founded on being competent and being able to weigh up information to act in a way that meets ethical expectations. One readily accessible framework for this is provided by Austin (2001) who describes the use of 'relational ethics' within a forensic psychiatric setting. This focuses on the interactions between the practitioner and the client and includes the core elements of engagement (e.g. showing interest and appropriate empathy and providing opportunity to engage); mutual respect (e.g. the demonstration of humanity and viewing the other's perspective) and attention to the environment (e.g. does the context and organisation facilitate ethical thinking and questioning). This latter aspect is important as Bonner (2006) warns of organisational and peer pressures which can result in a 'let it go' approach to ethical issues. In these situations, practitioners are discouraged from raising concerns or issues. Supervisors need to be aware of such processes if they are to help supervisees address possible issues within their own and others' practice. Further, Bonner (2006) advocates the administrative separation of mental health providers from custodial duties, however, whilst this may be possible (and desirable within a prison or correctional setting) it is generally not feasible within a forensic mental health setting or to extend the principles to many aspects of care and treatment within a probation setting. Indeed, some advocate that with very high risk offenders separating 'treatment staff' from 'custodial staff' can be the source of many problems and that the bringing together of treatment and corrections staff, not necessarily in the roles they carry out but in their attention to the differing tasks and functions can be vitally important (c.f. 'supportive authority', Jack Bush, personal communication).

Ward and Syversen (2009) provides a framework for ethical practice based on the central principles of human dignity and agency – the perspective that everyone has equal moral status and are accountable for their actions. Using this framework they show how dignity provides the 'conceptual glue' binding together the other principles of ethical practice (which they evidence through the examination of a professional code of ethics). Further, they argue that practitioners need to be encouraged to take a broader approach to ethics based on principles rather than rules to enable them to notice issues and problems that may have otherwise remained hidden. They also argue that practitioners shouldn't accept the values, rules and practices of the setting unquestioningly.

Many approaches to addressing ethical issues use some form of decision-making approach where the issue is identified and detailed, the context (including the setting, policies, legislation) is described, personal and professional values are discussed, possible plans and their consequences detailed, and an action is implemented and evaluated. For example, Barnao et al. (2012) suggest that solutions to ethical dilemmas should (a) generalise to others and (b) treat all involved with dignity. They present an 'Ethical Evaluation Guide' which is based on four clusters of questions concerning:

(a) Detection (e.g. what is the issue, what is the potential good or harm, what are the practitioner's duties, how does the system influence the issue).

(b) Dignity (e.g. whose dignity is (might be) affected and how, what is the individual's view).
(c) Equality (e.g. is equal consideration being given to all who are affected, what are the implications for others or potential future others).
(d) Generalisability (e.g. would the response being considered be the same for others such as those with similar needs but in other contexts).

Recognising ethical issues

Discussing practice will often lead to ethical issues being revealed, however there are a number of direct ways in which ethical issues might be signalled. These are outlined in Box ST2.1. These can also be used as questions by the supervisor to explore issues, e.g. how do you feel about your actions, your plan; what aspects of your practice are we not discussing today – is there anything we should be; what are you unsure about in your practice – anything you are concerned with?

> **BOX ST2.1: Spotting possible ethical dilemmas**
>
> Ethical dilemmas can show themselves in many ways, however there are a few indicators which supervisees should take as triggers to discuss an issue within supervision. These self-assessment prompts do not mean that you are definitely 'doing something wrong' but should be used as an indicator of a possible underlying ethical issue. Where these prompts are raised by activity within supervision, the supervisee and/or supervisor should discuss and seek outside consultation, supervision or advice.
>
> - What I'm doing doesn't feel right
>   e.g. I don't feel comfortable answering that question
> - If you want to keep what you are doing a secret
>   e.g. I'd better not tell anyone about this – they wouldn't understand
> - If a series of 'small steps' have taken you to a point that you wouldn't have had as an option at the start
>   e.g. Reading a client's 'life story' at home (I intended to read it in my office, I haven't had time, I need to read it before I see them tomorrow, I was taking other work home anyway . . .)
> - If someone challenged you by saying what you are doing isn't ethical
>   e.g. If your colleague questioned you
> - If you don't think your supervisor would do it
>   e.g. Would my supervisor suggest I take this course of action (or do it themselves)
> - If your action could be misunderstood or misconstrued by someone
>   e.g. a client has asked to borrow a small amount of money until they receive their benefits at the end of the week

> Remember – if your resources are depleted, for example if you have difficulties outside of work; many deadlines in work or you are feeling time pressured you may act in ways which you wouldn't normally do. These are times when your 'ethical safeguards' may be vulnerable and you may need to use supervision more explicitly to consider ethical issues.

Legal issues

In addition to ethical issues, those working in forensic settings also need to be aware of many legal issues. Some of these may relate to specific legal knowledge and practice (e.g. understanding the implications of a client being subject to specific mental health legislation; understanding the procedures for the protection of children or vulnerable adults; obligations in relation to the limits of confidentiality and the duty to protect or warn others) whilst others overlap significantly with ethics (e.g. issues of malpractice and liability). Supervisors should ensure that they are aware of the necessary legal and professional codes and should ensure that such awareness is promoted with supervisees. As described in the culture, context and legal issues competency framework by Davies et al. (2004), this might include respecting difference and avoiding stigma, the application of Human Rights, law and statutes and shaping local or national policy.

Conclusion

Ethical supervision can be achieved by ensuring that relevant issues are discussed within supervision but also that ethical consideration and practice is modelled and attended to within each supervision session. It is essential that both supervisor and supervisee use local and professional ethical codes within their practice and also make use of approaches to ethical issues which enable 'ethical blindness' to be avoided and the practitioner to be supported to engage in ethically sound practice.

References

Austin, W. (2001) 'Relational ethics in forensic psychiatric settings', *Journal of Psychosocial Nursing and Mental Health Services* 39(9): 12–17.

Barnao, M., Robertson, P. and Ward, T. (2012) 'Ethical decision making and forensic practice', *The British Journal of Forensic Practice* 14(2): 81–91.

Bernard, J. M. and Goodyear, R. K. (2014) *Fundamentals of Clinical Supervision* (5th edn), International Edition, London: Pearson.

Bonner, R. (2006) 'Ethical decision making for correctional mental health providers', *Criminal Justice and Behavior* 33(4): 542–64.

Davies, J., Tennant, A., Ferguson, E. and Jones, L. (2004) 'Developing models and a framework for multi-professional clinical supervision', *The British Journal of Forensic Practice* 6 (3): 36–42.

Haag, A. M. (2006) 'Ethical dilemmas faced by correctional psychologists in Canada', *Criminal Justice and Behavior* 33(1): 93–109.

Johns, C. (1993) 'Professional supervision', *Journal of Nursing Management* 1(1): 9–18.

Newman, A. S. (1981) 'Ethical issues in the supervision of psychotherapy', *Professional Psychology* 12(6): 690.

Overholser, J. C. and Fine, M. A. (1990) 'Defining the boundaries of professional competence: managing subtle cases of clinical incompetence', *Professional Psychology: Research and Practice* 21(6): 462.

Proctor, B. (1986) 'Supervision: a co-operative exercise in accountability', in M. Marken and M. Payne (eds), *Enabling and Ensuring*, Leicester: National Youth Bureau for Education in Youth and Community Work.

Ward, T. and Syversen, K. (2009) 'Human dignity and vulnerable agency: an ethical framework for forensic practice', *Aggression and Violent Behavior* 14(2): 94–105.

Wosket, V. and Page, S. (1994) *The Cyclical Model of Supervision*, Abingdon: Routledge.

Special Topic 3
Supervising group work

Many forensic practitioners are involved in providing groups of one type or another such as 'community meetings', those relating to formal therapy and skills or education groups. Providing any form of group is demanding, and for those supervising group work facilitators, attention is needed to the task (what the group is for); the individuals (both individual practitioners and group members); the group process (such as the interactions between the group members and the facilitators); and the relationship between the practitioners and the supervisor. Thus the group work supervisor needs to pay attention to multiple relationships, multiple individual needs, the task and other influences that may impact on the individuals or the functioning of the group! These are represented in Box ST3.1. Models such as the Process Model of Supervision (Chapter 4) may help the supervisor manage some of this. In the remainder of this special topic, the task, individuals and relationships will be considered in more detail.

BOX ST3.1: Supervising groupwork

Key: S – supervisor; F – facilitators; M – group members

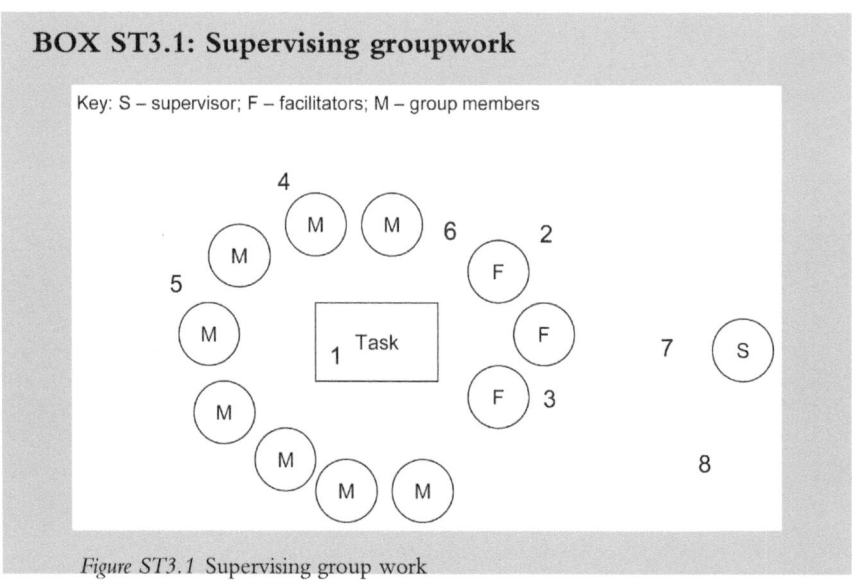

Figure ST3.1 Supervising group work

The supervisor needs to be able to attend to:

1. The task being undertaken by the group.
2. The needs of each facilitator.
3. The relationships between the facilitators.
4. Each group member's needs.
5. The relationships between group members.
6. The relationships between the group members and the facilitators.
7. The relationship between the facilitators and the supervisor.
8. Attention to relevant other factors (e.g. the wider system).

Task focus

The purpose of the group and the expected outcomes need to be carefully considered regardless of the nature and format of the group. Although responsibility for this lies with the members and facilitators of the group, the supervisor needs to understand these. It is important that the group members and facilitators are clear about the task (i.e. the reason for the group and what is expected of them etc). A contract based on such factors should be agreed and be regularly consulted within supervision. The supervisor's purpose in relation to the task is, in part, to ask 'is the group meeting its purpose?'.

Attention to the task. The supervisor needs to aid the facilitators to consider how the purpose of the group is being met during the session. In some groups, the structure of each session is relatively fluid with the use of a specific model or broad structure that allows freedom within the group to be reactive and led by the needs and issues brought by the members at the time. In such cases, it is necessary for the supervisor to be able to help the facilitators maintain an explicit focus on the task.

Programme Integrity and treatment adherence. In some groups, such as many of the accredited offending behaviour treatment programmes, the aims and the structure of the group will be detailed in a protocol or manual. In such cases, the role of the supervisor in relation to the 'task' will be to help monitor that the programme is being delivered according to the parameters laid down. This might include the sequence of material and the content of what is to be delivered. In such circumstances, the supervisor may be required to review recordings of group sessions and to follow a protocol within supervision. In groups using a specific form of therapy, supervision might include an assessment of adherence by the facilitators to the therapy model. Again there are often specific methods for this and recordings may be used to support the process. Where integrity or adherence are being monitored, it is the supervisor's job to identify drift from the programme or the treatment model and assist the facilitators to return to the model or materials. It is important, however, that the supervisor is not drawn into a simple 'administrative' role.

Focus on the group

In supervising groupwork, the supervisor generally needs to attend to two group processes – the 'supervision group' comprised of the supervisor and the facilitators (supervisees) and the 'task group' comprised of the facilitators and the group members. Although many of the skills and processes are the same, it is important that the supervisor attends to both of these. For both, the skills and ideas discussed in group supervision in Chapter 3 will be relevant. However, for the task group a focus on the group processes within the task group is a challenging yet vital aspect of group work supervision. The supervisor needs to facilitate discussion of the 'group process' comprised of the interactions between the group members, the interactions between the facilitators and the interactions between the facilitators and the group members. Attention should be given to 'roles' within the group (e.g. are there people who disrupt, are quiet, want to 'co-facilitate'), group development (such as the phases described by Tuckman, 1965; Tuckman and Jensen, 1977), and group processes (such as the relations between members of the group e.g. Bion, 1970; French and Simpson, 2010).

Focus on the individuals

Within supervision, the supervisor needs to attend to the needs of each of the supervisees. In general, the skills needed here are the same as those needed when providing any form of group supervision (see Chapter 3 and Special Topic 9). However, the one important feature that may differ from other group supervision is that the supervisees will have been part of the same group even though their perspectives, roles and individual needs may differ. This offers the opportunity for the supervisor to harness the recall, ideas and observations of the other supervisees to help meet the needs of each individual member.

The supervisor might also focus on the individual needs and experience of each of the group members as understood by the supervisees. This may reveal differences of view as well as consensus; and may reveal important factors such as group members who are 'liked or disliked' or for whom there are very different facilitator views. The supervisor needs to be able to help the supervisees discuss and address such issues. It is also important to review how the group is meeting individual needs, how individuals are responding and how to address any individual problems (e.g. individuals who arrive late or who miss or disrupt sessions).

Focus on other factors

A wide range of other factors may be pertinent to the supervision of groupwork, however many of these concern aspects of the wider system and others' understanding and expectations of the group. These might present in relation to support or undermining of the group and its purpose in both direct (e.g.

questioning the purpose) and indirect ways (e.g. making room booking difficult). They may also arise when issues from the wider context are discussed within the group or when there are tensions between the discussions, agreements or actions within the group and those outside the group (e.g. the expectation within the group for openness but agreement between prisoners not to talk to staff). The supervisor's role is to help highlight such difficulties and enable the facilitators to consider how these might be responded to or managed.

References

Bion, W. R. (1968) *Experiences in Groups: and Other Papers*, Abingdon: Routledge.
French, R. B. and Simpson, P. (2010) 'The "work group": redressing the balance in Bion's experiences in groups', *Human Relations* 63(12): 1859–78.
Tuckman, B. W. (1965) 'Developmental sequence in small groups', *Psychological Bulletin* 63(6): 384.
Tuckman, B. W. and Jensen, M. A. C. (1977) 'Stages of small-group development revisited', *Group & Organization Management* 2(4): 419–27.

Special Topic 4
Supervising non-client work: research, leadership and management activity

Within forensic settings and services, practitioners may be involved in a broad range of activity in addition to any role they have with clients. This may include audit, evaluation, research, management and leadership. Although many of the supervision ideas and principles contained within this book are equally applicable to these other tasks, this special topic considers some of the additional aspects that may be relevant when supervising some of these activities.

Supervising research, audit and evaluation

Research may be supervised through general supervision (i.e. research is one aspect of the range of work taken to supervision by the practitioner) or more commonly, by someone offering specialist supervision of the research activity alone. Similarly, workers may have research as their sole responsibility or as an aspect of their job. Although there is a great deal of overlap with supervision of other areas of practice, research supervision (like other competence-specific forms of supervision such as supervision for a specific therapy) has an additional set of skills, experience and knowledge which the supervisor needs to hold. In order to elucidate some of the key points, some evidence drawn from research supervision in academic settings (and therefore concerning students) will be explored.

Several authors have considered the functions of research supervision. For example, Jindal-Snape and Ingram (2013) highlight the dual functions of the 'academic' supervisor, namely, supervising the student's work (academic matters) and supporting the student's personal development (daily life matters). This suggests that supervising research requires knowledge of research methods and approaches (academic) and the ability to consider wellbeing. They suggest that supervisor and supervisee need to be explicit regarding their expectations of one another (and of supervision) and present the SuReCam model (Supervision Remit Compatibility) for this. This model has two axes: (1) daily life matters – ranging from freedom[1] to discuss daily life matters (vs no freedom); and (2) academic matters – ranging from freedom to discuss academic life matters (vs no freedom). They suggest that both supervisor and supervisee should discuss their expectations of both of these factors and share both their aspiration and their actual experience. Based on these two axes, they suggest that supervision can be one of four types. Two of these are unhelpful:

(1) Freedom to consider daily life matters but no freedom re academic matters: this is problematic because it is out of keeping with research supervision as there is no academic focus.
(2) No freedom on either domain: they consider this to be neglectful supervision as neither task is being attended to.

And two of which could be productive:

(1) Freedom re academic matters but no freedom to discuss daily life matters: here the focus is on the academic task and academic development and could be functional providing there are no daily life matters which the supervisee needs to address.
(2) Freedom to discuss both: here the supervisor recognises the possible interplay between daily life and academic matters. Their research (perhaps unsurprisingly) identifies this as the most desirable form of supervision.

It is possible to view these as similar to the formative and restorative functions of supervision (see Chapter 4), whilst their recommendation that supervisor and supervisee construct a written agreement to formalise expectations is directly paralleled within other aspects of supervision.

An adaptation of the 'supervision remit compatibility' model has been described for use in supervision more generally (Ingram, 2013). He suggests that the axis could be modified to represent (1) the degree of focus on the emotional elements of practice, and (2) the degree of focus on process vs practical issues on the other. As with the original version, Ingram suggests that this could be used when establishing or reviewing supervision to determine respective expectations and experience. Thus, the supervisee and supervisor could use the axes to rate their *aspirations*, which could then facilitate a *negotiation* leading to an *agreement* of approach which is later *reviewed* and *revised* as necessary. This would therefore provide a framework with which to co-create an agreed approach to supervision.

In a study of supervision as a form of teaching, Bruce and Stoodley (2013) found that the orientation of the supervisor could be described according to nine categories that were broadly defined, according to the core focus of the supervisor, under the following three headings:

(1) *a supervisor orientation* (supervisor promoting own interests, supervisor as expert, guardian of standards);
(2) *a student orientation* (student journey and learning, building on student's ability, enabling student development); and
(3) *a community orientation* (needs of the wider community, working collaboratively and part of a network, having a social impact).

They found that some supervisors were able to adopt more than one approach, or changed their approach with a supervisee over time. They suggest that their classification of supervisory teaching style may help supervisors: (a) to identify their style(s) and the impact of this on students; (b) to consider how they match their style to the supervisee; and (c) how this might need to change over time. They also suggest that the more alternatives a supervisor has, the more options they can choose from and therefore the more responsive they can be to individual needs. Although the classifications may not translate to other practice supervision, the idea of a repertoire of styles, models and approaches may be a common goal of all supervision.

External factors may also influence the nature of supervision and the styles adopted by the supervisor (Deuchar, 2008). For example, pressure to publish amongst academics might affect the nature, extent and types of research supervised and the ways in which supervisors engage with their supervisees. However, adopting the stance of research supervision as an apprenticeship, and the supervisor as a critical friend may be helpful, allowing roles to change and adapt as the relationship and research develop (Deuchar, 2008).

In the final study considered here, Wright, Murray and Geale (2007) identified two dimensions within supervision research; first – the approach to supervision itself (self-directed learning vs managed learning) and second – the main outcome being aspired to (complete the task, i.e. PhD vs new insights or discoveries). From this they described five supervisor 'roles':

(1) *Quality assurer* – task orientated, structured and focused on the goal (e.g. of student achieving their PhD).
(2) *Supportive guide* – focused on the task but also providing support to sustain the student.
(3) *Researcher trainer* – e.g. PhD as the route to being a researcher or academic and learning skills for this.
(4) *Mentor* – provide guidance rather than direct teaching, being part of a 'team'.
(5) *Knowledge enthusiast* – student as self-directed learner, supervisor – passionate, a motivator and facilitator.

Despite the ideas described above, Bingham and Durán-Palma (2013) suggest that research supervision is generally not well understood, however, they suggest that supervisors have a duty of care to balance equity (fair treatment) with efficiency (best use of resources). As can be seen, much of the research reported here focuses on the roles and functions of the supervisor, and how these might be used to a greater or lesser degree by supervisors to shape and mould what they provide to the supervisee. Each of the orientations and roles appear to serve a necessary function, however the impact of matching or failing to meet expectations is not yet known.

As with client work within forensic settings, those carrying out research and those who supervise them need to be attentive to the particular ethical issues which are present or can arise in forensic settings. The chapter by Ward and Willis (2012) provides a starting point for considering the ethical issues and ethical approaches to research in forensic settings. For those new to supervising research in forensic settings, the book by Sheldon, Davies and Howells (2012), and in particular the chapter by Davies, Sheldon and Howells (2012), is a possible place to start.

Leadership and management activity

Although leadership and management are distinct activities, they will be considered together here as it is common for people to hold both roles at the same time. In a review of the literature, Sirola-Karvinen and Hyrkäs (2006) found that supervision for (nurse) leaders and managers was important and it was able to support development in a wide range of areas including management skills; leadership skills; problem-solving skills; functionality in teams; self-management and internal management and led to professional growth and development, increased self-awareness and improved coping at work. They concluded that such supervision 'could be an efficient intervention and solution to the current challenges related to leadership skills' (p.607). Further, Johns and Graham (1994) describe the use of reflective practice for a nurse manager and some of the many issues that might be raised in this context. As they note, 'The potential for guided reflection to develop the practitioner's and manager's expertise and commitment to work is undoubted because it identifies, focuses and develops everyday aspects of practice that are significant in achieving effective performance in ways that pay attention to relevant and existing theory' (pp. 259–60).

Those in positions of leadership and management might want to consider some form of peer arrangement for supervision (Jindal-Snape and Ingram, 2013; McCormack and Hopkins, 1995). Such arrangements have been found to lead to positive long-term effects in relation to leadership, communication, coping and desire for self-development and self-knowledge (Hyrkäs, Appelqvist-Schmidlechner and Kivimäki, 2005; Ingram, 2013). In a study of nurse managers' experience of peer supervision, Hyrkäs et al. (2003) found that managers reported a number of factors each of which contained a hierarchy of elements:

Support. At the lowest level was sharing experiences and dispelling doubt about one's ability; then a 'feeling of togetherness' and at the top being able to give and receive support.
Reflection. Here the steps in the hierarchy were talking, then sharing, then joint reflection.
Personal growth. This moved from acceptance of oneself to increased self-esteem.
Leadership development. At the bottom of the hierarchy was clarification, then strengthening, then development and finally maturation.

In many ways the elements contained in the four areas above can be seen as moving from description, through sharing to integration.

For those providing or engaging in supervision with those newly in management and leadership positions, it is particularly important to note the developmental aspects that may be present. For example, at times of transition to a new role such as promotion to an advanced practice or leadership role, those features associated with the 'novice', e.g. insecurity, ambivalence, confusion and doubt may surface (see Bruce and Stoodley, 2013; Sharrock, Javen and McDonald, 2013). Aspects of the role of the supervisor are to help maintain a systemic perspective and to foster reflective practice through which the supervisee can 'learn to wear the new role comfortably' and engage in intentional actions through planning and mindful leadership practice (Sharrock et al., 2013).

The Clinical Leadership Template described by Johns (2003) provides a helpful summary of the possible tasks associated with leadership practice. In the Practice Leader Tasks (see Table ST4.1; adapted from this framework) three 'levels' of attention – the self, the staff and the unit or service – are presented in the rows whilst the three domains – practice, leadership and management – are in the columns. The table provides an indication of the types of task associated with each level and each domain. Johns (2003) notes that the supervisor's role is to assist the developmental process of 'becoming a leader' and to challenge and support the leaders. He also notes that group sessions may be beneficial as it enables practitioners to come together which can provide mutual empowerment and may even lead to the creation of a practice network. As with other aspects of supervision, he suggests there is a need to follow up previously planned actions to identify the outcomes from these. He suggests this can be supported through simple questions such as 'Did the leader take action as anticipated? What happened as a consequence? What factors constrained action?'

However, in Johns (2003) he suggested that the 'leaders had learned to be docile' (p. 30) and that supervision had limited effectiveness in supporting the leaders to move from a transactional to a transformational approach. He suggested this resulted from the context in which these leaders were relatively weak in contrast to other professionals. He identified five factors which acted as blocks that included an unsympathetic organisational culture and unrealistic

Table ST4.1 Practice leader tasks

	Practice	Leadership	Management
Self	Maintains practice expertise	Adopts leadership role	Maintain charisma and effectiveness
Staff	Facilitates accountability/ responsibility amongst staff	Staff support and competence development	Ensures quality of care
Unit/service	Develops and maintains practice vision	Facilitates practice development	Manages the unit effectively

Source: adapted from Johns, 2003.

expectations. Thus as with other forms of supervision, it is important to consider the readiness of the organisation before implementing supervision and reflective practice.

Finally, those supervising individuals in management and/or leadership positions may benefit from awareness of models, ideas and frameworks associated with these aspects of practice. There are many resources to choose from, however readers may find Adair (2013) helpful as a starting point especially as the notion of situation leadership has overlap with the developmental model of supervision and supervisory roles both discussed in Chapter 4. Understanding some of the key aspects of a functional team, such as the five outlined by Lencioni (2002), namely, trust, ability to engage in conflict, commitment, holding one another accountable, and a focus on collective results, can be very helpful when providing supervision to individuals in leadership and management positions.

Conclusion

Although there may be some specialist knowledge and experience required of the supervisor, supervising non-client work requires many of the same skills and abilities of the supervisor, and for the same key elements of supervision to be in place. In particular, and in common with supervision of other activity, having a clear agreement and being attentive to the developmental processes that may be present could be helpful.

Note

1 They appear to use the term 'freedom' to capture both having opportunity and this being seen as relevant.

References

Adair, J. (2013) *Develop Your Leadership Skills*, London: Kogan Page Publishers.

Bingham, C. and Durán-Palma, F. (2013) 'Research supervision', *Teaching in Higher Education* 19(1): 78–89.

Bruce, C. and Stoodley, I. (2013) 'Experiencing higher degree research supervision as teaching', *Studies in Higher Education* 38(2): 226–41.

Davies, J., Sheldon, K. and Howells, K. (2012) 'Conducting research in forensic settings', in K. Sheldon, J. Davies and K. Howells, *Research in Practice for Forensic Professionals*. Abingdon: Routledge, pp. 3–15.

Deuchar, R. (2008) 'Facilitator, director or critical friend? Contradiction and congruence in doctoral supervision styles', *Teaching in Higher Education* 13(4): 489–500.

Hyrkäs, K., Appelqvist-Schmidlechner, K. and Kivimäki, K. (2005) 'First-line managers' views of the long-term effects of clinical supervision: how does clinical supervision support and develop leadership in health care?', *Journal of Nursing Management* 13(3): 209–20, retrieved from http://onlinelibrary.wiley.com.eresources.shef.ac.uk/store/10.1111/j.1365–2834.2004.00522.x/asset/j.1365–2834.2004.00522.x.pdf?v=1&t=htfwnupa&s=5db693951e68fc555648dce5b07e6496f6f70506.

Hyrkäs, K., Koivula, M., Lehti, K. and Paunonen Ilmonen, M. (2003) 'Nurse managers' conceptions of quality management as promoted by peer supervision', *Journal of Nursing Management* 11(1): 48–58.

Ingram, R. (2013) 'Emotions, social work practice and supervision: an uneasy alliance?', *Journal of Social Work Practice* 27(1): 5–19.

Jindal-Snape, D. and Ingram, R. (2013) 'Understanding and supporting triple transitions of international doctoral students: ELT and SuReCom Models', *Journal of Perspectives in Applied Academic Practice* 1(1).

Johns, C. (2003) 'Clinical supervision as a model for clinical leadership', *Journal of Nursing Management* 11(1): 25–35.

Johns, C. and Graham, J. (1994) 'The growth of management connoisseurship through reflective practice', *Journal of Nursing Management* 2(6): 253–60.

Lencioni, P. (2002) *The Five Dysfunctions of a Team: A Leadership Fable*, San Francisco, CA: Jossey-Bass.

McCormack, B. and Hopkins, E. (1995) 'The development of clinical leadership through supported reflective practice', *Journal of Clinical Nursing* 4(3): 161–8.

Sharrock, J., Javen, L. and McDonald, S. (2013) 'Clinical supervision for transition to advanced practice', *Perspectives in Psychiatric Care* 49(2): 118–25.

Sheldon, K., Davies, J. and Howells, K. (eds) (2012) *Research in Practice for Forensic Professionals*, Abingdon: Routledge.

Sirola Karvinen, P. and Hyrkäs, K. (2006) 'Clinical supervision for nurses in administrative and leadership positions: a systematic literature review of the studies focusing on administrative clinical supervision', *Journal of Nursing Management* 14(8): 601–9.

Ward, T. and Willis, G. (2012) 'Ethical problems arising in forensic and correctional research', in K. Sheldon, J. Davies and K. Howells, *Research in Practice for Forensic Professionals*, Abingdon: Routledge, pp. 6–33.

Wright, A., Murray, J. P. and Geale, P. (2007) 'A phenomenographic study of what it means to supervise doctoral students', *Academy of Management Learning & Education* 6(4): 458–74.

Special Topic 5
Critiques of supervision and reflective practice

The focus of this book is on the role for supervision within forensic settings and how this might be provided safely, skilfully and for the benefit of the practitioner and the client. However, it is important to recognise that in the arena of clinical supervision and reflective practice there have been a few cautions and criticisms of supervision and especially of how it might be misused or misunderstood. This special topic focuses on the criticism of supervision as a surveillance, power and control mechanism used by organisations.

Surveillance control and power

Supervision as a mechanism for an organisation (or profession) to exert surveillance, power and control over individuals is a criticism that has been largely voiced from within the nursing field. Gilbert (2001) presents a critique of supervision based on the work of the philosopher, Foucault. He argues that supervision is a form of power that can be exerted through surveillance to monitor and influence how practitioners see, think, feel and behave. He describes supervision as a confessional act in which the supervisee reveals information about their practice (e.g. their performance, their beliefs, their ideas) which is used for *self-regulation* and *regulation by others*. Through this regulation, the existing dominant and prevailing views are perpetuated. In a simple way, there is a tension between two forces, complying and being autonomous.

Banks and colleagues (Banks *et al.*, 2012) also discuss how supervisees confess their actions (good and bad, positive and negative) and the surveillance to which they are subjected. Through this, and other forms of governance, the supervisee is 'helped' to conform to 'the direction required' (p. 598) and to construct their identity as a practitioner with reference to the 'expert'. From this viewpoint, supervision might be seen as both constraining (i.e. restricting new approaches and ways of working) and reductionist (i.e. there is one accepted way to do something). This could be thought of as 'thinking inside the box' and maintaining prevailing and existing understanding and practice(s) whilst excluding the new or different.

However, this is a two-way relationship with power being exerted from the 'top' and practitioners, through their training and other processes, learning and accepting the role of being 'uncritical doers' (Johns, 1993, p. 15). This can be seen as a process through which the 'practitioner has been socialised to be a competent yet docile practitioner' (Johns, 2001, p. 140), conforming rather than embracing responsibility and innovation. This is relevant to supervision as supervisors need to understand the position they hold (and the forces they may be subject to) and because such surveillance may result in 'a subordinate and disempowered practitioner who may struggle to respond to the opportunity of clinical supervision' (Johns, 2001, p. 140). The existing hierarchy and traditional structures often reinforce this, with organisations proclaiming that supervision is offered in the best interests of the practitioner, although actually it is being used as an organisational tool.

It is clear that supervision could act as a mechanism to monitor workers and suppress thoughts, plans or actions which might go 'against the grain', however this might be very subtle. For example, changes in supervisory practice have been reported in some disciplines. Manthorpe *et al.* (2013) report a shift in social work supervision away from the more traditional focus on the educational and support aspects of supervision and towards a more administrative focus. This might signal supervision being used for monitoring and management of practitioners' work.

Central to the arguments about monitoring and surveillance is an implication of harm through controlling and limiting the practitioners' thoughts, actions and behaviour. However, Clouder and Sellars (2004) raise a number of ideas relating to the notion of an intentional yet ethical form of surveillance. In this they suggest that surveillance and monitoring can form part of competence to practice, thereby helping to provide 'client protection' and practitioner accountability. In this regard supervision can act as a quality assurance mechanism (Mothersole, 2000) concerned with competence and outcomes. Clouder and Sellars (2004) argue that scrutiny and monitoring occur anyway and that supervision might provide a mechanism to support individual agency and individual accountability, aiding the practitioner to utilise their power, status and rights. What appears to be important is to try to separate the inevitable aspects of monitoring and control from the intent (is supervision being used explicitly or implicitly to enforce limits and maintain the dominant existing ways of working).

The balance of power. The supervisee is not passive and subservient, and it is worth remembering that there are many ways in which the supervisee could resist power. As reported by Clouder and Sellars (2004), the supervisee is generally able to engage in impression management should they wish to and is free to reveal or conceal, avoid, interpret and sanitise what is discussed. Evidence for non-disclosure is discussed in Chapter 7. Although it could be conceived that this is a form of self-surveillance, it is worth remembering that these are generally actions that have occurred and thus the surveillance is no deterrent to action!

Managing surveillance. There are several ways in which the organisation might develop supervision in order to intentionally 'compromise' attempts at supervision being used for surveillance. This starts with the stance and ethos of the service. Two points are relevant here. First, 'if we are concerned primarily with learning about our practice rather than learning about ourselves, then supervision takes on a different focus that does not entail any aspects of personal confession' (Rolfe and Gardner, 2006, p. 600). Second, where supervision is accepted as an activity that may be an end in itself and built on the best interests and needs of the practitioner not the organisation (Johns, 2001), the external direction of supervision might be removed along with notions of compliance. There are also a number of practical suggestions that have been made in response to the notion of supervision as surveillance. First, several authors have argued for separating professional development and professional regulation (e.g. Clouder and Sellars, 2004), which could be achieved by separating line management from professional supervision. In line with this, supervision should not be used as a tool for practice audit but should be a tool for exploration and critical analysis of practice (Morrison and Wonnacott, 2010). Second, Banks *et al.*, (2012) suggest that supervision be provided across professional groups (e.g. a psychologist supervising a nurse) and governance frameworks be developed to ensure that supervision is 'democratic, transparent and challenging' (p. 599). Finally Beddoe (2010) raises three helpful questions:

(1) How do supervision and line management differ?
(2) How do supervisors ensure their focus is on supervision rather than surveillance?
(3) How do supervisors resist the pressure to focus on 'compliance'?

Within the context of forensic practice the balance between surveillance and engagement is also an activity that the practitioner must balance, e.g. the monitoring of risk and the balance between custody and care. Such issues may well form part of the material for supervision.

Conclusion

Those concerned by the idea of supervision often voice ideas of being monitored and controlled through supervision of their practice. The notion that supervision is a form of surveillance has been argued by some, however the balance of power and the intent of supervision are important factors which might moderate this. It is for the reader to consider the relative merits and limits of these arguments about supervision. In forensic settings, colleagues watching your back may be no bad thing, however, where this becomes a method through which to constrain practitioners and demand conformity (either explicitly or implicitly) then it is likely that supervision is being misused or abused.

References

Banks, D., Clifton, A. V., Purdy, M. J. and Crawshaw, P. (2012) 'Mental health nursing and the problematic of supervision as a confessional act', *Journal of Psychiatric and Mental Health Nursing* 20(7): 595–600.

Beddoe, L. (2010) 'Surveillance or reflection: professional supervision in "the risk society"', *British Journal of Social Work* 40(4): 1279–96.

Clouder, L. and Sellars, J. (2004) 'Reflective practice and clinical supervision: an interprofessional perspective', *Journal of Advanced Nursing* 46(3): 262–9.

Gilbert, T. (2001) 'Reflective practice and clinical supervision: meticulous rituals of the confessional', *Journal of Advanced Nursing* 36(2): 199–205.

Johns, C. (1993) 'Professional supervision', *Journal of Nursing Management* 1(1): 9–18.

——(2001) 'Depending on the intent and emphasis of the supervisor, clinical supervision can be a different experience', *Journal of Nursing Management* 9(3): 139–45.

Manthorpe, J., Moriarty, J., Hussein, S., Stevens, M. and Sharpe, E. (2013) 'Content and purpose of supervision in social work practice in England: views of newly qualified social workers, managers and directors', *British Journal of Social Work*.

Morrison, T. and Wonnacott, J. (2010) 'Supervision: now or never', *In-Trac.Co.Uk*, retrieved 5 May 2014, from www.in-trac.co.uk/supervision-now-or-never/.

Mothersole, G. (2000) 'Clinical supervision and forensic work', *Journal of Sexual Aggression* 5(1): 45–58.

Rolfe, G. and Gardner, L. (2006) '"Do not ask who I am … ": confession, emancipation and (self)-management through reflection', *Journal of Nursing Management* 14(8): 593–600.

Special Topic 6
Overcoming problems in supervision

Supervision can run into difficulties despite the best intentions of the supervisor or supervisee, however these problems can often be resolved easily. Occasionally, more significant difficulties arise which are more complex to address; commonly these concern one of four issues: competence, confidence, ethics and the supervisory relationship. In this special topic we explore a number of specific challenges that can arise in supervision and consider how they might be prevented or overcome. Through these examples, the reader is encouraged to consider the general ideas that can be drawn in order to develop an approach (as supervisor or supervisee) to recognise and address difficulties in supervision.

Before considering possible problems it is worth revisiting the aspects of supervision that help it function and can mitigate against problems arising:

(a) regular, planned and protected time;
(b) agreement in place that is up to date and committed to by supervisor and supervisee;
(c) mutual trust and respect;
(d) clear expectations; and
(e) regular feedback and review.

The work by Ellis *et al.* (2014) on inadequate/harmful supervision and the 'minimum standards' discussed in Chapter 7 can also help ensure that the basic enabling components are in place; these should not be compromised if supervision is to have a chance to be functional. Ethical issues, malpractice and obligations such as the 'duty to protect' (e.g. vulnerable adults) that may arise in supervision are addressed more generally in the special topic on ethical issues.

Addressing specific problems

The following problems are examples of those that require prompt management or that can be more challenging to address. The suggestions of what might be done are intended as ideas to start the process of addressing the difficulty.

My supervision feels more like therapy

As discussed elsewhere, supervision is not a form of therapy for supervisees (Yegdich, 1998). Where supervision appears to be drifting in this direction it is important to raise this with the supervisor. Ways to maintain the interaction as supervision include ensuring that:

(a) there is a link between the discussion and the supervisee's practice;
(b) discussions about attitudes, emotions or life events and circumstances are:

   (i) relevant to the workplace;
   (ii) agreed as a topic for discussion;
   (iii) not a way to avoid focusing directly on the client work or tasks the supervisee is responsible for.

The supervisee doesn't use our discussions to inform their practice or is reluctant to provide feedback on previous actions

At the heart of solving this problem is identifying why supervision isn't translating into action (or development) or why this isn't reported upon. Common causes of this problem are:

(a) *I wasn't sure what was being suggested* – this problem might be simply overcome by the supervisee summarising the discussion and the actions they plan to take next. That way misunderstandings or lack of clarity can be addressed straightaway. Differences in learning styles (see Chapter 5) can contribute to this.
(b) *I didn't realise I needed to* – if supervision is useful it would be expected to have relevance to the work of the supervisee. A review of why this link isn't being made is needed along with possible adjustments to the agreement.
(c) *I am, you just don't know* – here the solution is to ensure that feedback on actions are on the 'agenda' so they can be discussed. Sometimes there is reluctance to do this where the supervisee feels that they have not done something 'properly' or don't want to provide feedback on something that hasn't worked. In such cases the supervisor may need to address the anxieties of the supervisee and build trust. This can be helped by ensuring there are clear, shared expectations summarised in the supervision agreement.

The 'agenda setting', 'bridge' and 'review' aspects of the supervision hour (see Chapter 4) are particularly relevant to addressing the above issues.

I'm worried about being evaluated negatively/the supervisee is failing to reach the required standard

In many supervision arrangements the supervisor will have the additional role of being an appraiser or evaluator of the supervisee's work. However, even when this is not the case, the supervisor will generally have a normative role (see Chapter 3). Although being evaluated and failing to reach the required level are different issues, they share some common responses. Fears about being negatively evaluated can give rise to supervisees trying to hide (or disguise) problems – see Chapter 7, or present positively skewed information. Further, it is often not possible and rarely desirable to separate supervision from appraisal where they co-exist. As noted by a participant in a study by Hair (2013), 'it is naïve and dangerous to separate the evaluative component from the other aspects of supervision … establishing a trusting relationship and setting ground rules for supervision can eliminate the false dichotomy related to supervision and evaluation' (p. 1574). A number of steps can be taken to prevent or address this problem such as:

(a) having clear ground rules and being explicit about what and how appraisal will be undertaken;
(b) the supervisor watching the supervisee at work;
(c) feedback and appraisal being regular features of supervision;
(d) the supervisor raising any concerns early and providing guidance on how they might be addressed; and
(e) involving others (e.g. course tutors or staff) where necessary.

There is more on approaches to providing feedback in Chapter 7.

My supervision doesn't meet my needs

There are many reasons why supervision may not be experienced as meeting the supervisee's needs. These include:

(a) *too much focus on management* – this issue is especially relevant where the supervisor is also the line manager and getting the balance right can be difficult. One approach to managing this is to allocate specific time to each function (i.e. management time; supervision time); another is to separate these functions by involving another person to take on one of the roles; and
(b) *differences in style* – sometimes there is a mismatch or misfit between the approach of the supervisor and the style of the supervisee. This may not always be problematic, for instance when the supervisee can use such a difference as a learning/developmental opportunity. However, mismatches can block supervision and discussion should take place to try to find ways to 'realign' styles so there is a better fit. However, it is important to recognise that 'differences in style' is often the 'symptom' of another problem rather than the problem itself.

As a general response to needs not being met, the supervisee and supervisor should review the supervision agreement and the agreed goals to ensure they are clear and still relevant. On rare occasions it may be necessary for the supervisee to change to a different supervisor – in such circumstances it is important to include someone else (a line manager, an experienced supervisor) in the discussions.

I'm having problems with my supervisor/supervisee

Such problems come in a wide range of 'shapes and sizes' – below are 8 examples all of which need to be raised within supervision in the first instance. Where this doesn't resolve things then it may be necessary to seek input, advice or action from others:

(a) *My supervisor/supervisee is always late/leaves early/is disinterested* – this needs to be addressed with reference to the supervision agreement, however it may be that a simple adjustment (e.g. to the timing, frequency or location) can resolve this. Sometimes this problem reflects a lack of organisational support for supervision (i.e. no protected time for supervision) – in such circumstances the supervisor and supervisee should work together to involve managers and others to help resolve the problem.

(b) *My supervisor/supervisee doesn't respect me* – lack of trust or respect challenge the very relationship on which supervision is based and requires immediate attention although this can be difficult to raise. It is important to have examples of why you experience your supervisee/supervisor in this way and to have some suggestions for how this might be overcome.

(c) *My supervisor/supervisee has unrealistic expectations of me* – this should be examined to discover why this might be the case. Is this based on expectations relating to your status/stage of development or the content of the supervision agreement for example? If this indicates 'below par' performance (as opposed to unrealistic expectations) the 'failings' need to be identified and methods proposed to address them at the earliest opportunity.

(d) *My supervisor/supervisee asks lots of personal questions* – this may be relevant in order for your supervisor to best meet your needs, however it may be based on a lack of clarity about the boundaries or purpose of supervision. Where this is problematic or intrusive (or takes a disproportionate amount of supervision time) this should be treated as the 'therapy' problem discussed elsewhere.

(e) *I want to change supervisor but don't want to hurt her/his feelings* – the possibility of change should form part of your initial agreement and therefore should be a part reviewing supervision. It is important to remember that supervision is centred on the supervisee and their practice (not the needs of the supervisor); therefore it is important to change supervisor when it seems appropriate. However, such a course of action should generally not be rushed into as first impressions and an initial 'settling in' period is needed whilst the supervision relationship is being established.

(f) *My supervisor focuses on their own needs and practice or discloses detailed personal information* – this is rarely appropriate and generally signals boundary problems and almost always signals that the supervisee's needs are not being addressed. Where possible, you should discuss this with your supervisor and where necessary your line manager or someone else in a senior position. It may also be useful to review the issues relating to boundaries in Chapter 8.

(g) *The supervisee doesn't prepare for supervision* – Lack of preparation may reflect such things as a lack of work, a lack of knowing how to prepare, a lack of confidence or resistance to supervision. It is important to identify the cause and function and take action including reviewing the agreement and involving the line manager where necessary. If not resolved, such experience can lead the supervisor to become dismissive or angry at the supervisee, further exacerbating the problem.

(h) *The supervisor or supervisee is avoiding supervision* – This suggests something very problematic at the heart of the supervision arrangement. It may be that the supervisor or supervisee doesn't want to engage (and is therefore 'voting with their feet') or that supervision is not seen as valuable. Where the issue is founded on feeling such as anxiety or inadequacy, or where the supervisee finds (or is anticipating finding) supervision unhelpful, uncomfortable, unreliable or unreasonable it is important to find a way to engage in supervision to raise this. In many cases this issue requires involvement from others (e.g. manager, peer consultant) but should be treated as requiring urgent attention.

Communication

Communication is a fundamental aspect of supervision, however sometimes problems arise in the ways this takes place. Where such difficulties occur it is important that the issue is raised in supervision as the most effective way to manage communication is by communicating! It is recognised that this can be difficult, especially if you are concerned that you might be judged or negatively evaluated (see earlier problem), however this must be overcome if the problem is to be resolved. Three examples of communication problems are:

(a) I don't understand some of what my supervisor talks about;
(b) my supervisor/supervisee talks too much/doesn't listen; and
(c) my supervisor/supervisee doesn't say much.

As with many other problems, these issues are best addressed by identifying the underlying cause(s) such as anxiety, not wanting to get 'it' wrong, or feeling inadequate in front of the supervisor. It may be possible to address this through giving permission to make mistakes, using other methods such as role play to check understanding, offering support, noticing successes and ensuring the supervisee and supervisor are clear on their roles (Bernard and Goodyear, 2014).

General prevention and response

Having considered a number of issues above, there are a range of preventative measures that can be taken and responses that can be used. These reflect many of the ideas that have been presented elsewhere within this text and are summarised in the two mnemonics contained in Box ST6.1.

BOX ST6.1: Preventing and responding to problems in supervision

To reduce the likelihood of problems – PREVENT:

P roactive approach to supervision
R elationship/alliance
E stablish an agreement
V alue each other's views and differences
E xplicit expectations
N otice difficulties early
T ake and give feedback

When problems arise a problem solving approach can be useful – RESPOND

R ecognise a problem exists
E xplore to identify causes
S peak to one another to consider options
P rioritise solutions and take action
O pen and respectful communication
N ote what helps or works
D on't avoid or ignore problems as they can fester and grow

References

Bernard, J. M. and Goodyear, R. K. (2014) *Fundamentals of Clinical Supervision* (5th edn), International Edition, London: Pearson.

Ellis, M. V., Berger, L., Hanus, A. E., Ayala, E. E., Swords, B. A. and Siembor, M. (2014) 'Inadequate and harmful clinical supervision: testing a revised framework and assessing occurrence', *The Counseling Psychologist* 42(4): 434–72.

Hair, H. J. (2013) 'The purpose and duration of supervision, and the training and discipline of supervisors: what social workers say they need to provide effective services', *British Journal of Social Work* 43(8): 1562–88.

Yegdich, T. (1998) 'How not to do clinical supervision in nursing', *Journal of Advanced Nursing* 28(1): 193–202.

Special Topic 7
Creative approaches to supervision

There are a wide range of creative techniques that can be used in supervision such as creative writing, audiotaping, music, dance, drawing, montage, painting and poetry (Taylor, 2010). Readings, stories and films can also be helpful for exploring issues and ideas. Many of these allow a problem, difficulty or idea to be explored in another way in the hope that such 'reconsideration' might lead to new insights, observations, options or actions. Creative approaches may draw upon a range of senses to help harness imagination and bring together experience, thought and learning. Creative supervision may be particularly useful where the 'supervisee is "stuck" or where there is resistance or a tendency to rationalize' (Lahad, 2000, p. 15), empowering and enhancing a sense of resourcefulness and control. In this special topic some of the common methods will be described, however, interested readers are encouraged to experiment and explore for themselves the 'world of creative approaches'.

It is important to remember that not all supervisees will be comfortable with these approaches (or may be willing to engage in and experiment with some and not others). Therefore, it is the supervisor's responsibility to gain agreement to use these approaches either generally or in specific situations in which they may be of benefit.

Metaphors can be thought of as 'indirect, yet powerful, vehicles for reframing experience from unusual or unexpected perspectives' (Owen, 2001, p. xv). As with many other creative approaches, they provide a mechanism for viewing a situation from a new direction or angle and offer the possibility of dealing with complex concepts and ideas in a more concrete form. Important qualities of a metaphor are that they can be readily used to consider the current situation without elaborate explanation or preparation (i.e. they must not be cumbersome or so complex as to require detailed discussion about their possible application). The metaphor uses the different but familiar to act as a precedent or proxy for an unfamiliar one (Schön, 1983). In this regard metaphor can be considered 'reflection on *seeing-as*' (p. 187). An example of a metaphor is provided in Box ST7.1.

> **BOX ST7.1: Use of flight as a metaphor of a service**
>
> This metaphor is taken from a supervision session in which discussions about power and influence within a forensic mental health setting had

been taking place. Attempts to explore this with a conventional approach, using the names and roles of members of the team, had been difficult as the 'expected hierarchy' (i.e. job titles as indicators of supposed power and influence) got in the way of exploring the complexity of the underlying relationships. The supervisor suggested that the system be looked at 'from a distance' to see what new insights might be given – the metaphor of an aeroplane flight was used to represent the journey from a client's admission to their discharge.

The supervisee was asked questions to explore key roles and responsibility, decision making and relationships. To begin, the supervisee was asked to identify who occupied the different roles e.g. the pilot, the co-pilot, the cabin crew, the baggage handler, the air traffic controllers and the ground maintenance staff. Then the supervisee was asked to consider those aboard the flight – who is in first class, who is scared of flying and who misses the flight. The supervisee was asked to ensure they were placed somewhere either on the plane or elsewhere. The supervisee was also asked to identify where the client was and some key issues such as who were they sitting with and how much say did they have over the destination.

Next the issue of shared goals was discussed by exploring who decides on the destination, does everyone know where they are going, is anyone 'just along for the ride' and whether everyone was going to the same place. This also included who was responsible for 'flight plans' – who drew them up, who authorised them, what if there was a disagreement etc. and who (if anyone) could make changes to the planned route. Questions were asked about 'behind the scenes' roles – who creates the rules, who 'investigates if something goes wrong'.

Key relationships were explored by asking the supervisee how the pilot and co-pilot got on, how the flight crew got on with air traffic control, who the supervisee had contact with and how the supervisee would get to speak with the captain if they wanted to.

As can be seen in this brief example, the supervisor was able to make assumptions (e.g. that the supervisee understood the different roles in the metaphor) which allowed them to begin the exploration without having to describe anything about the metaphor itself. Once the discussions had taken place the supervisor and supervisee 'translated' their observations and ideas back into the 'real situation' to consider any new insights or ideas triggered by this exploration.

Enacting covers a range of approaches such as sculpting and role plays. In individual supervision, sculpting (or a spectrogram) might use objects to represent features of the situation being brought to supervision, with the supervisee and supervisor discussing and exploring the representation. In a group format the other members of the group might be used to 'take on the role' of individuals relevant to the scenario, the members are then asked to comment on their perspective and observations (Scaife, 2013). The use of role play is familiar to most individuals as a method for skills practice and rehearsal, however its use as a creative approach can allow the supervisee to view the situation from different perspectives by 'seeing the situation from that viewpoint'. This might involve the supervisee changing their position when adopting these different roles (c.f. the empty chair technique within Gestalt therapy). It may be that different perspectives are explored within the actual situation or context or that the scenario is explored with a change to the setting or important aspects of the context.

Drawing and writing techniques can take many forms including prose and poetry, 'literal drawing' (e.g. creating a genogram) or metaphorical drawing (e.g. representing a staff team as animals). Supervisees can find drawing and 'creative writing' difficult because of fears of being judged — it is the supervisor's role to ensure that the task is not focused on 'picture quality' but on how the representations might be helpful. It is important to explore different materials and methods — a large piece of flip chart paper or a white board can enable space to be used and detail to be added. Similarly, 'tablets' or 'smart phones' with cameras can allow the completed work to be captured in an easy and portable format.

The six part story (Lahad, 2000) uses the framework of a fairy tale to explore ideas, beliefs and values in a structured way. The six parts of the story (which can be written or drawn in cartoon style) are based on six questions and is an approach to structured story telling:

1. Who is the main character in the story?
2. What is the mission or task that the main character is trying to achieve?
3. Who or what can help in this task?
4. What is the obstacle in the way (what needs to be overcome)?
5. How does the main character overcome the obstacle?
6. How does it end (what is the outcome?)

As with other methods the supervisor and supervisee can discuss and explore the resultant story.

Edward de Bono's *Six Thinking Hats* approach has been widely used both in the corporate world and in other settings such as education (De Bono, 1999). Within supervision this approach can provide a method for exploring problems, challenges, difficulties or opportunities from different directions. In brief, the approach describes six 'viewpoints' which can be taken, each of which might provide new information or new perspectives or insights. The hats can be summarised as:

- White — concerned with facts, e.g. 'what do you know about … '?
- Red — the emotional viewpoint, e.g. 'what do you feel about … '?
- Black — identifies weaknesses and difficulties, e.g. 'what might go wrong with … '?

- Yellow – positive thinking, e.g. 'what might be the benefits of … '?
- Green – creative and new ideas, e.g. 'what other possibilities might there be … '?
- Blue – organisational processes (the use of the other hats), e.g. 'what action will you take … '?

The supervisor might guide the supervisee using some or all of the different 'hats' in order to reach new understanding or a new way forward.

Conclusion

In this special topic a few creative approaches have been briefly described, however the main purpose of this special topic is to stimulate curiosity, creativity and experimentation. Interested readers might wish to consult the book *Creative Supervision* by Lahad (2000) or the chapter on 'creative approaches' by Scaife (2013) to develop these ideas further.

References

De Bono, E. (1999) *Six Thinking Hats*, London: Penguin Books.
Lahad, M. (2000) *Creative Supervision: The Use of Expressive Arts Methods in Supervision and Self-Supervision*, London: Jessica Kingsley Publishers.
Owen, N. (2001) *The Magic of Metaphor*, Carmarthen: Crown House Publishing Ltd.
Scaife, J. (2013) *Supervision in Clinical Practice*, Abingdon: Routledge.
Schön, D. A. (1983) *The Reflective Practitioner: How Professionals Think in Action*, New York: Basic Books.
Taylor, B. J. (2010) *Reflective Practice for Healthcare Professionals: A Practical Guide* (3rd edn), Buckingham: Open University Press.

Special Topic 8
Assessments and measures for use in supervision and research

There are many measures that have been used by supervisors and supervisees to inform supervision practice and by researchers to study it. Some of these measures were designed for other purposes (e.g. therapy outcome, workplace wellbeing), however there are a growing number that have been developed specifically for supervision purposes. This section provides a brief overview of a small selection of the measures developed for use in supervision, and is intended as a starting point for the interested reader. Measures using different approaches and assessing different aspects of supervision have been included. It is beyond the scope of this special topic to provide a detailed critique of the psychometric properties of the tools, therefore readers interested in using (or developing) measures in supervision should undertake a comprehensive search and evaluation of available tools in order to select the most appropriate for their purpose.

Supervision alliance

As we have seen in other chapters, the supervisory relationship or working alliance is an important aspect of supervision. There are a number of measures that have been developed to measure the supervisory relationship and alliance, a few of which are summarised here.

Working Alliance Inventory/Supervision (Bahrick, 1989), is a self-report measure adapted from an assessment of the working alliance in therapy. This tool consists of 36 items rated on a seven-point scale (never to always). There are three subscales relating to 'task', 'bond' and 'goal', and two parallel forms (one for the supervisor and another for the supervisee). Items include '[supervisor] and I agree about the things I will need to do in supervision' and 'We have established a good understanding of the kinds of things I need to work on'. This scale has been widely used and cited.

The Supervisory Relationship Measure (Pearce, Beinart and Clohessy, 2013) consists of 51 items rated on a seven-point scale (strongly disagree to strongly agree). It was designed to measure the supervisory relationship from the *supervisor's* perspective and includes items such as 'My trainee is reflective in supervision' and 'My trainee copes well with multiple demands'. In an initial study the researchers reported five subscales each with good reliability and validity. This is a newly developed tool, therefore its use so far has been limited. A related measure is the *Supervisory Relationship Questionnaire* (Palomo, Beinart and Cooper, 2010) which consists of 67 items rated on a seven-point scale (strongly disagree to strongly agree). It was developed to measure the supervisory relationship from the *supervisee's* perspective and includes items such as 'My supervisor treated me with respect' and 'Supervision sessions were focused'. In an initial study, six sub-scales were identified each with good reliability and validity. Although this is a newly developed tool, it has been used in a few published studies. Both these tools are based on the work of Beinart (2004).

Leeds Alliance in Supervision Scale (Wainwright, 2010) is a three-item sessional measure of the supervisory alliance designed to be used at the end of each supervision session. The three items concerning 'approach', 'relationship' and 'meeting my needs' are scored on a visual analogue scale. This scale is designed to promote supervisee to supervisor feedback and allows changes across time to be viewed.

Measuring facets of supervision

The *Manchester Clinical Supervision Scale* (MCSS; e.g. Winstanley and White, 2011) was developed from data collected as part of a large-scale supervision research project within the UK, and is reported as a measure of the effectiveness of clinical supervision. The original version of the scale had 36 items (Winstanley and White, 2003) with a revised version containing 26 items now available (Winstanley and White, 2011). This tool has a number of sub-scales (seven in the original and six in the shorter measure) which map onto the three functions of normative, formative and restorative as described by Proctor (Proctor, 1986). The MCSS is completed by the supervisee based on their perception of supervision using a five-point likert scale (strongly disagree to strongly agree). Items include 'My supervisor gives me support and encouragement'; 'I learn from my supervisor's experiences' and 'Other work pressures interfere with clinical supervision sessions'.

The scale has been widely used in research studies around the world, having been translated into several languages. Studies using the MCSS include Carthy, Noak and Wadey (2012); Hyrkäs (2005); White and Winstanley (2010). It is suggested that a total score threshold of 136 can be used to identify 'effective supervision' (White and Winstanley, 2010). The MCSS is widely used, has good psychometric properties and is linked to a model of supervision, however it is limited by only assessing the perceptions of the supervisee. As noted by White and Winstanley (2010), over time a link between 'operational definition, a conceptual model and a dedicated research instrument' (p. 154) has been shown.

Evaluation Process within Supervision Inventory (Lehrman-Waterman and Ladany, 2001) is a 21-item scale scored by the supervisee (in the original study these were psychology trainees) on a seven-point scale (strongly disagree to strongly agree). The tool has two sub-scales that relate to trainee perceptions of the degree to which 'goal setting' and 'feedback' are present in supervision. Items include 'My supervisor and I created goals that were realistic' and 'My supervisor's comments about my work were understandable'. The authors report validity and reliability information for the measure and it has been used in a number of other studies.

Supervisor Self-Disclosure Index (Ladany and Lehrman-Waterman, 1999) is a nine-item self-report measure rated on a five-point scale (not at all to often). The inventory assesses the level of supervisor disclosure as viewed by the supervisee and includes items such as 'My supervisor self-discloses information related to her or his past experiences'. Higher ratings on this index were found to be associated with a stronger working alliance between supervisee and supervisor.

A self-assessment strategy of competence and need is reported by Davies et al., (2004) who describe two complementary frameworks: the *Supervision Matrix: Clinical* and the *Supervision Matrix: Supervision*. Based on a developmental framework, this tool was developed within a forensic setting to enable some degree of supervisor-supervisee matching and the identification of supervisee strengths and needs.

Self-assessment Questionnaire for Supervisors (Hawkins and Shohet, 2006) is a framework to assist supervisors in appraising their competencies, capabilities and capacities. It is designed to provide a method for obtaining feedback from a range of individuals (e.g. supervisees) as well as self-assessment. Such a tool might be useful for monitoring change over time and to identify specific learning needs.

The *Taxonomy of Inadequate or Harmful Supervision* developed by Ellis et al. (2014) contains 37 supervision descriptors which are rated on a seven-point scale. This 'tool', whilst potentially relevant for a range of possible research (e.g. does training impact on the presence of these factors; is the supervision that is being investigated of a sufficient basic standard) also provides a useful checklist for supervisor and supervisee to potentially use to help frame and regularly evaluate their supervision.

The *Secure Unit Supervision Questionnaire* (Long et al., 2013) contained within the broader Clinical Supervision Questionnaire (Long, 2014) is a cross-sectional survey tool that enables services to gather information from staff about their use and experience of supervision. It includes items relating to supervision models, supervision frequency and supervision policy. These items are supplemented by a number of open-ended questions (e.g. 'What factors may prevent you from raising issues in supervision'). This tool may be useful for use when establishing or when reviewing supervision.

Regular monitoring

Another approach to evaluation is to use tools that enable you to monitor and scrutinise supervision on a regular basis (e.g. at the end of each supervision session). Such approaches have been used for measuring change in clients within forensic settings (Davies, 2010; Davies and Maggs, 2009) and can be readily adapted for use in supervision (see Box ST8.1). In the *Global Review Form: Supervision Version*, the idea is that 0 should represent acceptable/'good enough' supervision practice with +1 showing enhanced practice and -1 inadequate practice that needs attention. Newly added goals will commonly be rated as -1 (indicating a developmental need), and thus the expected change should be reflected over time by progression to 0 or even +1. Where goals relate to reflection (as opposed to skill acquisition per se), 0 is used to represent a functional level of reflective practice, with +1 highly functional and -1 problematic. In most cases no more than eight goals should be active at any one time, although these may relate to broad areas (see Lizzio and Wilson, 2002 in Chapter 5), however, in some cases it may be that a single goal is specified. From the ratings it is possible to plot the course of each of the domains over time.

BOX ST8.1: Regular monitoring – the Global Review Form: Supervision Version

Regularly monitoring aspects of supervision can be a helpful way of collaboratively 'taking stock' to ensure that supervision is functioning well and meeting the supervisee's needs. The framework presented here can be easily adapted to create a bespoke monitoring tool. The important principles are:

1. The anchor points for each point on the scale are defined and agreed before they are used. It is possible to develop the scale so that it covers up to seven points ranging from +3 to -3. Where appropriate other measures could be used to inform ratings (e.g. LASS to inform alliance).
2. Any areas that are below expectation (i.e. -1) require urgent attention. It maybe that the supervisor needs to discuss this in their own supervision and it may be useful to invite another experienced supervisor to provide input as necessary.
3. Goal 1; Goal 2 etc. should be specified based on your supervision agreement.
4. Learning goals that are consistently above expectation (i.e. +1) can be considered 'met' and may be replaced by new ones. Where the goal is based on reflective practice +1 indicates high functioning against this goal and may continue to be monitored.

Table ST8.1 Regular monitoring – the Global Review Form: Supervision Version

	Supervisor	Supervisee	Supervision facilities	Alliance	Goal 1	Goal 2
+1	Always prepared, on time, provides explicit information where relevant, facilitative, meets all of the supervisee's needs as agreed	Always prepared, on time, manages agenda, actively participates, responsive, provides feedback on supervision and agreed actions	Comfortable uninterrupted room. Necessary facilities always available. Access to resources (e.g. computer) as needed. Time etc. actively supported by manager	Strong working alliance with any 'ruptures' quickly identified and action taken to repair. Good match between supervisor and supervisee	Feedback from others (e.g. client) shows goal 1 is met. May include other evidence such as video-recording	Feedback from others (e.g. client) shows goal 2 is met. May include other evidence such as video-recording
0	Usually prepared and on time, generally provides explicit information where relevant and is facilitative, meets most of the supervisee's needs as agreed	Usually prepared and on time, generally manages agenda sometimes with support, actively participates, sometimes needs encouragement, generally responsive, provides feedback on supervision and agreed actions but usually needs to be asked	Facilities adequate but some interruptions on occasion or lack of some facilities that would aid supervision. Time etc. supported by manager	Working alliance generally fine but occasional difficulties which are difficult to repair but supervision still functions well	Self-report feedback from supervisee or supervisor that the goal is met or is being met	Self-report feedback from supervisee or supervisor that the goal is met or is being met
-1	Difficulties with one or more aspects e.g. poorly prepared, poor time keeping/many cancellations, overly didactic, doesn't facilitate development, not meeting supervisee's needs	Difficulties with one or more aspects e.g. poorly prepared, poor time keeping, defensive to suggestion, provides limited information about practice and action(s) taken since last supervision	Facilities inadequate, lack of space or privacy. Lack of basic resources needed. Lack of managerial/organisational support for supervision	Problems in the working alliance; mis-match between supervisor and supervisee (check task, goals and bond). Ruptures that are unresolved and that are in the way of supervision	Evidence that the goal is not being met either from self-report or other evidence. Review goal for appropriateness; review supervision methods being used	Evidence that the goal is not being met either from self-report or other evidence. Review goal for appropriateness; review supervision methods being used

Conclusion

This special topic has introduced a small selection of the many measures developed to assess some aspect(s) of supervision. The measures included here have generally been developed for 'clinical supervision', however, it is reasonable to assume that they could be used or easily adapted for forensic settings. There are also a growing number of measures that have been developed for therapy supervision (e.g. SAGE; Milne et al., 2011 – see Chapter 7) although these have not been discussed here. In addition, using client feedback to inform agenda setting and the focus of supervision has been promoted (e.g. Feedback Informed Supervision; *International Center for Clinical Excellence*, n.d.) and may be of interest to the reader.

References

Bahrick, A. S. (1989) *Role Induction for Counselor Trainees*, Columbus: Ohio State University.

Beinart, H. (2004) 'Models of supervision and the supervisory relationship and their evidence base', in I. Fleming and L. Steen (eds), *Supervison and Clinical Psychology: Theory, Practice and Perspectives*, Abingdon: Brunner-Routledge, pp. 36–50.

Carthy, J., Noak, J. and Wadey, E. (2012) 'Clinical supervision in a high secure hospital', *British Journal of Mental Health* 1(1): 24–32.

Davies, J. (2010) 'An individual approach to assessing change', in N. Gordon and P. Willmot (eds), *Working Positively With Personality Disorder in Secure Settings: A Practitioner's Perspective*, Oxford: Wiley & Sons.

Davies, J. and Maggs, R. (2009) 'Measuring individual change in a new low secure service: systems for individual and service evaluation', presented at the International Association of Forensic Mental Health Services 9th Annual Conference, Edinburgh.

Davies, J., Tennant, A., Ferguson, E. and Jones, L. (2004) 'Developing models and a framework for multi-professional clinical supervision', *The British Journal of Forensic Practice* 6 (3): 36–42.

Ellis, M. V., Berger, L., Hanus, A. E., Ayala, E. E., Swords, B. A. and Siembor, M. (2014) 'Inadequate and harmful clinical supervision: testing a revised framework and assessing occurrence', *The Counseling Psychologist* 42(4): 434–72.

Hawkins, P. and Shohet, R. (2006) *Supervision in the Helping Professions* (3rd edn), Buckingham: Open University Press.

Hyrkäs, K. (2005) 'Clinical supervision, burnout, and job satisfaction among mental health and psychiatric nurses in Finland', *Issues in Mental Health Nursing* 26(5): 531–56.

International Center for Clinical Excellence (n.d.) *International Center for Clinical Excellence*, retrieved 11 June 2014, from www.centerforclinicalexcellence.com/site.php?page=home.php.

Ladany, N. and Lehrman-Waterman, D. E. (1999) 'The content and frequency of supervisor self-disclosures and their relationship to supervisor style and the supervisory working alliance', *Counselor Education and Supervision* 38(3): 143–60.

Lehrman-Waterman, D. and Ladany, N. (2001) 'Development and validation of the evaluation process within supervision inventory', *Journal of Counseling Psychology* 48(2): 168.

Lizzio, A. J. and Wilson, K. L. (2002) 'The domain of learning goals in professional supervision', in M. Patton and W. McMahon (eds), *Supervision in the Helping Professions: A Practical Approach*, Frenchs Forest: Pearson Education Australia, pp. 27–41.

Long, C. (2014) *Clinical Supervision Questionnaire*, Northampton: St Andrew's Healthcare.

Long, C. G., Harding, S., Payne, K. and Collins, L. (2013) 'Nursing and health-care assistant experience of supervision in a medium secure psychiatric service for women: implications for service development', *Journal of Psychiatric and Mental Health Nursing* 21(2): 154–62.

Milne, D. L., Reiser, R. P., Cliffe, T. and Raine, R. (2011) 'SAGE: preliminary evaluation of an instrument for observing competence in CBT supervision', *The Cognitive Behaviour Therapist* 4(4): 123–38.

Palomo, M., Beinart, H. and Cooper, M. J. (2010) 'Development and validation of the Supervisory Relationship Questionnaire (SRQ) in UK trainee clinical psychologists', *British Journal of Clinical Psychology* 49(2): 131–49.

Pearce, N., Beinart, H. and Clohessy, S. (2013) 'Development and validation of the supervisory relationship measure: a self-report questionnaire for use with supervisors', *British Journal of Clinical Psychology* 52(3): 249–68.

Proctor, B. (1986) 'Supervision: a co-operative exercise in accountability', in M. Marken and M. Payne (eds), *Enabling and Ensuring*, Leicester: National Youth Bureau for Education in Youth and Community Work.

Wainwright, N. A. (2010) *The Development of the Leeds Alliance in Supervision Scale (LASS)*, Leeds: School of Medicine, University of Leeds.

White, E. and Winstanley, J. (2010) 'A randomised controlled trial of clinical supervision: selected findings from a novel Australian attempt to establish the evidence base for causal relationships with quality of care and patient outcomes, as an informed contribution to mental health nursing practice development', *Journal of Research in Nursing* 15(2): 151–67.

Winstanley, J. and White, E. (2003) 'Clinical supervision: models, measures and best practice', *Nurse Researcher* 10(4): 7–38.

Winstanley, J. and White, E. (2011) 'The MCSS-26©: Revision of the Manchester Clinical Supervision Scale© using the Rasch Measurement Model', *Journal of Nursing Measurement* 19(3): 160–78.

Special Topic 9
Team supervision

Team supervision is a specific form of group supervision that involves members of the same team (Hyrkäs, Appelqvist-Schmidlechner and Paunonen Ilmonen, 2002). This form of supervision has been reported in a number of general hospital settings and in education, however its use in custodial and forensic mental health settings is not known although it is probably relatively common. In an education context, Maxwell (2013) describes how team supervision can draw upon a wide range of models and approaches to help facilitate learning, development and solutions. He describes the use of solution circles (Forest and Pearpoint, 1996; McIntosh, 2012) – see Box ST9.1, 'functional analysis' and a contextual approach (viewing the world from the pupil's (client's) position) in order to facilitate team supervision. Through the use of these approaches and techniques such as analogies, metaphors and 'rich pictures' he describes the team evolving to a point where members saw each other as a resource.

BOX ST9.1: Building solutions in 30 minutes (adapted from Solution Circles: Forest and Pearpoint, 1996; McIntosh, 2012)

Building solutions has eight steps, which are worked through by the team. This approach is particularly helpful when an impasse is reached or the team is stuck rather than as an 'every session' approach to team supervision. Each step is time limited to allow focus to be maintained and actions to be generated within 30 minutes. Throughout the process, someone acts as note-keeper. It is possible for this process to be used when considering an individual client (although see Box ST9.2), however it is particularly useful with issues and problems facing the team.

1. Present the problem (4 minutes)

One of the group members has 4 minutes to present the key information about the problem. This is uninterrupted time during which everyone else listens and the note-keeper records information. If the person finished presenting information before 4 minutes has elapsed the group remain silent until the time is up.

2. Add information (2 minutes)

During this period the rest of the team can add anything they feel is important that has been left out.

3. Identify priorities (2 minutes)

The team agree on the main concerns or issues to focus on (maximum of 3). These should be written on a flipchart or board.

4. Generate solutions (5 minutes)

Everyone generates ideas and options, which the recorder captures or individuals write on paper or a flipchart. Anything that has worked previously should be captured along with any other ideas or possibilities. This process is creative and ideas or thoughts shouldn't be censored or their feasibility explored at this stage.

5. Consider options (10 minutes)

Discuss the options and ideas that have been generated. Focus on possibilities and positives . . . no problem or 'won't work' talk.

6. Decide on actions (5 minutes)

An action plan is developed and agreed based on those things that can be implemented readily (i.e. the individual who presented the problem or the team have the necessary resources). At least one action should be instigated within 24 hours. Someone is nominated to check that this has been done.

7. Brief reflection (2 minutes)

Each person in the group states what they found useful/will do to support the actions.

8. Follow up

The team agree when and how progress/outcomes will be reviewed.

As might be anticipated from the work of Tuckman (Tuckman, 1965; Tuckman and Jensen, 1977), Hyrkäs et al. (2002) found that initially, groups were slow and rigid but that over time they showed a sense of togetherness and a greater awareness of need. Although their study was based on investigating supervisor experiences of providing multi-professional team supervision in a general hospital setting, this process is likely to be common to team supervision in a forensic setting. As with other forms of supervision, Hyrkäs et al. (2002) note that there needs to be a contract stating the nature, objectives, methods and goals of the group. They found that some participants dropped out over time and suggest that who will participate and the level and type of commitment expected is clarified from the start. Supervisors commented that having two supervisors per group was helpful and reported improvements in ways participants dealt with grievances over the course of the group. In a separate study based on the same team supervision service initiative, Hyrkäs and Appelqvist-Schmidlechner (2003) interviewed groups of individuals who had attended team supervision some 4–6 months after it ended. The impact of the supervision was summarised through four themes:

(1) Togetherness (sense of solidarity).
(2) Communication and expression of opinions (openness vs restrictiveness; frankness vs sensorship).
(3) Team relationships (increased coherence; tensions).
(4) Team working methods and work motivation (changed decision making, motivations and frustrations).

The authors concluded that when team supervision was successfully implemented, it had a positive effect upon communication between team members. For this service, Hyrkäs and colleagues (Hyrkäs, Lehti and Paunonen Ilmonen, 2001) also attempted to provide a methodology for a cost-benefit analysis of team supervision. They applied their financial costing approach to a single ward and concluded that 'team supervision was a profitable investment on Ward A' (p. 267).

In a focus group study of team supervision in acute hospital settings in Australia, O'Connell and colleagues (O'Connell et al., 2013) found that team supervision was positively appraised. Participants reported that team supervision provided a forum to debrief and address work issues; improved communication; reduced stress/enhanced well-being; enhanced problem solving skills; and empowered staff. They also reported that the qualities of effective supervisors were being relaxed; informal; encouraging; independent; objective (being at a distance from the ward/managerial issues) and having the ability to listen. They identified the importance of preparation through providing pre-reading material, having team supervision ambassadors and ensuring an effective method to organise practicalities such as a meeting time.

Within a forensic setting, team supervision, especially where there is a multi-professional team, can be useful for a number of different reasons. These include:

(a) fostering a multi-professional focus to clients;
(b) building the team ethos and identity;
(c) promoting a shared understanding based on different viewpoints and roles;
(d) allowing reflection on complex issues such as team dynamics, managerial issues, boundaries etc.; and
(e) managing 'drift' to ensure consistency and clarity between members of the team.

Some of these reasons reflect the four themes reported by Hyrkäs and Appelqvist-Schmidlechner (2003) above. This form of *open team supervision* can be very beneficial. Within a secure forensic mental health setting in the UK, Long et al. (2013) have reported the intention to make this form of group supervision mandatory with an expectation that by providing weekly sessions every member of the team attends at least monthly. This form of group supervision can be facilitated in a variety of ways, however Box ST9.2 provides a broad template for fostering discussion in relation to the clients the team work with. This can be supplemented by other approaches to foster reflection and support (see Chapter 5).

> **BOX ST9.2: Template for client discussions within team supervision**
>
> This template provides a general outline for facilitating team discussions in relation to individual clients. It is based around a one hour supervision session and assumes that the members in the team supervision know one another (in particular their roles within the team), know the service setting (including rules and procedures) and have some knowledge of the client being discussed.
>
> 1. Agree a client to focus on.
> 2. Outline basic information (e.g. time in the service).
> 3. Describe the challenges and difficulties faced by staff and the client.
> 4. Explore possible reasons for the difficulties.
> 5. Discuss how each member experiences the client and the boundaries each sets (and how these are responded to).
> 6. Describe the client's aspirations and goals.
> 7. Discuss discharge/release options and routes and what would need to change/happen to facilitate this.
> 8. Describe risk issues (including behavioural, legal, ethical and interpersonal).
> 9. Discuss what works, client successes/positives.
> 10. Identify possible solutions/decisions/actions to take.
> 11. Share with the wider team.
> 12. Future review.
>
> A record of the meeting should be kept by the staff team and as shown in point 11, discussion is needed at the end of the session to ensure that the contents (and especially the solutions/develops and actions) are shared with the rest of the team. As with other forms of supervision the discussion ends by considering what will be monitored and how this will be reviewed (e.g. feedback in a future team supervision session).

As with all forms of supervision, it is important to consider the possible limitations of this form of supervision. Because of the potential for 'transient' group membership, this form of supervision may bring with it a reluctance for participants to self-disclose, an absence of focus and the potential for repetition of content (Cleary and Freeman, 2005). Those providing this form of supervision should be mindful of these possible limitations and the impact this may have on what is or isn't discussed.

Conclusion

Team supervision can offer a helpful way to bring together members of a team to review and reflect on their work. It is a very flexible arrangement, enabling members to participate when they are able to, whilst providing a regular 'reflective' or 'learning' space within the setting. It is particularly useful for reviewing team difficulties and facilitating discussions about specific clients.

References

Cleary, M. and Freeman, A. (2005) 'The cultural realities of clinical supervision in an acute inpatient mental health setting', *Issues in Mental Health Nursing* 26(5): 489–505.

Forest, M. and Pearpoint, J. (1996) 'Solution circle: getting unstuck', *Inclusion Press*, retrieved 10 May 2014, from www.inclusion.com/ttsolutioncircle.html.

Hyrkäs, K. and Appelqvist-Schmidlechner, K. (2003) 'Team supervision in multiprofessional teams: team members' descriptions of the effects as highlighted by group interviews', *Journal of Clinical Nursing* 12(2): 188–97.

Hyrkäs, K., Appelqvist-Schmidlechner, K. and Paunonen Ilmonen, M. (2002) 'Expert supervisors' views of clinical supervision: a study of factors promoting and inhibiting the achievements of multiprofessional team supervision', *Journal of Advanced Nursing* 38(4): 387–97.

Hyrkäs, K., Lehti, K. and Paunonen Ilmonen, M. (2001) 'Cost–benefit analysis of team supervision: the development of an innovative model and its application as a case study in one Finnish University Hospital', *Journal of Nursing Management* 9(5): 259–68.

Long, C. G., Harding, S., Payne, K. and Collins, L. (2013) 'Nursing and health-care assistant experience of supervision in a medium secure psychiatric service for women: implications for service development', *Journal of Psychiatric and Mental Health Nursing* 21(2): 154–62.

Maxwell, T. (2013) 'A reflection on the work of an Educational Psychologist in providing supervision for a team of community based support workers, supporting families with vulnerable adolescents at risk of exclusion from school', *Pastoral Care in Education* 31(1): 15–27.

McIntosh, S. (2012) 'Solution circles – a creative problem solving tool', *One Education*, retrieved 10 May 2014, from https://docs.google.com/a/oneeducation.co.uk/viewer?a=v&pid=sites&srcid=b25lZWR1Y2F0aW9uLmNvLnVrfGVwLWNvbm5lY3R8Z3g6NDZhNDRlZTA5ZmI0M2RmOQ.

O'Connell, B., Ockerby, C. M., Johnson, S., Smenda, H. and Bucknall, T. K. (2013) 'Team clinical supervision in acute hospital wards: a feasibility study', *Western Journal of Nursing Research* 35(3): 330–47.

Tuckman, B. W. (1965) 'Developmental sequence in small groups', *Psychological Bulletin* 63(6): 384.

Tuckman, B. W. and Jensen, M. A. C. (1977) 'Stages of small-group development revisited', *Group and Organization Management* 2(4): 419–27.

Special Topic 10
Reflective practice

Reflective practice is an approach to learning and development, which can be used within supervision. It's concerned with reviewing experience either as it happens – reflection in action; at a later time – reflection on action (Schön, 1983); or before it takes place – reflection before action (Greenwood, 1993) and can be undertaken alone or with a 'guide'. Reflection in action has an overlap with the concept of the internal supervisor (Casement, 1985). For the purposes of this special topic, the focus is limited to guided reflection 'before' or 'on' action described as prospective analysis and retrospective reflection (Schön, 1983; Wilson and Lizzio, 2009). In doing so, several approaches to reflective practice will be considered, however the reader is also encouraged to review the material contained in Chapter 5.

Reflective practice

What is reflective practice?

Reflective practice (RP) carries with it an air of mystery and reverence, possibly because of the philosophical debates that often surround it. However, RP is simply an approach to learning and development that seeks to combine 'knowledge' with 'experience'. For the purpose of this special topic, reflection is defined as an active 'process of reviewing an experience of practice in order to describe, analyse, evaluate and so inform learning about practice' (Reid, 1993, p. 305). It therefore involves an active and deliberate critical evaluation of practice and experience in order to achieve effective and desirable future practice (Johns, 1995; Duffy, 2007). Reflective practice is said to have many positive effects including developing critical thinking, highlighting poor practice and improving patient care. This focus on action, learning and development results in reflection being more than just thoughtful practice (Jarvis, 1992). This might be by relating experience to other knowledge such as a formal evidence, however it is important that in this process the research is fitted to the situation not the situation to evidence (Johns, 1995). RP also requires the ability to consider the whole situation (including consequences) rather than just specific components.

As a result of the growth of interest in reflective practice, especially within nursing, there are many texts written on reflective practice such as those by Johns (2010c); Rolfe, Jasper and Freshwater (2011) and Taylor (2010).

Guided reflective practice

Although reflection can take place alone, guided reflection is a process by which 'people can learn through their everyday experiences to become who they want to be' (Johns, 2010b, p. 2). It has been suggested that reflection is at the heart of supervision (Scaife, 2013) and that RP and supervision are synonymous (Johns, 1993); indeed, Carpenter *et al.* (2012) describe 'reflective supervision' as a key process within social work and social care. Thus, it could be argued that supervision provides the formal structure with reflection as the enabling process (Fowler and Chevannes, 1998). One reason for guided RP is that actions can be subject to habituation through which they can become ritualised and 'unthinkingly' applied (Jarvis, 1992). This can be exacerbated when the individuality of the client is lost and replaced by some collective grouping such as prisoners or patients; or client work is seen solely as a target to be met. As Jarvis (1992) observes, 'When people become objects then the danger of actions moving from the carefully planned to the taken-for-granted is enhanced but, by contrast, when professionals treat their patients as unique human beings then the danger of the practice becoming mindless decreases and the level of consciousness required by practice remains high' (p.177). Thus guided RP can help the practitioner to remain responsive, thoughtful and humane and able to deliver a high-quality service. However, learning from experience, and making changes to practice can be challenging for the individual and the service and this can lead to 'sanctions' in order to bring practice or people 'back in line' (Johns, 1999). Although the intent is to 'uncover and expose thoughts, feelings and behaviours that are present in a period of time' (Driscoll and Teh, 2001, p. 96) in order to become more effective/improve future actions, the process of RP can be very challenging as it may lead to challenging one's own actions in order to bring about changes to practice. As a result of the potential personal and organisational challenge, there is a danger that RP is accommodated to fit the culture rather than change it (Johns, 1999). Supervisors therefore need to be attentive to the needs of the supervisee and to supporting the outcomes that might arise from the process of reflection.

Supporting reflective practice requires a facilitative stance from the supervisor. This might be in the form of a guide who is able to balance high challenge with high support (Johns, 2010a) or even an 'enlightened guide' (Rolfe and Gardner, 2006) who can foster awareness of practice, the process of critical reflection and assist the practitioner to harness evidence generated from practice (cf. practice-based evidence Davies, Jones and Howells, 2010). The supervisor might also be seen as a critical friend (Taylor, 2010); someone who can offer an external perspective and who is prepared to ask probing and important questions which might lead to perceptions, actions and assumptions for practice being challenged. In order to take on such roles it is important that the supervisor is trusted and respected; an anxious supervisor can become controlling and directive towards the supervisee undermining the process of reflection (Johns, 1999).

In a study of reflective practice within nursing, Paget (2001) found that the majority of respondents found it useful and believed that a significant specific change had occurred in their practice as a result of reflective practice and that this change had been integrated into their practice. Some, however, noted intentions to make changes but reported organisational blocks to achieving these. Most considered the facilitator to be 'very important' to the effectiveness of reflective practice. They found some indication that those who were more experienced perceived less benefit from reflective practice but that benefits were found at all levels and argue that RP is relevant across all levels of experience and practice. They suggest that 'the skill of reflecting, once learned, can be a medium for constant reviewing of professional practice' (p. 209).

Planning for reflection

Engaging in reflection can be challenging for the supervisor and supervisee as it encourages a detailed focus on practice in order to facilitate learning. As a result, it has been argued that supervisees need to be minimally defensive and willing to work in collaboration for it to be successful (Bégat et al., 2003). In addition, Atkins and Murphy (1993) suggest that supervisees need to be motivated and open-minded in order to engage in RP; and need to be self-aware, able to describe, and able to engage in critical analysis, synthesis and evaluation. However, it should be borne in mind that these skills and abilities will also be developed and shaped through the process of RP itself.

Some have suggested that guided reflective practice may not suit all supervisees (Jones, 2006), that some may not be able to do it (Fowler and Chevannes, 1998) and that it may be more difficult for beginning practitioners (Mackintosh, 1998). Other practitioners report that they are 'already doing it' (Reid, 1993) outside of formal supervision. This reinforces the need for the supervisor and supervisee to establish a supervision agreement in which the use of reflective practice within supervision is clearly established.

For those wishing to engage in guided RP within supervision, Taylor (2010) presents what she refers to as the REFLECT model of reflection. However, it is probably more accurate to think of this as a broad template of the necessary conditions:

(a) Readiness – create time, space etc.
(b) Exercise thought – express self freely, remain open to ideas.
(c) Follow systematic processes – use a framework to reflect.
(d) Leave yourself open to answers – don't force answers to 'appear'.
(e) Enfolding insights – develop ideas over time.

(f) Changing awareness – develop learning.
(g) Tenacity in maintaining reflection – create a habit, nurture reflection.

There are many ways to identify material on which to reflect. These might be through questioning why an outcome has occurred (or by comparing actual outcomes against an anticipated outcome or theoretical expectations) or by reviewing those aspects of practice that are taken for granted or have become routine (Jarvis, 1992). Johns (2003) also notes that emotion may act as a trigger for reflection and action and thus emotion may be a useful starting point. Additionally, it may be useful to consider how intended action and actual action differed (Wilson and Lizzio, 2009), and to have a range of prompts such as something that:

(a) went well;
(b) puzzled or confused me;
(c) made me feel (stupid, happy, professional, angry, vulnerable, proud);
(d) concerned me about my (or someone else's) practice;
(e) I would change about what I did; and
(f) I tried that I haven't done before.

(based on Driscoll, 2007)

Models and approaches to reflective practice

Many models and frameworks have been described to help guide and structure reflective practice. At the most general, RP can be used to consider broad questions such as 'is it safe? is it right? is it kind?' (Butterworth *et al.*, 2008), however most frameworks for reflection provide a more stepped process. A number of these are briefly presented below.

Three types of reflection (Taylor, 2010)

Taylor details three types of reflection although she emphasises that reflection need not be categorised (and thus constrained) to just one – a combination may be used together or sequentially:

(a) *Technical* – this form of reflection makes use of an objective approach using rational, scientific and deductive methods to determine evidence for practice, develop policies and procedures and find practical answers to practice problems (e.g. what impact would changing [this practice] make?). The three steps in this type of reflection can be summarised as:

   (i) assessing and planning – initial assessment of the problem or event leading to a hypothesis;
   (ii) implementing – develop an argument by analysing the issues and assumptions; consider possible consequence; and

(iii) evaluation – reconsider the problem in the light of the new information, what are the conclusions, what do you 'recommend' as an action?

(b) *Practical* – in this approach, a systematic questioning process is used to increase awareness of human interaction (and communication) through making sense of/understanding experience – values, thoughts and feelings within a context (e.g. why did I react in that way to [the client]?). The steps in this form of reflection are:

(i) experiencing – describe the detail of what happened including feelings, others' actions, sights, sounds, smells etc. (it may be helpful to imagine yourself back in the situation);
(ii) interpreting – clarify and explain the meaning of the situation – what were my hopes, how were these (and/or my values) communicated in the situation; and
(iii) learning – what can I learn from the situation about myself and others (and my expectations of myself and others); what learning can I take from the situation?

(c) *Emancipatory* – this type of reflection requires a systematic analysis of one's own practice, 'taken-for-granted' assumptions, 'oppressive forces', and constraints to engage in transformative action (e.g. why didn't I raise my concerns with the management plan?). The four steps in this type of reflection can be summarised as:

(i) constructing – a description of the situation or event;
(ii) deconstructing – what power or 'political' forces were at play, how might my actions be viewed by an 'interested observer';
(iii) confronting – a critical analysis of practice – where do the ideas informing my practice stem from, what power relations are involved, what cultural, social and personal constraints are evident;
(iv) reconstructing – what can I do differently, how might I bring about change, how might I work differently?

The What? Model of Structured Reflection (Driscoll, 2007)

In this model, selected aspects of a practice experience are considered in order to draw out possible learning and inform future action. The model to guide this is based on three simple questions:

(1) *What* – a description of the event or experience (questions such as what happened? what did I say or do? how did I react?).
(2) *So what* – an analysis of the event or experience (questions such as how did I feel at the time? are my feelings any different now? what were the effects of my actions?).
(3) *Now what* – proposed actions arising from the reflection (questions such as what would I do differently if the same happened again? what is the

main learning I can take from this reflection? how will I action the results of my reflections?).

Gibbs's experiential learning cycle (Gibbs, 2013). This model is comprised of six steps shown below with associated cue questions:

(1) *Description* (what happened?).
(2) *Feelings* (what were your reactions and feelings?).
(3) *Evaluation* (what was good or bad about the experience?).
(4) *Analysis* (what sense can you make of the situation?).
(5) *Conclusions* (what can be concluded (a) generally from these experiences and your analysis, and (b) about your own specific situation or way of working?).
(6) *Personal action plans* (what are you going to do the same/differently in this type of situation next time?).

In this model it is important not to make judgements or interpret information until step 3.

Reflective Learning Model of Supervision (Beddoe and Davys, 2010)

his model is based on a four stage cycle:

(1) *Event* (awareness of experience, clarify the supervision issue).
(2) *Exploration* (of impact on the supervisee and implications for the client, organisation, policies etc.).
(3) *Experimentation* (testing the viability of the ideas, possibilities and learning generated during the exploration).
(4) *Evaluation* (testing whether the 'issue' is resolved, identifying new learning needs or issues arising from the discussion).

In an ongoing piece of work, Johns has developed a series of models for structured reflection. Although this is an evolving process, two of the 'editions' are presented as they offer different anchor points from which to consider reflection.

(1) *Model for Structured Reflection* (5th edn: Johns, 1993):
    (a) *Phenomenon* – provide a description of the experience;
    (b) *Causal* – what are the contributing factors;
    (c) *Context* – what is the background;
    (d) *Reflection* – on intentions, actions, feelings, outcomes;
    (e) *Alternative actions* – then and now; and
    (f) *Learning* – what have I learned, how do I feel now.
(2) *Model for Structured Reflection* (10th edn: Johns, 1995). This is based on 'ways of knowing' as shown in each of the 'cue questions':
    (a) *Aesthetics* – (practitioner response – what was I trying to achieve, why did I do what I did?).

(b) *Personal* – (practitioner feelings – how did I feel, what internal factors were influencing me?).
(c) *Ethics* – (what is 'right and wrong' – how did my action fit with my beliefs, why did I act in an incongruent way?).
(d) *Empirics* – ('learned knowledge' – what knowledge did or should have informed me).
(e) *Reflexivity* – (connecting – how does this fit with past experience, how do I feel now, what would I do next time?).

Each of the models presented above offer the supervisor and supervisee some structure by which experiences can be processed and considered. Box ST10.1 presents a range of questions which might be helpfully used to aid reflection.

BOX ST10.1: Questions to aid reflection

The following questions have been drawn from the authors in this special topic, personal experiences of providing and receiving reflective supervision and suggestions from participants at training events. They can be used alongside many of the models and frameworks described in this special topic. They are written as if spoken by the supervisor for application to a past event but a change of tense would allow most to be applied to a future action or event. The questions in Box 7.2 might also be useful.

What do you want from discussing this situation?
What were your goals/what were you trying to achieve?
What were the outcomes?
Where did you learn this from?
What does this tell you about your expectations of yourself/others?
What influenced you at the time (social rules, policies, others around you)?
What have you done in similar situations in the past?
What were you thinking at the time?
What power factors might be relevant?
What worked well?
What needs to change?
What do others think and why?
What do you need to do next?
How did you feel?
How did the client feel?
What would happen if you did nothing?
What conclusions have you reached?
What have you learned about yourself?
What other choices did you have at the time?
What choices would you have next time?
What would be the possible outcomes/consequences of these choices?

Conclusion

Guided reflective practice can be used within supervision to build understanding, learning and development through reviewing what has happened (reflection on action) or before undertaking a task (reflection before action). There are many ways in which this can be done, however the key role for the supervisor is to facilitate thinking and review.

References

Atkins, S. and Murphy, K. (1993) 'Reflection: a review of the literature', *Journal of Advanced Nursing* 18(8): 1188–92.
Beddoe, L. and Davys, A. (2010) *Best Practice in Professional Supervision*, London: Jessica Kingsley Publishers.
Bégat, I., Berggren, I., Ellefsen, B. and Severinsson, E. (2003) 'Australian nurse supervisors' styles and their perceptions of ethical dilemmas within health care', *Journal of Nursing Management* 11(1): 6–14.
Butterworth, T., Bell, L., Jackson, C. and Pajnkihar, M. (2008) 'Wicked spell or magic bullet? A review of the clinical supervision literature 2001–', *Nurse Education Today* 28(3): 264–72.
Carpenter, J., Webb, C., Bostock, L. and Coomber, C. (2012) 'Effective supervision in social work and social care', *SCIE Research Briefing*, available at www.scie.org.uk/publications/briefings/files/briefing43.pdf.
Casement, P. (1985) *On Learning From the Patient*, London: Tavistock Publications Ltd.
Davies, J., Jones, L. and Howells, K. (2010) 'Evaluating individual change', in M. Daffern, L. Jones and J. Shine, *Offence Paralleling Behaviour: A Case Formulation Approach to Offender Assessment and Intervention*, Oxford: Wiley & Sons.
Driscoll, J. (2007) *Practising Clinical Supervision*, Oxford: Elsevier Health Sciences.
Driscoll, J. and Teh, B. (2001) 'The potential of reflective practice to develop individual orthopaedic nurse practitioners and their practice', *Journal of Orthopaedic Nursing* 5(2): 95–103.
Duffy, A. (2007) 'A concept analysis of reflective practice: determining its value to nurses', *British Journal of Nursing* 16(22): 1400–407.
Fowler, J. and Chevannes, M. (1998) 'Evaluating the efficacy of reflective practice within the context of clinical supervision', *Journal of Advanced Nursing* 27(2): 379–82.
Gibbs, G. (2013) *Learning by Doing*, Oxford: Oxford Centre for Staff Learning and Development, Oxford Brookes University.
Greenwood, J. (1993) 'Reflective practice: a critique of the work of Argyris and Schön', *Journal of Advanced Nursing* 18(8): 1183–7.
Jarvis, P. (1992) 'Reflective practice and nursing', *Nurse Education Today* 12(3): 174–81.
Johns, C. (1993) 'Professional supervision', *Journal of Nursing Management* 1(1): 9–18.
——(1995) 'Framing learning through reflection within Carper's fundamental ways of knowing in nursing', *Journal of Advanced Nursing* 22(2): 226–34.
——(1999) 'Reflection as empowerment?', *Nursing Inquiry* 6(4): 241–9.
——(2003) 'Clinical supervision as a model for clinical leadership', *Journal of Nursing Management* 11(1): 25–35.
——(2010a) 'Deepening insights', in C. Johns, *Guided Reflection: A Narrative Approach to Advancing Professional Practice*, Oxford: Wiley-Blackwell, pp. 51–65.
——(2010b) 'The basic scheme', in C. Johns, *Guided Reflection: A Narrative Approach to Advancing Professional Practice*, Oxford: Wiley-Blackwell, pp. 1–26.

Johns, C. (ed.) (2010c) *Guided Reflection: A Narrative Approach to Advancing Professional Practice* (2nd edn), Oxford: Wiley-Blackwell.

Jones, A. (2006) 'Clinical supervision: what do we know and what do we need to know? A review and commentary', *Journal of Nursing Management* 14(8): 577–85.

Mackintosh, C. (1998) 'Reflection: a flawed strategy for the nursing profession', *Nurse Education Today* 18(7): 553–7.

Paget, T. (2001) 'Reflective practice and clinical outcomes: practitioners' views on how reflective practice has influenced their clinical practice', *Journal of Clinical Nursing* 10(2): 204–14.

Reid, B. (1993) '"But we're doing it already!" Exploring a response to the concept of reflective practice in order to improve its facilitation', *Nurse Education Today* 13(4): 305–9.

Rolfe, G. and Gardner, L. (2006) '"Do not ask who I am … ": confession, emancipation and (self)-management through reflection', *Journal of Nursing Management* 14(8): 593–600.

Rolfe, G., Jasper, M. and Freshwater, D. (2011) *Critical Reflection in Practice* (2nd edn), London: Palgrave Macmillan.

Scaife, J. (2013) *Supervision in Clinical Practice*, Abingdon: Routledge.

Schön, D. A. (1983) *The Reflective Practitioner: How Professionals Think in Action*, New York: Basic Books Inc.

Taylor, B. J. (2010) *Reflective Practice for Healthcare Professionals: A Practical Guide* (3rd edn), Maidenhead: Open University Press.

Wilson, K. L. and Lizzio, A. J. (2009) 'Processes and interventions to facilitate supervisees' learning', in N. Pelling, J. Barletta and P. Armstrong, *The Practice of Clinical Supervision*, Samford Valley: Australian Academic Press, pp. 138–64.

11 The end of the beginning
Summary, observations and future directions

In many respects, this text reflects the influences on my own experience of supervision as a supervisee, supervisor, researcher and trainer. It is also shaped by the things I wished I'd known when embarking on supervision, the things that continue to present a challenge and the gaps I have sought to 'plug' in my own skills and understanding as issues and opportunities have arisen. This text is intended as a foundation for the reader, providing a resource which distils a range of information that is potentially relevant to those providing, receiving, planning and researching supervision. As with many areas of practice, to become competent in supervision requires knowledge and skill (experiences). This text should assist with the former and act as a signpost to other resources, allowing the interested reader ways to develop, expand or explore ideas further.

Writing a book on supervision for forensic practitioners raises many challenges at a practical and theoretical level. These include finding the correct tone and style and ensuring adequate coverage of key issues, ideas and evidence. A great deal of this has been harnessed, borrowed, translated and adapted from other fields – especially therapy, nursing and mental health. There is an on-going need to scrutinise the ways in which aspects of supervision can be generalised from elsewhere, however, from personal experience, anecdote and the limited research evidence, drawing from other settings appears appropriate at this time. It remains to be seen how theories, models, research and practice might be shaped and developed over the next 20 years. However, the task of seeking to establish a basis for forensic supervision and evidence to support this, reveals the enormous opportunities for development in this field.

As outlined in Chapter 1, a guiding factor in the structure of this text has been the attempt to be inclusive to reflect the diversity of professional groups, the vast array of forensic settings, and to include those with or without professional training for the work they do. There is a history of giving the least focus, training, support and attention to our least qualified staff. Supervision offers a chance to address this problem and invest in the workforce at all levels. This text also addresses several groups including those providing supervision, those receiving supervision and those in a position to develop supervision strategies and influence supervision practice within their workplace or organisation. Ideally, such groups will work together within services to develop local strategies and policies to embed supervision.

As described in the opening pages of this book, the work undertaken by forensic practitioners can be demanding, challenging and enjoyable, however, the need for support, development and monitoring of practice are important. In such settings, it can be easy to overlook the 'real life of the person' within the practitioner – they may themselves have been a victim of a crime, have particular values and aspirations about forensic work and will vary in their resources and capacity to respond to the multitude of emotional demands placed upon them by working in this field. These factors are likely to be dynamic, changing with the individual's experience both inside and outside work. Supervisors need to be attentive to this if they are to meet the changing needs of the supervisee.

Practitioners in forensic settings are also required to consider a wide range of factors such as multiple risks, complex processes (such as the mental health – criminal justice interface); specialist regulation (such as penal codes and frameworks), the challenge of fostering positive risk taking and the potential for boundary difficulties and breaches. This might include the use of frameworks such as the 'Triangle of Boundary Maintenance' (see Box 8.1), approaches to ethics (Special Topic 2) or positive risk taking (Chapter 8). However, such principles will be 'personalised' based on the service specific factors and unique individual factors if they are to be of maximum use. As discussed in Chapter 8 and Special Topic 2, supervision provides a mechanism to help to maintain a balance between self-care and a focus on others and their tasks, attending to the broad issues of boundaries, risk and ethics. Supervision can assist supervisees to understand and modify their responses so as to avoid becoming over-involved or detached when faced with these complexities. In this way supervision may offer safeguards through external support, early identification and protection to the supervisee.

As well as having the potential to provide support and foster learning, there is a potential for supervision to be of poor quality and to be misused. This includes the potential for dual relationships between the supervisor and the supervisee as discussed in Chapter 8 and the failure to appreciate the complexities relating to power and responsibility within supervision. To minimise the likelihood of these, training of supervisees and supervisors, outside scrutiny, policies, governance arrangements and a culture of empowering of staff (not only through supervision) can provide important safeguards for those receiving and delivering supervision. Individuals and those overseeing supervision policy and practice within an organisation should be familiar with the issues associated with lousy and harmful supervision discussed in Chapters 6, 7 and 8. In addition, supervisors, trainers and managers need a good understanding of supervisor competence and how this might be promoted and assessed. Indeed, given the possibility of poor supervision as discussed above, supervisors have a duty to be competent if they are to undertake the role. A number of frameworks have begun to emerge that describe the core values and appropriate general and supervision specific competencies associated with effective supervision. For example, good supervisor practice draws upon what works, makes use of supervision agreements to specify purpose, expectations and responsibilities, is responsive to the supervisee and is flexible; drawing on models and frameworks as they are needed. As with all forms of interaction, the alliance between the 'participants' needs to be fostered creating a bond that is built on trust, respect and collaboration. Thus effective supervisors pay attention to core conditions such as the supervisory alliance. The content of Chapters 3, 4 and 7 provides a wealth of information relevant to supervisor competence regardless of the type (e.g. individual or group) or form (e.g. peer, expert) of supervision being undertaken.

One method for supervisors to review their competence is to periodically undertake a self-assessment of their professional and supervision practice competence, skills and needs. By discussing this with their supervisor and line manager they can use the information to inform their own supervision and development. Individuals (or services) might also wish to engage in a 360° appraisal process in which feedback is obtained from supervisees, managers, supervisors and relevant others. Again this can be used to identify good practice and areas for development. There are many ways to do this, however, as a start, supervisors may wish to revisit some of the exercises within earlier chapters in this book (e.g. Box 1.2). Further, the existing competency frameworks such as those discussed in Chapter 7 provides a starting point based on current best practice.

Learning about one's practice and oneself can be challenging and feedback can be difficult, however it should be a core aspect of supervision. Instilling a 'feedback culture' within supervision fosters learning and development and provides a basis on which to address issues of competence and difficulties that will inevitably arise from time to time such as issues relating to boundaries or conflict. However, as well as formative and summative feedback within the supervisory relationship (see Chapter 7) feedback needs to be extended to the wider system. The system needs to invest in understanding what works and what needs to be changed through local audit and evaluation. This would enable a 'learning organisation' to engage in a recursive/iterative process to improve supervision within the organisation.

The aspiration to empower and support an individual to enhance their practice is well founded. However, the supervisor needs to be aware of the power dynamics in both the alliance and 'supervision content and process' if they are to enable supervisees to develop and experiment rather than to constrain and restrict practitioners.

In developing supervision practice we need also to consider the allied activities of consultation and training. Consultation is commonly driven by the need to resolve a specific issue, develop a formulation or seek an 'outside' opinion. The need for training is typically triggered by common learning needs across a staff group. However, their relationship to supervision is both direct (one may lead to the other) and indirect (they share some common skills, methods and frameworks). It is essential that with all these activities, attention is paid to the needs of the recipients, the purpose, expectations and anticipated outcomes, and the most effective ways to provide these. Whilst this text is principally concerned with supervision, the chapter on learning (Chapter 5) is relevant to training, whilst Chapter 3 and Special Topic 9 is relevant to consultation.

Adult learning and development theory is relevant and helps to identify what to focus on and how. Learning goals may be benchmarked against other frameworks identifying what can be achieved with assistance, what has been learned (through review and reflection on successes and mistakes) – seeking to identify how new learning and experience has been integrated either through assimilation or accommodation (see Chapter 5).

From this text, their own practice, and discussions with others, supervisors should consciously build up their own personalised 'toolkits and resources' for use in supervision. This might include questions, frameworks, exercises and learning methods (e.g. the questions in Box 7.2) and creative and experimental ways of considering problems and issues (e.g. Special Topic 7).

Where next?

In considering next steps there are three broad areas of practice supervision in need of attention and development, namely: organisation/practice; training/development and research. The remainder of this chapter will consider each of these. In many of the elements here there are parallels between action needed at the organisational level and at the level of supervision practice itself.

Organisation/practice

It is essential that supervision is not an island detached from practice, but it is a central element of practice, informed by and informing how the practitioner approaches and carries out their work. At the level of supervision practice, this requires that a link is made between the content of supervision and the attitude, actions or ideas that the supervisee will carry back to their practice (see Figure 4.2). However, such links also need to be recognised by the service as essential to successful practice. Further, organisations need to concern themselves with outcomes of supervision at the client, worker and service level. If this is accepted then the ways supervisors are identified and supported, and the emphasis given to supervision will need to change. At present, the role of the supervisor is typically one that is acquired by default. This sets supervision apart from many of the other aspects of service delivery such as risk assessment and management, formulation, running groups, delivering therapy or teaching and training others. For each of these roles, formal routes to skills development exist (even if they are not used!). Given the potential for supervision to meet many practitioner needs and service goals, it is surprising that so little has been invested in this area of practice thus far. In order to bring about change, organisations need to ensure that supervision is understood and that it is given sufficient priority by managers in order to stand a chance of it having an impact at the individual and organisational level. Part of this will be the necessity to ensure that all those involved feel ownership of supervision and believe in its value. This change will also require training and development of staff, and investment to create and foster a 'supervision savvy' workforce. Such preparation for supervision at an organisational level is paralleled by the preparatory activity of individual supervisees prior to each supervision session (see Chapter 6). Such preparation at all levels is vital if supervision is to live up to expectation. Services and supervisors should orientate supervisees, however this requires the organisation to empower supervisees, allowing them to have ownership and control of their development and practice, and investing in and trusting supervisors to deliver this appropriately and safely (see Special Topic 5).

As already indicated, services have a vital role in setting the context within which supervision can flourish or stagnate. The level of managerial interest and support is essential to embedding supervision within an organisation. Indicators of support for supervision will be reflected in how it is prioritised, audited and the degree to which supervisors themselves receive adequate supervision of their portfolio of work including supervision. Developing a service approach to supervision may be one indication of a 'learning organisation' willing to develop, support and scrutinise in order to improve what is done and how.

Training

It is evident that there is a great deal of scope to develop a range of supervision training options. To have the greatest impact, these need to be based on some form of hybrid model where the 'teaching of knowledge' is coupled with 'learning through experience' (see Chapter 10). It is also likely that this will need to be at a range of levels, from introductory 'in-service' training through to post-graduate programmes. Training will also need to be constructed with different audiences in mind, at minimum this might be the supervisor, the supervisee and the service managers.

Supervisor development and the learning 'education and reflection' that takes place within supervision itself needs to be based on an adult learning approach. The philosophy and approach is well captured by Benjamin Franklin who, over 200 years ago, stated 'Tell me and I forget. Teach me and I remember. Involve me and I learn'. From a training perspective, this means that attention will need to be paid to the different ways in which supervision skills may be developed, as didactic methods are unlikely to be sufficient. Therefore, consideration to individualised learning styles and needs as well as different methods such as modelling and skills practice (Chapter 5) and creative methods (Special Topic 7) are likely to be required.

At this stage in the development of forensic practice supervision, the supervisor pool at the highest level of skill and experience may be limited. This has several implications such as the availability of expertise to develop training and help services develop strategy. It may also mean that there are restricted options for the development of students, trainees and newly qualified staff to shape and develop their supervision practice. Therefore, it may be necessary to see such training and service development over a three to five or even 10-year period, with a developmental trajectory towards an experienced and expert system over time. However, establishing training now, even if this is in a basic format, will enable the supervision resource to grow over time. Additionally, with careful evaluation, a better understanding of what competencies are required and what forms of training and development might be best suited for supervisor development can be gained.

Research and evaluation

Research is needed to establish the evidence base for such things as the impact of supervision on staff, services and clients; the competencies needed to provide adequate supervision; how these might be acquired, and how problematic supervision might be identified. At present, the research on supervision in forensic practice has been relatively neglected despite the clear need for this to be undertaken. This means that practitioners and researchers have many opportunities to engage in research that could have a significant impact on the field. It is important to recognise, however, that a combination approach is required – gathering evidence from *within* practice itself (practice-based evidence produced by practitioner-researchers) and systematic programmes of investigation conducted by researchers *on* practice. Both of these are important and offer the mechanisms to answer different questions and address different problems.

Determining what works in supervision and establishing evidence to link supervision with impacts on supervisees, the client or the service being provided, is seen by some as the Holy Grail for supervision research. However, how to design research that can help understand, specify and quantify the impact of supervision is difficult, especially as some impacts may be indirect (e.g. impacting on a supervisee's resilience to stress in the workplace); subtle (e.g. changes to aspects of practice or an attitudinal change) or of a cumulative nature (e.g. gradual change built over time rather than a step change in skill or approach). Alongside new areas of research and evaluation, it may be important to undertake some 'simple replication' of research that has been conducted elsewhere (e.g. the association between self-reported burnout and perceived supervision quality) or extensions of these (e.g. burnout, quality and a rating of supervisor competence). There is also the potential for building upon studies that have sought to measure the impact of supervision on client outcomes by comparing different supervision models and approaches. Whatever the research, researchers should be aware of and influenced by the problems that have been highlighted in supervision and, more importantly, the ways these could be overcome (see Chapter 2).

In some areas, the volume of supervision research is offset by the highly variable quality of the studies undertaken so far. As a result of the reviews of supervision research in other areas, there is an opportunity for forensic practitioners and researchers to learn lessons from other areas and to engage in high quality evaluation and research in supervision from the outset. As noted in Chapter 2, research using a range of methods including single case, mixed methods, qualitative and quantitative approaches will all have their place to examine, understand and develop supervision practice. Researchers need to be mindful not only of the study design but also the methods and tools they are using. However, there is opportunity to use innovative research designs and methods in this area. To complement this, supervisors should consider how they might routinely gather information, data and evidence with which to evaluate their own practice. This also needs to be considered at a service level. This could include using simple rating or feedback processes (see Special Topic 8), collecting information through periodic supervision reviews or commissioning evaluation or research more formally.

Conclusion

Supervision for forensic practitioners is a relatively new field that deserves more systematic attention than it has received to date. There is a great deal that can be drawn from other areas, however, much work is needed to support the implementation of high quality supervision. Managers, practitioners, researchers and (would-be) supervisors should work together to meet the challenge of developing this nascent field.

Author index

Abraham, A. J. 24
Adair, J. 40, 203
Adams, J. 20, 24
Adams, L. 79
Allen, B. 140–41
Allenby, A. 158, 161
Altman, D. G. 113
Anderson, B. J. 41
Angelone, E. O. 88
Appelqvist-Schmidlechner, K. 20, 24, 25, 41, 89, 156–57, 161, 162, 171, 201, 226, 227, 228–29
Armstrong, A. 8
Armstrong, P. 81, 85, 115
Arvidsson, B. 39, 112
Aston, L. 38
Athlin, E. 20, 115
Atkins, S. 54, 233
Atkinson, C. 50
Austin, W. 139, 142, 144, 188, 189, 190
Ayala, E. E. 29, 104, 105, 209, 221
Ayer, S. 52, 174
Azar, S.T. 24, 66, 116, 117–18, 121, 130–31, 132, 177

Bahrick, A.S. 219
Balshaw-Biddle, K. 135, 136–37
Bambling, M. 22, 28, 29, 109, 174
Banks, D. 205, 207
Barnao, M. 188–89, 190–91
Barnes, K. L. 44, 109–10, 111, 115, 125–26
Barnhill, M. B. 135, 136–37
Baxter, T.D. 38
Bazerman, M.H. 117, 145
Beddoe, L. 2, 5, 40, 61,132–33, 161, 207, 236
Bégat, I. 8, 24, 233
Beinart, H. 219, 220

Benner, P. 79–80
Bentley, N. 122
Bell, L. 22, 25, 29, 30, 158, 159, 234
Berg, A. 17, 24
Berger, L. 29, 104, 105, 209, 221
Berggren, I. 113–14, 233
Berman, J. J. 110, 111
Bernard, J.M. 2, 25–26, 27, 28–29, 39, 40, 50, 58, 61, 68, 71, 75, 88, 186, 187, 188, 213
Bingham, C. 200
Bion, W.R. 40, 196
Bishop, V. 134, 158, 160
Bjones, I. 108, 114, 169, 170, 171
Bjørk, I. T. 87–88
Black, N. 27
Black, S. 122
Bland, A.R. 146
Bluglass, R. 7
Bober, T. 25, 116, 151
Bogo, M. 26
Bøhler, A. 108, 114, 169, 170, 171
Bond, M. 2, 3, 39, 40
Bonner, R. 186, 187, 190
Borders, L. D. 67
Bordin, E.S. 22, 53, 98, 106, 115
Bosta, D. 140–41
Bostock, L. 19, 23, 29, 107, 232
Bradley, G. 163
Bradshaw, T. 21
Brocklehurst, N. 160
Bruce, C. 199, 202
Brock, M. E. 54
Bubner, S. 121
Buckley, M. R. 54
Bucknall, T. K. 228
Burkard, A. W. 124
Burke, W. R. 106, 119
Burns, R. 77, 78, 82, 88, 89

Burnard, P. 20, 24
Bush, Jack 190
Butterworth, A. 21
Butterworth, T. 18, 22, 24, 25, 29, 30, 50, 134, 158, 159, 160 183–84, 234

Carpenter, J. 19, 23, 29, 107, 232
Carrington, G. 75
Carson, J. 18, 24, 134, 158, 160, 183–84
Carthy, J. 156, 157, 158, 220
Casement, P. 231
Chauhan, R. S. 54
Cheater, F.M. 6, 20, 151, 153, 157, 159, 165
Chevannes, M. 50, 232, 233
Chur Hansen, A. 124
Clarke, J. 10
Clark, J.J. 146–47, 147–48
Clarke, P. 67, 87
Clarke, R. D. 124
Cleary, M. 39, 174, 230
Clements, A. 18, 24, 134, 158, 160, 183–84
Cliffe, T. 28, 29, 114, 224
Clifton, A. V.205, 207
Clohessy, S. 219
Clouder, L. 206, 207
Coffey, M.151
Coleman, B. 38
Coleman, M. 151, 171
Collie, R. M. 50
Collins, L. 23, 153, 156, 160, 165, 221, 229
Collins, M. 130, 143
Coomber, C. 232
Cooper, L. 20, 24
Cooper, M. J. 220
Corbett, M. M. 42, 116
Cornish, J. A. E. 26, 113, 127, 174, 175–76, 176–77
Cottrell, S. 151–52, 157
Coyle, D. 20
Crawshaw, P. 205, 207
Cushway, D. 109
Cutcliffe, J.R. 2, 35, 38, 50, 160, 162, 169, 172, 173

Daffern, M. 10, 141
Dall'Alba, G. 79, 80, 89–90
Daniels, G. 7
Davies, J. 27–28, 29, 30, 38, 51, 58, 59, 61, 122, 157, 161, 162, 164–65, 169, 171, 174, 175–76, 177, 178, 192, 201, 221, 222, 232

Davies, S. 130, 143
Davys, A. 2, 5, 40, 61, 161, 236
Day, A. 2, 3, 28, 84–85, 121, 157, 159, 160, 163
De Bono, Edward 217–18
Deuchar, R. 200
Devine, A. 38
Dilworth, S. 28
Driscoll, J. 232, 234, 235
Duffy, A. 231
Durán-Palma, F. 200

Edwards, B. 7
Edwards, D. 20, 24
Ekstein, R. 5, 82
Ellefsen, B. 24, 233
Elliott, W.N. 140
Ellis, M. V. 18, 26, 29, 104, 105, 209, 221
Epstein, R.S. 146
Evans, A. L. 44, 109–10, 111, 115, 125–26
Evershed, S. 136, 137, 139, 141, 142, 143, 144, 145, 146, 147–48

Falender, C. A. 26, 115, 119, 123, 126, 113, 127, 159, 170 174, 175–76, 176–77
Fallon, P. 7
Faulkner, C. 136, 139, 141, 142, 147–48
Fawcett, T. N. 38
Ferguson, E.51, 58, 59, 161, 162, 164, 174, 176, 192, 221
Fleming, I. 2
Flesaker, K. 87
Foley, P. 8
Forest, M. 226–27
Foucault, Michel 205
Fowler, J. 2, 6, 40, 50, 51, 53, 75, 163–64, 174, 232, 233
Francis, Q.C., Robert 7
Frazier, S. L. 20, 50, 51, 85, 119
Freeman, A. 39, 174, 230
Freitas, G. 26, 30, 123, 124
French, R.B. 40, 196
Freshwater, D. 3, 13, 42, 104, 151, 153, 157, 158, 159, 232
Fothergill, A. 20
Fridlund, B. 39, 112

Gabbard, G.O. 134, 136, 146
Gallimore, R. 81, 86–87
Gardner, L. 8, 124, 207, 232
Gatward, R. 10
Geale, P. 200
Gibbs, G. 236
Gilbert, T. 205

Giordano, A. 67
Gollwitzer, P.M. 57
Goodyear, R. 2, 25–26, 27, 28–29, 39, 40, 50, 58, 61, 68, 71, 75, 88, 106, 113, 119, 127, 174, 175–76, 176–77, 186, 187, 188, 213
Gordon, A. 121
Gordon, K. 121–22, 172
Graham, J. 201
Greenwood, J. 231
Grist, S. 172
Gu, D. 121
Gutheil, T.G. 134, 136, 146
Guzzard, C. R. 106, 119

Haag, A.M. 186, 187, 188
Haataja, R. 20, 24, 25, 89, 156–57, 161, 162, 171
Hair, H.J. 6, 34, 38, 52, 109, 160, 162, 169, 170, 172, 211
Hale, C. 6, 20, 151, 153, 157, 159, 165
Hallberg, I. R. 17, 21, 24, 109, 118–19
Hall-Lord, M. L. 20, 115
Hamer, D. 123
Hamilton, L. 143
Hannigan, B. 20, 24
Hansen, G. S. 108, 114, 169, 170, 171
Hansson, U. W. 17, 24
Hanus, A. E. 29, 104, 105, 209, 221
Happell, B. 153–54
Harding, S. 23, 153, 156, 160, 165, 221, 229
Harkness, D. 7, 21, 122–23
Hatcher, R. 26, 113, 127, 174, 175–76, 176–77
Hawkins, E.J. 28, 29
Hawkins, P. 51, 62, 66, 110, 154–56, 183, 221
Health, Department of 3
Heber, S.A. 136, 141–42, 147–48
Heckman-Stone, C. 124
Hensley, H. 7, 21, 122–23
Higgins, I. 28
Hill, C. E. 42, 116, 123, 124
Hoffman, M. A. 123, 124
Höjer, S. 163
Holland, S. 2, 3, 39, 40
Holloway, E.L. 69
Hollyoake, K. 123
Holmes, S. E. 123, 124
Holton, E. F. III 75, 77–78, 80, 81, 85, 86
Hopkins, E. 37, 201
Houston, G. 66–67
Howe, H. E. 110, 111

Howells, K. 27–28, 29, 30, 121, 201, 232
Hussein, S. 21, 102, 162, 206
Hyrkäs, K. 3, 16,20, 24, 25, 38, 39, 40, 41, 72, 89, 156–57, 159,161, 162, 169, 171, 172, 201, 220, 226, 227, 228–29

Ingram, K. M. 172
Ingram, R. 121, 198, 199, 201
Inskipp, F. 3, 39, 40
Inman, A. G. 124

Jackson, C.22, 25, 29, 30, 158, 159, 234
James, I. A. 81, 85, 115
Jarvis, P. 231, 232, 234
Jasper, M. 232
Jauncey, S. 121
Javen, L. 202
Jeacock, J. 18, 24, 134, 158, 160, 183–84
Jenkins, E. 54, 153
Jensen, M.A.C. 40, 196, 227
Jindal-Snape, D. 198, 201
Johns, C. 68, 102, 106, 116, 118, 186, 201, 202, 206, 207, 231, 232, 233, 234, 236–37
Johnson, S. 228
Johnston, L.H. 58, 111, 114
Jolly, B.C. 3, 20, 28, 114, 171
Jones, A. 29, 34, 43, 75, 88, 161, 165, 171
Jones, L. 10, 27–28, 30, 141
Jones, P.R. 117
Joyce, L. 51, 52, 58, 59, 161, 162, 164, 174, 176, 192, 221
Juggessur, T. 24
Juhnke, G.A. 70
Justice, L. 113

Kadushin, A. 50–51, 52, 53, 54, 95
Kagan, H. 87
Kagan, N.I. 87
Karpman, S. 64–65
Kaslow, N. J. 26, 113, 127, 174, 175–76, 176–77
Kelly, B. 28
Kenny, A. 158, 161
Kenrick, C. 123
Kilminster, S.M. 3, 20, 28, 114, 171
King, D. 177
King, R. 22, 28, 29, 109, 174
Kitchener, K.S. 134–35
Kivimäki, K. 201
Kivlighan, D. M. 88
Knibbs, J. 109
Knight, S. 52, 174
Knudsen, H. K. 24

Kolb, D.A. 86
Knowles, M. S. 75, 77–78, 80, 81, 85, 86
Knox, S. 124
Koivula, M. 3, 16, 38, 40, 72, 169, 172, 201
Krengel, M. 18, 26

Ladany, N. 18, 26, 42, 61, 112, 116, 220–21
Lahad, M. 215, 217, 218
Lambert, M.J. 28, 29
Lambert, W. 22, 28, 29, 174
Landmark, B. T. 108, 114, 169, 170, 171
Larsen, D. 87
Larsen, K. 87–88
Lehti, K. 38, 40, 159, 201, 228
Lehrman-Waterman, D. 220–21
Lencioni, P. 203
Leventhal, G. 26, 113, 127, 174, 175–76, 176–77
Lewis, R. 157, 161
Lizzio, A.J. 81, 82–84, 85, 95, 118, 119–20, 124, 222, 231, 234
Long, C. G. 23, 153, 156, 160, 165, 221, 229
Love, C.C. 136, 138, 139, 141–42, 145, 146, 147–48
Lowe, L. 160
Lützén, K. 23
Lynch, L. 153–54

MacDonald, F. 27, 30, 61, 171, 178
MacDougall, A. E. 54
Mackintosh, C. 233
Maggs, R. 157, 161, 222
Magnusson, A. 23
Magnuson, S. 111–12
Mairs, H. 21
Manthorpe, J. 21, 102, 162, 206
Marie-Blackburn, I. 81, 85, 115
Marquart, J. W. 135, 136–37, 139, 140
Marrow, C. E. 123
Maruna, S. 132
Maxwell, T. 226
McCormack, B. 37, 201
McDonald, S. 202
McIntosh, S. 226–27
McKnight, K. 26
McLean, S. 124
McNeill, B.W. 29, 51, 59–61,110, 111, 125 178
Mehr, K. E. 61, 112
Mehta, T. G. 20, 50, 51, 85, 119
Meltzer, H. 10

Mezirow, J. 82
Milne, D. 2, 3, 28, 29, 58, 71–72, 81, 85, 111, 114, 115, 224
Molassiotis, A. 38
Moore, E. 139, 143, 144, 146, 147–48
Mor Barak, M. E. 22, 28, 51, 52, 174
Morgan, M.M. 27, 29, 51, 68, 69
Mori, Y. 61, 112
Moriarty, J. 21, 102, 162, 206
Morris, G. H. 126
Morrison, T. 207
Mothersole, G. 5, 10, 13, 30, 75, 115, 132, 133, 141, 151, 156, 160, 161, 206
Mullarkey, K. 53, 66
Mullings, J. L. 139, 140
Murphy, K. 54, 233
Murray, J. P. 200

Nagi, C. 122
Nelson, M. L. 44, 109–10, 111, 115, 125–26
Newman, A.S. 186, 188
Nielsen, C. 87–88
Nightingale, V. 52, 174
Noak, J. 156, 157, 158, 220
Norem, K. 40, 111–12
Nutt, E. A. 42, 116

Ockerby, C. M. 228
O'Connell, B. 228
O'Donoghue, K.B. 29, 54–55, 56, 57, 58
Office for National Statistics (ONS) 10
Olding, C. 172
Overholser, J.C. and Fine, M.A. 131, 187, 189
Owen, N. 215

Page, S. 51, 54–55, 187
Paget, T. 158, 233
Pajnkihar, M. 22, 25, 29, 30, 158, 159, 234
Palomo, M. 220
Parker, V. 28
Paunonen, M. 3, 16, 72, 169, 172
Paunonen-Ilmonen, M. 38, 40, 41, 159, 201, 226, 227, 228
Paustian-Underdahl, S. C. 113
Payne, K. 23, 153, 156, 160, 165, 221, 229
Pearce, N. 219
Pearpoint, J. 226–27
Peternelj-Taylor, C.A. 135–36, 139, 140, 143, 147–48, 149
Petrie, T. 62, 110, 111, 172, 173–74, 175, 176
Phelps, D. L. 124

Phillips, B.T. 8
Pilling, S. 175–76
Playle, J.F. 53, 66
Power, A. 177
Power, S. 134
Pratt, D.D. 80–81, 89
Proctor, B. 3, 16, 35, 38, 39, 40 50, 51, 52, 53, 54, 95, 169, 172, 173, 187, 220
Pross, C. 25
Purdy, M. J.205, 207
Pyun, H. 22, 28, 51, 52, 174

Rafferty, M. 171
Raine, R. 114, 224
Rankine, M. 39, 40
Ratliff, D. A. 126
Raue, P. 22, 28, 29, 174
Regehr, C. 25, 116, 136, 139, 141, 142, 147–48, 151
Reichelt, S. 41
Reid, B. 231, 233
Reiser, R. P. 28, 29, 114, 224
Richards, K. 23, 28
Robertson, P. 188–89, 190–91
Rogelberg, S. G. 113
Rogers, C. 82
Rolfe, G. 8, 79, 124, 207, 232
Roman, P. M. 24
Rossen, E.K. 146
Roth, A. 175–76
Russell, R.K. 62, 110, 111, 172, 173–74, 175, 176

Salmon, A. 27, 30, 61, 171, 178
Sandberg, J. 79, 80, 89–90
Scaife, J. 2, 3, 58–59, 68, 88, 124, 175–76, 217, 218, 232
Scanlon, C. 22, 158, 160, 161
Schacht, A. J. 110, 111
Schafer, P. 142, 145, 146
Schult, D. 18, 26
Schweitzer, R. 22, 28, 29, 174
Schoenwald, S. K. 20, 50, 51, 85, 119
Schön, D.A. 79, 215, 231
Scott, C. W. 113
Scott, K. J. 172
Sellars, J. 206, 207
Severinsson, E. 8, 23, 24, 109, 113–14, 118–19, 233
Shanley, M.J. 3, 54, 59, 68
Shanock, L. R. 113
Sharpe, E. 21, 102, 162, 206
Sharrock, J. 202
Sheldon, K. 27, 29, 201

Shernoff, E. S. 20, 50, 51, 85, 119
Shine, J. 10, 141
Shohet, R. 51, 62, 66, 110, 154–56, 183, 221
Siembor, M. 29, 104, 105, 209, 221
Simon, R.I. 146
Simpson, P. 40, 196
Singleton, N. 10
Sirola-Karvinen, P. 201
Skjerve, J. 41
Sloan, G. 159
Smenda, H. 228
Smith, N. G. 172
Snow, R. W. 41
Sommer, I. 87–88
Sprenkle, D.H. 27, 29, 51, 68, 69
Steen, L. 2
Stege, R. 87
Stevens, M. 21, 102, 162, 206
Stevenson, C. 3, 54, 59, 68
Stoltenberg, C.D. 51, 59–61, 178
Stoodley, I. 199, 202
Storey, L. 3, 42, 104, 151, 153, 157, 158, 159
Strom-Gottfried, K. 136–37
Swafford, K. G. 88
Swanson, R. A. 75, 77–78, 80, 81, 85, 86
Swords, B. A. 29, 104, 105, 209, 221
Syversen, K. 186, 187, 190

Taylor, B.J. 215, 232, 233, 234
Taylor, K. N. 172
Teasdale, K. 160
Teh, B. 232
Tennant, A. 51, 58, 59, 157, 161, 162, 164, 174, 176, 192, 221
Tharp, R.G. 81, 86–87
Theander, K. 20, 115
Thom, N. 160
Titterton, M. 132
Todd, G. 13
Travis, D. J. 22, 28, 51, 52, 174
Triantafillou, N. 70–71
Triggiano, P. J. 44, 109–10, 111, 115, 125–26
Tuckman, B.W. 40, 196, 227
Turner, J. 28

Vitanza, S. A. 172
Vygotsky, Lev 81

Wadey, E. 156, 157, 158, 220
Wainwright, N.A. 220

Walker, R. 146–47, 147–48
Wallerstein, R.S. 5, 82
Walsh, L. 3, 42, 104, 151, 153, 157, 158, 159
Wampler, K. S. 126
Ward, T. 50, 132, 186, 187, 188–89, 190–91, 201
Watkins, C.E. 52
Webb, C. 19, 23, 29, 107, 232
Weir, W.S. 22, 158, 160, 161
Wells Parker, E. 41
Westergaard, J. 50
Wheeler, J. 116
Wheeler, S. 23, 28, 177
White, E. 2, 16, 18, 19, 20, 24, 108, 134, 156, 157, 158, 160, 162, 163, 165, 166, 183–84, 220
Whitehead, P. R. 50
Whyte, D. A. 38
Wilcoxon, S. A. 40, 111–12
Williams, C. 164–65
Williamson, P. 121
Willis, G. 201
Wilson, K.L. 44, 81, 82–84, 85, 95, 118, 119–20, 124, 222, 231, 234
Willson, L. 38
Winstanley, J. 2, 16, 19, 20, 108, 156, 157, 158, 162, 163, 165, 166, 220
Wong, S. C. P. 121
Wonnacott, J. 207
Woods, K. 50
Worley, R. 139, 140
Worthen, V. 29, 110, 111, 125
Wosket, V. 51, 54–55, 187
Wright, A. 200

Xie, B. 22, 28, 51, 52, 174

Yegdich, T. 5, 54, 210
Yonge, O. 135–36, 139, 140, 143, 147–48, 149

Zeni, T. A. 54
Zorga, S. 75, 81, 85

Subject index

acceptance, fostering of 153
accident, risk of 137
acclimatisation to workings of supervision 92–96, 106–7
accreditation of supervisors 162
action planning 106
active boundary management 146–47
active supervision methods 122
acute hospital setting, focus group study in 228
addressing risk issues in supervision 132–33;
adult learning: adult learning model (andragogy) 77–78; direction and support in 80–81; theories of 77–82, 243
agenda: supervisee being supervised 106; types of supervision, forms and tasks 45–46
agreements and contracts 43–45
alliance 106; 219–20; quality of 109
apprenticeship learning 88–89
Ashworth Hospital Inquiry (1999) 7
assessments and measures 219–24; *Evaluation Process within Supervision Inventory* 220–21; *Feedback: Informed Supervision* (International Center for Clinical Excellence) 224; *Global Review Form: Supervision Version* 222–23; *Leeds Alliance in Supervision Scale* 220; *Manchester Clinical Supervision Scale* (MCSS) 220; measurement of facets of supervision 220–21; regular monitoring 222–23; *Secure Unit Supervision Questionnaire* 221; *Self-assessment Questionnaire for Supervisors* 221;
supervision alliance 219–20; *Supervision Matrix* 221; *Supervisor Self-Disclosure Index* 221; *Supervisory Relationship Measure* 219–20; *Taxonomy of Inadequate or Harmful Supervision* 221; *Working Alliance Inventory* 219
assisted learning: approaches to 86–87; Zone of Proximal Development (ZPD) and 81
audit 156, 164–65; clinical supervision routine audit event record, example of 164–65
autonomy 58, 60, 81, 111, 135, 188
avoidance, dealing with 213

background information, gathering of 121–22
balance in supervision, achievement of 102
balance of power 206
barriers, anticipation, identification and addressing of 155
behaviour of supervisors 111–13
benificence 187
bias 35, 71, 76, 85, 117, 145, 159
boundaries: active boundary management 146–47; client and the practitioner, boundaries between 135–38; crossing boundaries 136; forms of boundary breach 136; inattention to 136; interpersonal demand and 10; maintenance of 188; maintenance of, quick guide to 147–48; management through supervision of 134–48; recognition of problem of 146; Triangle of Boundary Maintenance

143–44, 241; *see also* risk and boundaries, management of; violation of boundaries
boundary maintenance, quick guide to 147–48
British Psychological Society, Division of Clinical Psychology 9
burnout, impact of 24–25

case work, supervision of 121–23
child secure care unit, example of 184–85
child welfare services, impacts on staff in 23
client factors 140–41
client-focused supervision 21–22; questions concerning 122–23
client outcomes, research on impact of supervision on 28–29
client-related action plan, development of 122
client risks, supervision and 130–31
client/task: benefits of supervision 7–8; outcomes, evaluation of 20–22
Clinical Leadership Template 202
commitment, establishment of 153
common factors approach 68–69
communication, dealing with problems of 213
competence: conceptual competence 83; core values and competences 241–42; maintenance of 188, 190; quality of 109
conflict, dealing with 125–27
consultation 41–42; practice supervision and 242–43
contextual differences 163
contextual information, gathering of 121–22
core features of successful supervision 157
core skills and knowledge for supervisors 108–27; active supervision methods 122; alliance, quality of 109; background and contextual information, gathering of 121–22; behaviour of supervisors 111–13; bias 117; case work, supervision of 121–23; client-focused supervision questions 122–23; client-related action plan, development of 122; competence, quality of 109; conflict, dealing with 125–27; 'disciplinary supervision' 125; establishment of supervision 115–19; ethical, legal and diversity issues 127; feedback, provision of 123–25; focus, deciding on 122; 'good' supervisors, qualities of 109–10; 'homework' setting 122; interpersonal stance 126; learning and development, promotion of 119–20; original question, determination of addressing of 122; personal qualities of supervisors 110; perspective, differences of 125–27; preparation for supervision 113–15; problems, identification of examples of 122; provision of supervision 119–25; question being asked, identification of 121; questions for supervisors 120–21; reflective preparation 126; relevant background and contextual information, gathering of 121–22; 'remote' supervision, provision of 123; role clarity, establishment of 115–16; ruptures in relationship, management of 119; strains in relationship, management of 119; student and trainee supervision 114–15; supervisee burnout 117–18; supervisee current understanding, checking on 122; supervisee non-disclosure 116–17; supervisor competence 113; supervisor qualities 109–13; supervisor social skills 109; supervisory relationship 118–19; technical approach 126; training for supervision 115; understanding the supervisee 116–18
core values and competences 241–42
cost considerations 159
counselling 5–6
creative approaches to supervision 215–18; creative techniques, range of 215; De Bono's *Thinking Hats* 217–18; drawing 217; enacting 216–17; metaphors 215–16; six-part story 217; writing 217
Creative Supervision () 218
cross-discipline supervision 160–61

De Bono's *Thinking Hats* 217–18
decision-making 11; focus, deciding on 122
definitions: clinical supervision 3; forensic practitioner 1–2; practice 4; practice supervision 2–5, 6; range of 4; reflective practice 231–32
delivery method 161–62
democracy in supervision 207
development of supervision: in forensic practice 1–2, 151–66;
developmental and educational needs, engagement with 185
developmental model 58–62
dignity, respect and 187

Subject index 255

directional conformity 205
'disciplinary supervision' 125
discussion of work 11; discussions within supervision 93
disempowered practice 206
disinterest, dealing with 212
domains of learning 82–85
drawing, creative supervision and 217
dual relationships 136
due process 188

efficacious supervision 96–104
emancipatory reflection 235
emotional distress 145, 185; hurting feelings 212
enacting, creative supervision and 216–17
environment factors (context) 141–42
establishment of supervision 115–19
ethical issues 186–92; autonomy 188; boundaries, maintenance of 188; competence, maintenance of 188, 190; due process 188; ethical, legal and diversity issues 127; 'ethical blindness' 188–89; ethical dilemma frameworks 189–91; ethical expectations 187–89; ethical issues, recognition of 191–92; ethical judgement 83–84; ethical supervision 186–92; ethical surveillance 206; legal issues 192; responsibility 188; spotting possible ethical dilemmas 191–92; training and expertise, practice within scope of 188
ethical judgement 83–84
evaluation 156, 164, 165–66; criteria for 17–19
Evaluation Process within Supervision Inventory 220–21
evidence-based supervision: evidence base for and impacts of practice supervision 16–30; models of supervision, frameworks and 71–72
expectations: discussions about 97; first supervision session, expectation from 94; lack of realism in 212
experience: experienced practitioner 96; learning from 86
experiential learning cycle 86
explicit teaching 85–86
external factors, influences on supervision of 200

factors: for consideration in supervision, wide range of 241; pertinent to group work 196–97

feedback: feedback culture, need for 242; learning organisation, feedback within 242; provision of 123–25; reluctance to provide 210
Feedback: Informed Supervision (International Center for Clinical Excellence) 224
finding a supervisor 104
first supervision session 94
focus, deciding on 122
forensic mental health inpatient service, example of 184
forensic practice, development of supervision in 1–2. 151–66; barriers, anticipation, identification and addressing of 155; supervision routine audit event record, example of 165; contextual differences 163; cost considerations 159; group delivery 161–62; implementation of supervision, barriers and pitfalls in 151–53; initial training and information 155; interest of stakeholders, development of 154; Lynch Model of Implementation 153–54; managerial support, importance of 157–58; maximisation of success, thoughtful implementation and 163–64; practical factors 153; preparation and training of staff 161; problem alliances 152–53; professional requirements 162–63; service strategy, development of 153–63; staff engagement 151–53; staff ownership for successful supervision, importance of 157; stakeholder engagement 154; strategic support, importance of 157–58; support for on-going supervision training and development 155–56; understanding and harnessing what is already in place 154
forensic supervision, future research in 27–30
formalised relationship within practice supervision 3–4

Gibbs' experiential learning cycle 236
Global Review Form: Supervision Version 222–23
glossary of supervision terms 105–6
goals of forensic practice supervision 98–99
goals and, reviewing supervision in context of 103–4
good practice, role of supervision in 6–7
'good' supervisors, qualities of 109–10
group consult model 40–41
group delivery in forensic practice 161–62

group supervision 39–41
group work, supervision of 194–97; factors pertinent to 196–97; group focus 196; individual focus 196; Process Model of Supervision 194; programme integrity 195; task focus 195; treatment adherence 195
guided reflective practice 232–33, 238

'homework' setting 122
hybrid model of training and development 171

impact of supervision, arguments concerning 158–59
implementation of supervision, barriers and pitfalls in 151–53
individual focus in group work 196
individual supervision 39; individual delivery 161–62; individual supervision agreement, example of 45
influence of supervisee and supervisor, research on 27–28
informal supervision 21, 93
integrity 188
interest of stakeholders, development of 154
International Center for Clinical Excellence 224
interpersonal attributes, incompetence due to difficulties with 189
interpersonal challenges 185
interpersonal demand and boundaries 10
Interpersonal Process Recall (IPR) 87
interpersonal stance 126
intervention, earliness of 146

job satisfaction, impact of 24–25
judgement, incompetence due to lack of 189
justice 188

KEN (Knowledge, Experience, Need) exercise 12–13
knowledge: incompetence due to lack of 189; provision of supervision training, knowledge about 172–73; *see also* core skills and knowledge for supervisors

lateness, dealing with 212
leadership: forensic practice, development of supervision in 158; non-client work, supervision of 201–3

learning in supervision, approaches to 75–90; adult learning, theories of 77–82; adult learning model (andragogy) 77–78; apprenticeship learning 88–89; assisted learning and the Zone of Proximal Development (ZPD) 81; assisted learning approaches 86–87; conceptual competence 83; direction and support in adult learning 80–81; domains of learning 82–85; experience, learning from 86; experiential learning cycle 86; explicit teaching 85–86; Interpersonal Process Recall (IPR) 87; learning to learn 89; personal awareness and development 84; problem-based learning 88; promotion of learning 85–89; role efficacy 83; specific skills learning 87–88; stages of learning 79–80; supervision as learning 75–77; supervisor as assessor 89; systemic competence 83; taking stock 76–77; technical competence and proficiency 84; unhelpful learning roles and styles 82; 'whole-part-whole' approach 86
Leeds Alliance in Supervision Scale 220
legal issues 192
limitations of team supervision, consideration of 230
line management 106; differences from supervision 94; supervision and 162
local strategies and policies 240–41
'lone working,' risk associated with 184
lovesickness 137
loyalty, sense of ownership and 153
Lynch Model of Implementation 153–54

maintenance of appropriate boundaries, role of supervision in 142–48
management: managerial support, importance of 157–58; non-client work, supervision of 201–3; too much focus on 211
Manchester Clinical Supervision Scale (MCSS) 19, 20, 24, 108, 156, 157, 158, 220
metaphors in creative supervision 215–16
methodological research traps 16–17
minimally adequate supervision 104–5
models of supervision, frameworks and 50–72; common factors approach 68–69; developmental model 58–62; evidence-based supervision 71–72; overview of models 50–52; process model 62–68; reflective practice, models and approaches to 234–37; research on 29;

solution-focused supervision 70–71; supervision functions and dimensions 52–54; supervision hour 54–58
monitoring 5, 7, 18, 37, 99, 113, 132, 142, 146, 184, 206–7, 241; staff-monitoring system 6; regular monitoring 222–23
multi-professional teams 228
mutiny, dealing with 152

naïveté 137
natural progression 169–70
needs: documentation of 11; from supervision for supervisee being supervised 97–98
negative evaluation, concern about 210–11
NHS Foundation Trust Public Inquiry (2013) 7
non-client work, supervision of 198–203; Clinical Leadership Template 202; developmental aspects, importance of recognition of 202; external factors, influences on supervision of 200; leadership 201–3; management 201–3; peer supervision 201; Practice Leader Tasks 202; research, supervision of 198–201; research supervision, dimensions of 198–99; SuReCam model (Supervision Remit Compatibility) 198–99;

open team supervision 229
operation of practice supervision 10–12
opinions, communication and expression of 227–28
organisation and practice, future developments 243–44
organisation of supervision, supervisee being supervised 94
organisational responses to risk 142
original question, determination of 122
outcomes 34, 35–36, 195, 202, 206, 232; anticipation of 57, 243; benefits of supervision and 159; costs and 159; differences in client outcomes 71; educational outcomes 132; feedback on 46; goals and, reviewing supervision in context of 103–4; impact of supervision on client/task outcomes 166; practice supervision and 4–5, 6, 8, 11, 16–17, 18, 20, 21–22, 24, 26, 27, 30; researching the impact of supervision on client outcomes 28–29; supervisee outcomes 82–83

peer consultation 38
peer supervision: non-client work, supervision of 201; types of supervision, forms and tasks 37
personal awareness and development 84
personal considerations about practice supervision 12–13
personal information: disclosure of 212–13; supervisor requirement for 94–95
personal qualities of supervisors 110
personal questioning 212
perspective, differences of 125–27
policy use to set tone 144
political differences 163
Positive Risk Taking (PRT) 132
post-qualification supervision 160
power: balance of power 206; disempowered practice 206; power dynamics in context of practice supervision 242; surveillance control, power and 205–7; two-way relationship with 205–6
practical reflection 235
practice, definition of 4
Practice Leader Tasks 202
practice supervision: adult learning theory 77–82, 243; assessments and measures 219–24; boundaries, interpersonal demand 10; Boundary Maintenance, Triangle of 241; client/task, benefits to 7–8; consultation and 242–43; core skills and knowledge for supervisors 108–27; core values and competences 241–42; creative approaches to 215–18; critiques of supervision and reflective practice 205–7; decision-making 11; definition of 2–5; development of supervision in forensic practice 151–66; ethical issues 186–92; evidence base for and impacts of 16–30; formalised relationship within 3–4; good practice, role of supervision in 6–7; group work, supervision of 194–97; KEN (Knowledge, Experience, Need) exercise 12–13; learning in supervision, approaches to 75–90; as life-long development 6; models of supervision, frameworks and 50–72; non-client work, supervision of 198–203; practice, definition of 4; practitioner, benefits to 8; dealing with problems of 209–14; professional standards 9; rationale for 6–10; reflective practice 231–38; risk and boundaries, management of 130–49;

self-assessment 242; setting, impact on supervision of 183–85; supervisee being supervised 92–107; team supervision 226–30; training and 242–43; training and development for supervisors and supervisees 169–78; types of supervision, forms and tasks 34–48
pre-emptive action 143–44
predators 137
preparation for supervision: core skills and knowledge for supervisors 113–15; preparation and training of staff 161; supervisee being supervised 100–102; supervision problems, dealing with 213
PREVENT 214
problem alliances 152–53
problem-based learning 88
problems, identification of examples of 122
problems in supervision, dealing with 104–5, 209–14
Process Model of Supervision 62–68; group work, supervision of 194; setting, impact on supervision of 183
professional requirements 162–63
professional standards in practice supervision 9
professional supervision 37
programme integrity, group work and 195
promotion of learning 85–89
provision: of supervision 119–25; of training and development 173–77
psychology supervision, identification of competencies in 26

questions for supervisors 120–21
questions to aid reflection 237

rationales for: practice supervision 6–10; training and development 171–73; use of supervision 92–93
reciprocal supervision 37
recognition of risk 139–40
record keeping 46–47
REFLECT model of reflection 233–34;
reflecting team approach 41
Reflective Learning Model of Supervision 236
reflective practice 231–38; definition of 231–32; emancipatory reflection 235; Gibbs' experiential learning cycle 236; guided reflective practice 232–33, 238;
models and approaches to 234–37; planning for reflection 233–34; practical reflection 235; questions to aid reflection 237; REFLECT model of reflection 233–34; Reflective Learning Model of Supervision 236; Structured Reflection, models for 236–37; What? Model of Structured Reflection 235–36. *See also reflective practice, critiques of supervision and*
reflective practice, critiques of supervision and 205–7; democracy in supervision 207; disempowered practice 206; ethical surveillance 206; monitoring 206–7; power, two-way relationship with 205–6; regulation by others 205; self-regulation 205; surveillance control, power and 205–7; surveillance management 206–7; transparency in supervision 207
registration 9
'remote' supervision, provision of 123
research on practice supervision: approaches to 29–30; burnout, impact of 24–25; child welfare services, impacts on staff in 23; client-focused supervision 21–22; client outcomes, research on impact of supervision on 28–29; client/task outcomes, evaluation of 20–22; evaluation criteria 17–19; forensic supervision, future research in 27–30; influence of supervisee and supervisor, research on 27–28; job satisfaction, impact of 24–25; methodological research traps 16–17; models of supervision, research on 29; research and evaluation, future developments 245–46; self-esteem, confidence and 21; staff, evaluation of impacts on 22–25; supervisee, research on impact of supervision on 28; supervision, research on approaches to 29; supervision of research, non-client work and 198–201; supervision quality, evaluation of 19–20; supervisors, evaluation of effects on 25; theoretical research traps 16–17; workplace wellbeing, evaluation of impacts on 23–25
research, supervision of 198–201
resistance, dealing with 152
resources for supervision 43
respect, dealing with lack of 212
RESPOND 214
responsibility 103, 188
reviewing supervision 43, 103–4

Subject index 259

risk and boundaries, management of 130–49; active boundary management 146–47; addressing risk issues in supervision 132–33; boundary inattention 136; boundary maintenance, quick guide to 147–48; boundary maintenance, triangle of 143–44; boundary management through supervision 134–48; boundary problem recognition 146; client and the practitioner, boundaries between 135–38; client factors 140–41; client risks, supervision and 130–31; crossing boundaries 136; dual relationships 136; early intervention 146; environment factors (context) 141–42; forms of boundary breach 136; intervention, earliness of 146; lovesickness 137; maintenance of appropriate boundaries, role of supervision in 142–48; naïveté 137; organisational responses 142; policy use to set tone 144; Positive Risk Taking (PRT) 132; pre-emptive action 143–44; predators 137; recognition 139–40; risk management through supervision 130–33; sexual contact 137; staff factors 138–40; sub-optimal performance, management of risks associated with 131; supervisee safety and wellbeing through supervision 131–32; supervision, boundary maintenance within 144–45; supervisor and supervisee, boundaries between 134–35; tone setting using policy 144; violation of boundaries 136; violation of boundaries, factors associated with 137–38; violation of boundaries, management of 147; vulnerability, continuum of 145; wellbeing of supervisee through supervision 131–32
role clarity, establishment of 115–16
role efficacy 83
ruptures in relationship, management of 119

safety in practice 42
Secure Unit Supervision Questionnaire 221
self-assessment 242
Self-assessment Questionnaire for Supervisors 221
self-determination (choice) 188
self-directed learning 170
self-esteem, confidence and 21
self-regulation 205

service strategy, development of 153–63
setting, impact on supervision of 183–85; child secure care unit, example of 184–85; developmental and educational needs, engagement with 185; emotional distress 185; forensic mental health inpatient service, example of 184; interpersonal challenges 185; 'lone working,' risk associated with 184; probation service, example of 184; Process Model of Supervision 183
sexual contact 137
skills: incompetence due to lack of 189; specific skills learning 87–88; *see also* core skills and knowledge for supervisors
Social Work Reform Board 9
Social Work Task Force in England 9
Solution Circles 226–27
solution-focused supervision 70–71
specialist supervision 36–37
specific skills learning 87–88
staff: evaluation of impacts on 22–25; ownership for successful supervision, importance of feelings of 157; preparation and training of 161; risk and boundaries, staff factors 138–40; staff engagement 151–53
stages of learning 79–80
stakeholder engagement 154
standards, concern about failure to reach 210–11
steps in developing and implementing supervision 154–56;
strains in relationship, management of 119
strategic support, importance of 157–58; strategy and policy development 155
Structured Reflection, models for 236–37
student and trainee supervision 114–15
style differences 211
sub-optimal performance, management of risks associated with 131
successful supervision: features of 156–57; implementation of, maximisation of 153–63
supervisee being supervised 92–107; acclimatising to workings of supervision 92–96, 106–7; action planning 106; agenda 106; agreement 106; alliance 106; balance, achievement of 102; contributing to supervision, what you should take 99–100; discussions within supervision 93; efficacious supervision

96–104; expectations of supervision, discussions about 97; experienced practitioner, practice supervision and 96; finding a supervisor 104; first supervision session, expectation from 94; glossary of supervision terms 105–6; goals of forensic practice supervision 98–99; idea of supervision, daunting nature of 95–96; informal supervision 93; line management, differences from supervision 94; line management 106; minimally adequate supervision 104–5; needs from supervision 97–98; organisation of supervision 94; personal information, supervisor requirement for 94–95; preparation for supervision 100–102; problems in supervision, dealing with 104–5; rationale for use of supervision 92–93; reasons for needing supervision 93; reflection 106; responsibilities in context of supervision 103; reviewing supervision 103–4; supervision methods and approaches 95; supervision relationship, development of 102; trainee/new practitioner, practice supervision and 96; uncertainty about wanting supervision 95–96; understanding supervision 92–96; useful things to remember about supervision 96
supervisee burnout 117–18
supervisee current understanding, checking on 122
supervisee non-disclosure 116–17
supervisee safety and wellbeing through supervision 131–32
supervisee training 173
supervision: boundary maintenance within 144–45; core conditions for 42–43; functions and dimensions 52–54; implementation of, barriers and pitfalls in 151–53; as learning 75–77; maximisation of success in, thoughtful implementation and 163–64; methods and approaches, supervisee being supervised 95; research on approaches to 29; service and workforce benefits, forensic perspective on 9–10; steps in developing and implementing 154–56; successful supervision, core features of 157; supervising the supervisors 177–78; supervision agenda 45–46; supervision agreement 43–45; supervision alliance 219–20; supervision competence, areas of 174; supervision hour 54–58; as tool for exploration and critical analysis of practice 207; useful things to remember about 96; *see also* successful supervision
Supervision Hour 54–58
Supervision Matrix 221
supervision not meeting needs 211–12
supervision problems, dealing with 209–14; addressing specific problems 209–13; avoidance 213; communication 213; disinterest 212; expectations, lack of realism in 212; feedback, reluctance to provide 210; lateness 212; management, too much focus on 211; mitigation against problems arising 209; negative evaluation, concern about 210–11; personal information, disclosure of 212–13; personal questioning 212; preparation for supervision 213; PREVENT 214; prevention and response 214; respect, lack of 212; RESPOND 214; standards, concern about failure to reach 210–11; style differences 211; supervision not meeting needs 211–12; supervisor needs, concentration of 212–13; supervisor/supervisee problems 212–13; therapy, supervision feeling more like 210
supervision record, example of 47;
supervision relationship, development of 102
supervision routine audit event record, example of 165;
supervision tasks 42–47
supervisor as assessor 89
supervisor choice (and within and cross-discipline supervision) 160–61
supervisor competence 113
supervisor development paradigms 169–71
supervisor qualities 109–13
Supervisor Self-Disclosure Index 221
supervisor social skills 109
supervisor/supervisee problems 212–13
supervisors: as assessor 89; evaluation of effects on 25; supervisee and, boundaries between 134–35
supervisory relationship 118–19
Supervisory Relationship Measure 219–20
Supervisory Relationship Questionnaire 220
support for on-going supervision training and development 155–56
SuReCam model (Supervision Remit Compatibility) 198–99
surveillance control, power and 205–7
surveillance management 206–7

suspicion 152
Swedish study of district nurses and mental health care practitioners 23
system factors 153
systemic competence 83

taking stock 76–77
task focus in group work 195
taught course model 170–71
Taxonomy of Inadequate or Harmful Supervision 221
teaching, supervision as 199–200
team supervision 226–30; acute hospital setting, focus group study in 228; client discussions within, template for 229; limitations of 230; multi-professional teams 228; open team supervision 229; opinions, communication and expression of 227–28; Solution Circles 226–27; team relationships 227–28; togetherness (solidarity) 227–28; types of supervision, forms and tasks 41; working methods 227–28
technical competence and proficiency 84
technology, use of 163
theoretical research traps 16–17
therapy: practice supervision and 5–6; supervision feeling more like 210
togetherness (solidarity) 227–28
tokenism 152
training and development for supervisors and supervisees 169–78; delivery of training 176–77; hybrid model 171; natural progression 169–70; providing supervision training, knowledge about 172–73; provision of training and development 173–77; rationale for training and development 171–73; self-directed learning 170; supervisee training 173; supervising the supervisors 177–78; supervision competence, areas of 174; supervision training programme outline 175–76; supervisor development paradigms 169–71; supervisor training 173–77; taught course model 170–71; training, competencies to include in 174–75
transparency in supervision 207
trauma, prevention of 25
treatment adherence 195
trust: in relationships 42; sense of control and 153

types of supervision, forms and tasks 34–48; agenda 45–46; agreements and contracts 43–45; basic standards for supervision 43; consultation 41–42; core conditions for supervision 42–43; forms of supervision 34, 38–41; group consult model 40–41; group supervision 39–41; individual supervision 39; individual supervision agreement, example of 45; peer consultation 38; peer supervision 37; professional supervision 37; reciprocal supervision 37; record keeping 46–47; reflecting team approach 41; resources for supervision 43; safety in practice 42; specialist supervision 36–37; supervision agenda 45–46; supervision agreement 43–45; supervision record, example of 47; supervision tasks 42–47; support staff supervision 36; team supervision 41; training supervision 35–36; trust in relationships 42; types of supervision 34–38

uncertainty about wanting supervision 95–96
understanding in supervision: harnessing what is already in place and 154; supervisee being supervised 92–96; understanding the supervisee 116–18
unhelpful learning roles and styles 82

Victoria Climbie Inquiry (2003) 6–7
violation of boundaries 136; factors associated with 137–38; management of 147
vulnerability, continuum of 145

wellbeing: of supervisee through supervision 131–32; workplace wellbeing, evaluation of impacts on 23–25
What? Model of Structured Reflection 235–36
'whole-part-whole' approach to learning in supervision 86
Working Alliance Inventory 219
working methods for team supervision 227–28
writing in creative supervision 217

Zone of Proximal Development (ZPD) and 81

eBooks
from Taylor & Francis

Helping you to choose the right eBooks for your Library

Add to your library's digital collection today with Taylor & Francis eBooks. We have over 50,000 eBooks in the Humanities, Social Sciences, Behavioural Sciences, Built Environment and Law, from leading imprints, including Routledge, Focal Press and Psychology Press.

Choose from a range of subject packages or create your own!

Benefits for you
- Free MARC records
- COUNTER-compliant usage statistics
- Flexible purchase and pricing options
- 70% approx of our eBooks are now DRM-free.

Benefits for your user
- Off-site, anytime access via Athens or referring URL
- Print or copy pages or chapters
- Full content search
- Bookmark, highlight and annotate text
- Access to thousands of pages of quality research at the click of a button.

Free Trials Available

We offer free trials to qualifying academic, corporate and government customers.

eCollections
Choose from 20 different subject eCollections, including:
- Asian Studies
- Economics
- Health Studies
- Law
- Middle East Studies

eFocus
We have 16 cutting-edge interdisciplinary collections, including:
- Development Studies
- The Environment
- Islam
- Korea
- Urban Studies

For more information, pricing enquiries or to order a free trial, please contact your local sales team:

UK/Rest of World: **online.sales@tandf.co.uk**
USA/Canada/Latin America: **e-reference@taylorandfrancis.com**
East/Southeast Asia: **martin.jack@tandf.com.sg**
India: **journalsales@tandfindia.com**

www.tandfebooks.com